Teach Yourself

The Israeli-Palestinian Conflict

Stewart Ross

For UK order enquiries: please contact Bookpoint Ltd, 130 Milton Park, Abingdon, Oxon OX14 4SB. *Telephone:* +44 (0) 1235 827720. *Fax:* +44 (0) 1235 400454. Lines are open 09.00–17.00, Monday to Saturday, with a 24-hour message answering service. Details about our titles and how to order are available at www.teachyourself.com

For USA order enquiries: please contact McGraw-Hill Customer Services, PO Box 545, Blacklick, OH 43004-0545, USA. *Telephone:* 1-800-722-4726. *Fax:* 1-614-755-5645.

For Canada order enquiries: please contact McGraw-Hill Ryerson Ltd, 300 Water St, Whitby, Ontario L1N 9B6, Canada. *Telephone:* 905 430 5000. *Fax:* 905 430 5020.

Long renowned as the authoritative source for self-guided learning – with more than 50 million copies sold worldwide – the *Teach Yourself* series includes over 500 titles in the fields of languages, crafts, hobbies, business, computing and education.

British Library Cataloguing in Publication Data: a catalogue record for this title is available from the British Library.

Library of Congress Catalog Card Number: on file.

First published in UK 2007 by Hodder Education, part of Hachette UK, 338 Euston Road, London NW1 3BH.

First published in US 2007 by The McGraw-Hill Companies, Inc.

This edition published 2010.

Previously published as *Teach Yourself the Israeli–Palestinian Conflict*

Typeset by MPS Limited, A Macmillan Company.

Printed in Great Britain for Hodder Education, an Hachette UK Company, 338 Euston Road, London NW1 3BH, by CPI Group (UK) Ltd, Croydon, CR4 0YY.

Impression number 10 9 8 7

Year 2018

Contents

Credits

Front cover: © bluemagenta/Alamy

Back cover: © Jakub Semeniuk/iStockphoto.com, © Royalty-Free/Corbis, © agencyby/iStockphoto.com, © Andy Cook/iStockphoto.com, © Christopher Ewing/iStockphoto.com, © zebicho – Fotolia.com, © Geoffrey Holman/iStockphoto.com, © Photodisc/Getty Images, © James C. Pruitt/iStockphoto.com, © Mohamed Saber – Fotolia.com

Note from the author

Asked by an anxious worshipper when there would be peace between the Israelis and Palestinians, Allah paused for a moment before replying, 'Never... at least, not in my time.'

[Joke current in the Middle East, 2006]

I beseech you, in the bowels of Christ, think it possible you may be mistaken.

Oliver Cromwell

The Arab–Israeli conflict is at the same time vitally important yet fiendishly difficult to explain in clear, unbiased language. This is not for want of trying: a quick book or web search reveals masses of material on the subject. Closer examination, though, soon shows that much of it tries, wittingly or otherwise, to defend a particular point of view, whether it be Israeli, Palestinian, Arab, American, etc.

That the conflict is of crucial importance hardly needs explaining, as in almost every capital city from Washington to Brussels and Beijing governments accept that it is a festering sore from which poison has seeped into every corner of the region and beyond. Time and again politicians of every persuasion say that healing this ugly and open wound would lead to a swift improvement in the political health of the entire Middle East. To have some understanding of the course of the Israeli–Palestinian impasse is, therefore, essential for anyone wishing to cast a reasonably educated eye over the modern world.

The complexity of the story is similarly self-evident. As you read on, you will see how it is not – and never has been – a simple one-side-versus-another situation. Both 'Israeli' and 'Palestinian' are portmanteau words enclosing vast ranges of opinion and belief, some sufficiently mutually hostile, apparently, to justify killing. Add to the mix fervent religious belief, a long heritage of anguish and behind-the-scenes support for every form of extremism, and one begins to get some idea of the intricacy of this troubled history.

For the reasons suggested above, the subject of this book raises the fiercest of passions. Although, as a neutral observer, I have made every effort to be objective and even-handed, I am all too aware that it is impossible to produce an account that pleases all sides. Therefore, if my reading of events is not yours, I crave your indulgence.

The Middle East c. 1918.

Only got a minute?

In the later part of the nineteenth century, the balance of the Arab community living between the Mediterranean and the River Jordan was upset by the arrival of several thousand Jewish immigrants. After 1918, with this 'Holy Land' under British control, Jewish immigration increased and inter-community violence flared. While the Jews wanted an independent homeland, the Arabs were determined to prevent Palestine's partition.

The Jewish homeland – Israel – emerged with the United Nations' endorsement in 1948. In four major wars (1948–9, 1956, 1967 and 1973) the Arab world fought in vain to crush the new nation. By the end of the Six Day War (1967), Israel occupied all the territory the UN had allocated to Israel and Palestine.

The majority of Palestinians were now refugees living in UN-managed camps. The Palestine Liberation Organization (PLO), led by Yasser Arafat, head of the militant Fatah, gave voice to these peoples' anger and aspirations, and conducted operations against Israel that provoked ferocious reprisals.

Arab unity was broken when Egypt (1978) and Jordan (1994) agreed terms with Israel. With the PLO exiled in distant Tunis, in 1987 the West Bank and Gaza erupted in a popular uprising – the Intifada – against the occupiers. Amid the chaos, the Islamists of Hamas added a religious strand to Palestinian resistance.

The USA, Israel's principal backer, brokered an agreement in 1994–5 by which the PLO renounced violence, Israel undertook to withdraw from Palestinian areas and a Palestinian National Authority was established to govern Gaza and the West Bank. Extremists on both sides rejected the deal and tit-for-tat violence restarted. Desperate, the Palestinians rose up in a second intifada.

The talks-breakdown-violence pattern reoccurred during the first decade of the twenty-first century. Reconciliation was made harder when, after Arafat's death (2004), Fatah and Hamas openly split and Hamas seized control of Gaza.

5 Only got five minutes?

Holy Land

From Roman times onwards, the Jews were a people without a land. Then, in the late nineteenth century, their scattered communities in Europe began to dream of 'Zion' – a Jewish homeland in the Holy Land at the eastern end of the Mediterranean. Before World War I, several thousand Jews emigrated there, upsetting the balance of the local Arab community. After the war, Britain governed Palestine as a mandate of the League of Nations. Jewish immigration increased and inter-community violence grew. Eventually, the British decided that the territory was best divided into Jewish and Arab states. While delighting the Jews, the idea horrified the Arabs.

Israel triumphant

The horror of the Holocaust swung Western opinion strongly behind the idea of a Jewish homeland, and Israel was formed after World War II with the endorsement of the United Nations. In the war that followed (1948–9), the Arab states failed to crush the new nation. The result was a disaster for the Palestinian Arabs, who lost all the territory originally assigned to Palestine. It was now they, not the Jews, who were a people without a land.

Most Palestinians became refugees in Egypt-controlled Gaza, the Jordan-controlled West Bank or further afield. Many lived in UN-managed camps. Their position deteriorated further after a brief war in 1956 and even more after Israel occupied Gaza and the West Bank during the Six-Day War (1967). Resistance to Israel and the campaign for a Palestinian homeland were spearheaded by the Palestine Liberation Organization (PLO). Its charismatic head, Yasser Arafat, also led Fatah, a militant guerrilla Palestinian group.

Enter Islam

Following a fourth Arab–Israeli war (1973), Egypt made peace with Israel. Jordan followed suit 16 years later. In 1967, Israel had forced the PLO to leave its original bases. Arafat and his followers were then driven from Jordan (1970) and Lebanon (1982), and ended up exiled in distant Tunis. Meanwhile, ordinary Palestinians of the West Bank and Gaza grew more and more desperate until, in 1987, they began a popular uprising against the occupiers; the First Intifada. With Arafat and the PLO leadership in Tunisian exile, a new brand of Islamist-led resistance emerged. Hamas transformed and re-invigorated the 40-year-old conflict by combining nationalism with militant Islam.

The First Intifada ended when the USA, Israel's principal backer, brokered a deal (the Oslo Agreement, 1994–5) by which the PLO renounced violence, Israel undertook to withdraw from Palestinian areas, and a Palestinian National Authority (PNA) was established to govern Gaza and the West Bank. Extremists on both sides rejected the compromise and soon tit-for-tat violence had restarted. Palestinian militants used bombs and fired mortars and short-range rockets into Israel. Israel responded by moving into Palestinian areas with disproportionate force.

Impasse

When further talks broke down in 2000 and the PNA proved intolerably corrupt, a Second Intifada broke out. All the while, the Israeli policy of building settlements in occupied East Jerusalem and the West Bank made reconciliation less possible. Some of these encroachments were defended by the massive 'security fence' by which Israel separated its citizens from the West Bank.

The death of Arafat (2004) and the election of Mahmoud Abbas to head the PNA gave new hope of a deal. So did an Israeli withdrawal from Gaza (2005) and the progress of a flexible Road Map peace plan. Set against this was a split between Fatah and Hamas, and the latter's seizure of control of Gaza in 2007. This weakened the Palestinian position and put power in the hands of those to whom the very idea of a compromise was anathema. Impasse resulted.

10 Only got ten minutes?

Historic roots

The land between the Mediterranean and the River Jordan has always been considered holy. After classical times, the territory was inhabited mainly by Muslims of Arab stock, with some Jews, Christians and others. In the later nineteenth century, Jews emigrated there in growing numbers. Their motives were mixed. Some believed they were returning to a promised land, others simply wanted a new life safe among people of their own kind.

The indigenous inhabitants had gradually developed a common identity that on occasion expressed itself as 'Palestinian'. Inevitably, tensions arose between these indigenous Arabs and the Jewish immigrants.

Between the wars, Britain governed Palestine as a League of Nations mandate. When its administrators failed to reconcile the two communities, they decided that the territory should be divided into Jewish and Palestinian states. The USA approved this plan, and after World War II, so did the newly formed United Nations.

Israel

The Jews welcomed the two-state idea, especially as the proposed State of Israel would give them far more land. The Palestinian Arabs objected strongly, as the proposal would legitimize the loss of much Arab land. Desultory fighting developed into all-out warfare when the Jews pre-emptively announced the formation of the State of Israel in 1948. It was the better-organized and better-equipped Israelis who triumphed.

During the fighting (1948–9), the Israelis extended the frontiers of their new country dramatically, creating hundreds of thousands of Palestinian refugees. The war also saw Gaza and the West Bank occupied by Egypt and Jordan respectively. Palestinians now found themselves under Israeli or Arab occupation or living in exile. This set the scene for one of the longest running and most bitter conflicts of modern times.

War

Western governments, suffused with guilt over the Nazi Holocaust and under pressure from Jewish lobbies, tended to support Israel. Arab nations endorsed the Palestinian cause, though more in their words than in their actions. During the era of the Cold War, the USA backed Israel, while the Soviet Union was generally pro-Palestine. Thus the Israel–Palestine question became an issue of global importance.

The dispossessed Palestinian Arabs found a powerful voice in the Palestine Liberation Organization (PLO, founded in 1964) and its charismatic chairman Yasser Arafat. Meanwhile the Israelis implemented their resolution never to be persecuted again by building up large, well-equipped and well-organized armed forces. These enabled it to come out on top in three more wars against its Arab neighbours (1956, 1966 and 1973). In the second of these, the Six-Day War, the Israelis overran Gaza and the West Bank and took the Golan Heights from Syria. This brought even more Palestinians under direct Israeli rule.

The Islamic ingredient

Now that Israel controlled all the territory originally allocated to Israel and Palestine, as well as the Golan Heights, the PLO took refuge in neighbouring Jordan. They soon fell out with the government of King Hussein and were driven north into Lebanon in 1970.

Here too the PLO proved a destabilizing influence. In 1982, Israel became involved in Lebanon's long-running civil war, invading the country and besieging the PLO in Beirut. Arafat and his supporters had to move again, this time to Tunis. Meanwhile, to the chagrin of the Arab world, Israel had made peace with Egypt (Camp David Agreement, 1978). Reconciliation with Jordan followed in 1994.

Arafat's organization, Fatah, was essentially nationalist and secular. The picture became infinitely more complicated when Fatah's leadership was challenged by Islamist organizations, most notably Hamas. This had emerged during a spontaneous upsurge of Palestinian resistance to Israeli domination know as the First Intifada (1987–91). With the Fatah leadership in exile, the Sunni militants of Hamas won support through their grass-roots activities.

Oslo and beyond

Arafat eventually returned home to a very different world. Under the terms of the Oslo Accords (1994), Israel recognized the PLO, which in turn renounced violence. An elected Palestinian National Authority (PNA) was set up to govern in the West Bank and Gaza, and Israel agreed to withdraw from certain occupied areas as a prelude to a comprehensive settlement.

Oslo was rejected by powerful interests on both sides. Many Palestinians baulked at a compromise that left them still stateless and governed by President Arafat's Fatah-dominated, scandalously corrupt PNA. In Israel, right-wing and religious groups refused to accept the surrender of conquered land. Such views led to the assassination of Prime Minister Yitzhak Rabin (1995). Israel countered Palestinian terrorist-style attacks on civilian targets with disproportionate force, sweeping into areas they had withdrawn from and assassinating Palestinian militant leaders.

Fragmented pictures

By 2000, the population of Israel had grown to around 5,700,000, more than a million of whom were what the Israelis called 'Arabs' but whom others referred to as 'Israeli Palestinians'. Most were settled but perhaps 250,000 were still considered refugees within Israel.

Jewish Israelis were known as either Ashkenazim (loosely those of western European origin) or Sephardim or Mizrahim (loosely those of eastern origin). Their religious persuasions varied from the secular, to Reform, Orthodox and Ultra-Orthodox branches of Judaism. In the israeli electoral system, politics and religion overlapped and intertwined to make the rational course of government rarely the most practicable.

The Palestinian picture was similarly fragmented. No one knew exactly how many there were. By 2000, there were just over 1 million Palestinians inside Israel and perhaps another 1,850,000 or more in the West Bank and Gaza. Beyond that, in the refugee camps and suburbs of Syria, Lebanon and Jordan, working around the Gulf and elsewhere, no one knew. Several estimates offered a figure of between 1.5 and 2 million.

Wherever they were, Palestinians shared a common heritage of a lost land and an exile culture of poetry, song and story. From the 1980s onwards, their human tragedy was increasingly mixed with religious war.

On and on ...

Before he left office, US President Bill Clinton came close to brokering a two-state peace settlement. When the talks eventually broke down, a Second Intifada erupted (2000), this time bearing a distinctly Islamic hue. The situation became still more chaotic as Fatah and Hamas drifted further apart until, following Arafat's death in 2004, they were in open conflict. Turning their back on a negotiated settlement, the Israelis began a policy of unilateral disengagement and withdrawal behind defence barriers along their frontiers.

Peace initiatives from the Arab world (2002 onwards) and the West (the Roadmap, 2002 onwards) came and went, but still the cycle of attack and counter-attack continued. After Israel withdrew its Gaza settlements in 2004, Hamas seized control there and the rocket bombardment of Israel intensified. Israel retaliated with a massive invasion of the territory in 2009. Three years earlier, it had launched a similar retaliatory assault on the Shia Islamist group Hezbollah operating out of southern Lebanon.

All the while, Israel maintained its 'facts on the ground' policy of expanding settlements in East Jerusalem and on the West Bank. Mahmoud Abbas, Arafat's PNA replacement, held numerous talks, some of which offered hope of a settlement, but each time the soft centre of moderate opinion was incapacitated by the hardliners on both sides. One day this dreadful deadlock will come to an end, as all things must, but quite how it is impossible to say.

1

Biblical beginnings 2500 BC to the nineteenth century

In this chapter you will learn:

- ***the origins of the terms 'Palestine' and 'Israel'***
- ***about Palestine in classical times***
- ***about Crusader and Ottoman Palestine***
- ***about the religions of Judaism and Islam.***

This is a story of two peoples and one land. Throughout the twentieth century and beyond, the Palestinians and the Israelis have fought bitterly over a small strip of territory, about 192 kilometres long, that lies between the shore of the eastern Mediterranean and a line, about 64 kilometres further east, marked by the River Jordan, Lake Galilee (Tiberias) and the Dead Sea. The conflict has caused countless deaths and brought immeasurable suffering and hardship. Moreover, for more than 60 years, it has destabilized the entire Middle East.

The historical origins of this tragic impasse lie in the nineteenth century. Its complexity, ferocity and longevity, however, cannot really be understood without some knowledge of migrations and struggles as ancient as human civilization itself.

Philistines and Jews

THE FERTILE CRESCENT

The land with which we are concerned was once part of what scholars term the 'Fertile Crescent' (see Figure 1.1). Around 10,000 years ago, in this broad arc stretching from the Rivers Tigris and Euphrates to the Nile Valley, some of the earliest human civilizations emerged. Considering the region's low rainfall, made worse by its underlying porous limestone and hot, harsh summer weather, the decision of our distant ancestors to build their first permanent habitations here might appear almost perverse. However, at the time, closer by some ten millennia to the end of the last Ice Age, the Earth was cooler than today and the fruitful crescent was greener and its climate more clement.

Under these favourable circumstances farming flourished, allowing settled rather than nomadic communities to develop. One of the first permanently inhabited sites was on a small hill, just north of the Dead Sea and less than 16 kilometres west of the River Jordan, which received a plentiful supply of fresh water from a lively spring. By *c.* 8000 BC, it had become one of the world's first towns. Enclosed within its massive stone defensive wall, some 2,500 people lived. The site, abandoned and resettled many times over the millennia, approximates to the modern town of Jericho.

The natives of the earliest Jericho have long since disappeared and their city and the land around it has served as home to many other peoples. Some called it a 'promised land', a 'land of milk and honey', although it was not just fertility that over the years made this scrap of coastal plain and inland hills so attractive. It was, and still is, of considerable strategic importance from both a military and commercial point of view. Its main roads link Egypt to Syria, and the Mediterranean to Jordan and Iraq. Whoever controlled this vital thoroughfare had great power.

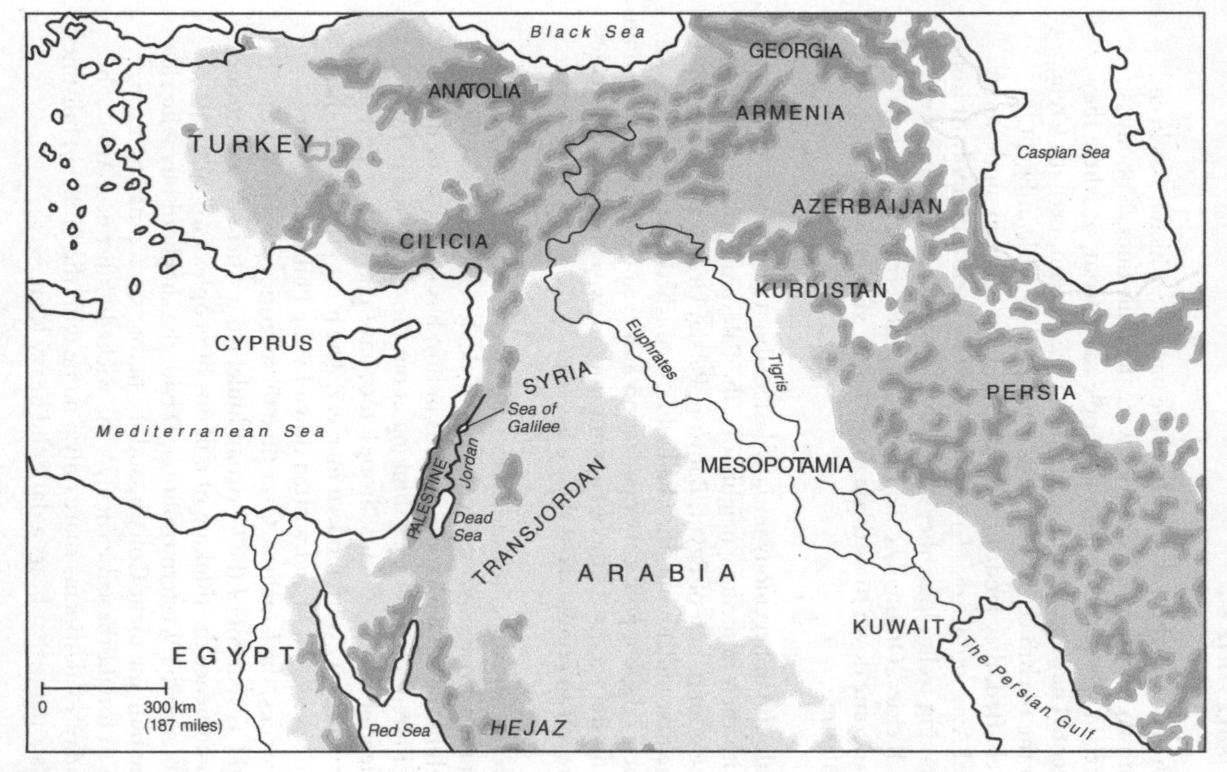

Figure 1.1 The geography of the Middle East; the darker areas indicate high ground.

PALESTINE

The people who gave this land the name by which it has been known for most of its history were the Philistines. Nobody is certain where these vigorous people came from, or where they went. They emerged, it seems, from the Aegean, perhaps Crete, in the twelfth century BC, and attempted to settle in Egypt. Rebuffed, they landed on the coastal strip between modern-day Tel Aviv and Gaza. Here, empowered by their monopoly of iron-making technology, they established themselves and built five rich cities. Originally called 'Philistia', the territory they inhabited has come down to us through the Greek version of its name – Palestine.

Palestinian hegemony initially lasted about 300 years. After conflict with their immediate neighbours, the Palestinians later fell under the domination of Egypt, Babylon, Persia, Greece and Rome. By the first millennium, they had all but vanished as a distinct people: their religion, political organization and even their language remain a mystery to us. Little but a name and a few semi-historical stories are left to remind us of their existence.

Nevertheless, names and stories are potent cultural symbols. In the Christian West, a cruel linguistic development has linked 'philistine' to barbarity, and this in turn has subconsciously coloured some people's thinking about those who today call themselves Palestinians. Stories, too, have played their part in creating awkward modern imagery. The most powerful of these stories were told and written down by the Philistines' great enemies, the Israelites. Over time these stories passed into the Old Testament of the Christian Bible, from where they continue to influence the thinking of millions of people. Two cultural icons of the Western tradition, David, the shepherd boy who slew the bullying giant Goliath, and the heroic strong-man Samson, both fought the same enemy – the wicked Philistines. Although today's Palestinians share only a name with the Biblical Philistines, it's a name that bears a dark and heavy legacy.

Insight

German students once used the term 'Philistines' pejoratively to mean outsiders i.e. townspeople not at their university. The nineteenth-century English writer Thomas Carlyle was among the first to employ the term to denote someone who was thought to be uncultured.

ISRAEL

If the Palestinian name presents difficulties, they are as nothing compared with those surrounding the second group that here concerns us, the Israelis. We begin with a Semitic people who called themselves 'Hebrews'. Interestingly, 'Hebrew' seems to be related to the word 'Habiru', meaning an outsider or bandit. The Hebrews may have been part of the band of warriors whom the Egyptians beat off – the future Philistines. In other words, the Hebrews and the Philistines might have a common ancestry. Other scholars claim that DNA testing shows the Hebrews to be more closely related to the peoples of the northern part of the Fertile Crescent, such as Kurds, Turks and Armenians.

'Hebrew' is the same as 'Yehudi', which the Romans wrote in Latin as 'Judaeus' and from which derives the French 'Juif', the German 'Jude' and the English 'Jew'. The Hebrews, divided into 12 tribes, were said to be descended from Jacob, who was also known as 'Israel', meaning 'standing with God'. In about 1200 BC, these 12 Hebrew or Jewish tribes of Israel settled the land between the Mediterranean and the River Jordan. To cut short a long and extremely complicated story, they fought the Philistines, with varying degrees of success, and also fell out among themselves, splitting into northern and southern kingdoms. The north was conquered and its scattered citizens largely absorbed into other peoples of the region, although some survived as a distinct group in Persia. The southern Hebrews remained a separate entity in an area that others knew as the Kingdom of Judah (of the Jews) but which the Jews themselves came to refer to as the Land of Israel.

Bound together by their powerful and distinctive religion, which taught that they were the people chosen by the one god, Yahweh, the Jews of the Land of Israel maintained their identity despite periodic repression and deportation by Assyrians, Babylonians, Persians and the Hellenistic (Greek-style) Seleucids. Their state was based around the city of Jerusalem, at the heart of which lay the great temple. Despite this focus, however, by the second century BC, the Jews were already known as a scattered people found in most countries of the Middle East and beyond. The diffusion of the Jews is known by the Greek word 'diaspora', meaning 'dispersal' (see p. 15).

Conquest, Christianity and Islam

ROME

During the first century BC, Rome extended its power across the Mediterranean world and beyond. To begin with, its control over Judea was tactful and light-handed. This changed following serious revolts against Roman rule in 66–73 AD and 132–5 AD. Legions sent to restore imperial control razed Jerusalem to the ground and utterly destroyed its new temple, slew or exiled thousands of Jews, and established Roman colonies in their former homeland. Even the name 'Judea' went, replaced by the Roman province of 'Palaestina'. Jerusalem was rebuilt as Aelia Capitolina, a city that no Jew was allowed to enter. Those remaining in the region lived further north, in and around Galilee. Hebrew all but disappeared as a spoken language.

By 150 AD, therefore, the Jewish state, like the Philistine one before it, was nothing but a fading memory. Yet the Judean land – Palaestina, or Palestine as it will henceforth be called – continued to flourish because of its strategic, commercial and religious importance. It flourished even more when the Roman Empire formally adopted Christianity in the fourth century. Almost overnight, from being a troublesome outpost of empire, Palestine became its religious heartland. Pilgrims and others seeking spiritual solace flooded into the 'Holy Land'. Many new churches were built, including the Church of the Holy Sepulchre in Jerusalem. Towns grew and agriculture expanded as Palestine enjoyed what has become known as a 'golden age'. Some say that not until the twentieth century would the land again enjoy such prosperity.

BYZANTIUM

The Roman Empire was by now divided in two, the Western part remaining under the rule of Rome and the Eastern owing allegiance to an emperor based in the ancient city of Byzantium (soon renamed Constantinople; nowadays Istanbul). Palestine came under Byzantine control and for administrative purposes was also divided in two.

With one eye on the twentieth century, when two peoples would claim that Palestine belonged to them by right, we may wonder who lived in Palestine at this time. Precise ethnic or racial definitions are impossible to ascertain; even if they were, they would be largely irrelevant to a society that did not think in our terms of nation or race. Instead, there were three principal cohesive bonds: the empire and its local manifestation in the form of the governor or prince; family and tribe; and religion.

By these criteria, the Palestine of the early seventh century AD bore little relation to the modern region. The overarching allegiance was to Constantinople. As the land had been peopled by a variety of conquerors and settlers for thousands of years, its family and tribal pattern was extremely complex. There was a handful of Arabs – Arabic-speaking desert peoples who worshipped a variety of gods – and there were probably a few dozen Jewish communities. The great majority of those living in Palestine (the modern term 'Palestinian' would be anachronistic) were Christians who spoke Aramaic, although Latin, Greek and other languages were also used. A few pockets of paganism remained in which ancient deities such as the fish-god Dagon were worshipped. It was all a very long way from the explosive mixture that would detonate so forcefully 1,300 years later.

ISLAM

A major ingredient of the twentieth-century conflict was added in the 630s. Byzantine power was already under threat. Early in the century, a Persian army had overrun Palestine and destroyed its churches. Understandably, but perhaps unwisely, the Jews had sided with the invaders, so the recapture of the province by the Byzantines was accompanied by a retaliatory slaughter of the Jews. Seven years later, the Byzantines were driven out again, this time for good.

Insight

Arabs and Jews (along with several other Middle Eastern peoples) are probably both descended from Semite ancestors who migrated north from the Arabian peninsula around 2500 BC.

The latest wave of invaders were Arabs inspired by a new religion, Islam. The conquest was launched by Abu Bakar, the first caliph (successor to the Prophet Mohammed), who united Arabia and announced a Holy War – Jihad – to spread Islam further afield. His successor, Caliph Umar, executed the same policy with dramatic success. Under his leadership, the Muslim Empire expanded east into Persia, north into Armenia and west into Libya. Palestine was taken in 636, although Jerusalem held out for two more years. Umar's successors of the Umayyad Dynasty made Damascus the capital of their empire and maintained Palestine (Filastin), with a capital at Ramlah, as an administrative district of the province of Syria.

MUSLIM PALESTINE

The new conquest did not immediately alter the face of Palestine all that much. There were two reasons for this. First, the conquering Arabs were very few in number and had to rely on native peoples to maintain their empire's administration and agricultural and commercial life. Second, the Umayyad Muslims, whose dynasty lasted until 750, showed considerable tolerance towards other 'people of the book' – Christians and Jews who shared Islam's monotheistic heritage.

Over time, however, the situation changed. The Umayyads were succeeded by the Abbasids (750–1258), whose capital was Baghdad. Needing a power base to the west, they paid special attention to Palestine and encouraged large-scale conversion to Islam. As Arabic was (and still is) the language of Islam, it gradually spread as the province's common language. Simultaneously, there was a steady influx of Arab people from the more arid lands to the east and south. Jerusalem was adorned with remarkable new Islamic architecture (see pp. 16–17). At the same time, a small Jewish community re-established itself in the city – Muslims did not share the Christian antipathy towards those supposedly responsible for the death of Jesus Christ.

The Palestinian battlefield

CRUSADERS

Palestine was rarely at peace during the Abbasid Caliphate. Invasion, oppression and massacre were frequent, lending the land more the aspect of a battlefield than a place of habitation. The population, which in the heyday of Byzantine peace and prosperity may have reached 1 million, fell to perhaps a quarter of that.

In the tenth and eleventh centuries, Palestine was conquered first by the Fatimid Dynasty from Egypt, then by the Seljuqs (Turks from south-west Asia) and finally by Christian crusaders from Western Europe. The latter, who took Jerusalem in 1099 and the following year established the Christian Kingdom of Jerusalem, were a rag-bag coalition led by kings and princes on the make. No doubt some of their number were fired by a genuine wish to see the holy places of the Bible in Christian hands, but the motives of many were a great deal less idealistic. Conquest is rarely an altruistic undertaking.

Insight

When al-Qaeda leader Saed Elshari said he would 'cut the tails of the crusaders' and 'destroy the dreams of crusade' (*Al Jazeera*, February 2010), it was simply one of numerous examples of Islamists using the powerful 'crusader' image to inspire support for their campaign against the West.

Palestine was in Christian hands until the emergence of Salah al-Din Yusuf ibn Ayyub, a formidable warrior and administrator of Kurdish extraction. Better known in the West as Saladin, he smashed the crusaders in battle and took Jerusalem. Although the Europeans fought back and managed to recapture the city, by 1244 it was back under Islamic governance and remained so for the next 700 years.

Sadly for Palestine, the end of the crusader kingdom did not bring peace. The next power to take control were the Mamluks – a dynasty descended from the slave warriors, mostly of Turkish origin, who had played a key role in Islamic armies. In the later thirteenth century, having defeated a force of invading Mongols, the ex-slaves killed the sultan and established themselves as a ruling dynasty in Cairo.

OTTOMANS

The last power to seize and hold Palestine before modern times were the Ottoman Turks. Named after their first notable leader, Osman, the Ottomans were a nomadic Turkman people whose military prowess was encouraged by their being sandwiched between two much larger powers, the Mongols in the east and the Byzantine Empire in the west. Finding the Byzantines the weaker of the two, the Ottomans began a series of conquests that took them into Arabia and Egypt and even to the gates of Vienna. In the process, they swallowed up Palestine (1516).

For most of the next 400 years, Palestine remained more or less under Ottoman rule. For administrative purposes it was divided into three: the districts of Nabulus and Acre (modern-day

Akko or Akka), which were subordinated to Damascus; and Jerusalem, which was under the direct control of Istanbul, the Ottoman capital. Under these arrangements, which gave leading local families (the 'notables') a great deal of power, the various inhabitants of Palestine lived for some three centuries.

The majority of the population were Arabic-speaking Muslims, and therefore came under the loose definition of 'Arab'. Christians made up perhaps a fifth of the population, depending on the degree of toleration being shown at the time, and there were always several thousand Jews. Relations between the communities flared periodically into violence, and the history of the period is punctuated by bouts of civil turmoil and war.

SIGNS OF CHANGE

Ottoman rule was not without its advantages. In the sixteenth century, Jerusalem benefited from major public works, which included a new water system and massive surrounding walls. During the eighteenth century, trade and urban life picked up after a century of decline. Nevertheless, early modern Palestine was an isolated, backward and surprisingly unvisited land. Few pilgrims went there and the handful of European visitors who made the journey were shocked at the dilapidated state of its buildings and historic monuments. When the Frenchman Constantin Volney travelled to Palestine five years before the French Revolution, he declared that Jerusalem was in such a sorry state that he had difficulty recognizing it.

The first catalyst for change came when Emperor Napoleon invaded Egypt and marched into Palestine with the intention of establishing a French empire in the Middle East. Disease, the British fleet, and Ottoman arms put an end to these unrealistic dreams. Nevertheless, a legacy survived. In a vain effort to rally local support, Napoleon had said he would restore Jerusalem to the Jews if they helped him in his conquest of Palestine. The offer was rejected. Even so, the French not only opened Palestine to the outside world, but also sowed an imperial idea that would take root and grow in other minds. The French might not have settled in Palestine, but in the next century others would. Their arrival had consequences few could have foreseen.

The land of faith

JUDAISM

Judaism was the only one of the three major Middle Eastern religions linked to a specific people – the Jews (Islam was espoused to a language, Arabic, but not to a race). At Judaism's heart lay the belief that the one God – creator of the universe and the embodiment of divine love and divine justice – had chosen the Jews to be the vehicle of His way: 'For you are a people consecrated to the Lord your God: of all the peoples on earth the Lord your God chose you to be His treasured people' (*Book of Deuteronomy*).

The Jews' very personal God had made a pact or covenant with them: in return for being His chosen people they were to obey His pattern and structure of life set out in His teaching, in the Biblical Torah and the post-Biblical Mishna. This led to a division between Orthodox Jews, who took the Torah literally and interpreted it strictly, and Reformed Jews who adopted a more liberal, individualistic approach. Nevertheless, both believed that one day their efforts would be crowned by the arrival of the Redeemer, the Messiah, whose brilliance would allow all other people to recognize God's ways and adopt them. Then the whole earth would bear witness to the love, peace and justice of God.

Another part of God's covenant involved giving His people a specific 'Promised Land' – 'Judah' or 'Israel' – with its sacred capital of Jerusalem. However, after the Diaspora (see p. 15) very few Jews actually lived in their former kingdom and only a few went back there on pilgrimage. Until the nineteenth century, most Jews understood 'returning to the Promised Land' in a non-literal way, meaning the establishment of perfect peace and harmony on earth.

ISLAM

Islam, which means literally 'surrender' (to God or 'Allah'), is the historical successor to Judaism and Christianity. Inheriting aspects of both, it accepts the Biblical figures of Noah, Moses and Jesus as true prophets. It reserves the position of last and greatest prophet for Mohammed, a seventh-century inhabitant of the Arabian town of Medina who, Muslims believe, received God's word via the Angel Gabriel. Mohammed had God's word written down in the Koran. Hence the basic Muslim profession of faith: 'There is no god but God; Mohammed is the prophet of God.'

The Koran, backed up by early traditions set out in the Hadith, forms the basis of the Muslim faith. This incorporates a set of specified religious practices and, more widely, an entire way of life. These link Islam to politics so that, before the twentieth century, the idea of an Islamic country with a non-sectarian government was an anathema.

Insight

On his way home after his first revelation of the word of Allah, the prophet Mohammed saw a vision of the angel Gabriel against a wholly green sky. The colour remains that of the Muslim faith to this day.

Islam's blunt simplicity gave believers certainty and self-confidence: they had accepted the right way and so were destined for a heaven redolent with physical as well as spiritual delights. The unwavering rituals of prayer five times a day, the annual fast and the once-in-a-lifetime pilgrimage to Mecca, placed the lives of believers within a secure and reassuring framework. The faith's emphasis on community – the essential equality of all believers and the need for the wealthy and fortunate to support those less well-positioned than themselves – helped it to acquire a mass following.

From the beginning, Islam displayed undertones of violence that distressed adherents of more pacific beliefs and philosophies. Much of the faith's early expansion was carried out by a Holy War (*Jihad*), and from time to time since then, more extreme Muslim groups have resurrected the concept of *Jihad* to justify armed resistance to perceived oppression.

Insight

Jihad, one of Islam's most contentious teachings, is interpreted variously as military war or as a battle with the demons within one's erring soul.

Despite the precise nature of many of its teachings, Islam has had its fair share of schisms and splits. The largest and most enduring of these began with a dispute over the leadership of the movement and the two sides went on to adopt distinctly separate theological positions. The majority, including most Arab Muslims, are the Sunni. The minority, based originally in Iran (Persia), are the Shia.

Toleration and conflict

For centuries Jews and Muslims were generally much more tolerant of each other than Christians were towards either. From the point of view of the Palestinian Arabs, from the mid-nineteenth to mid-twentieth centuries their conflict with immigrant Jews was not primarily a matter of religion but of land. The same was not true of all Jews, however. As we shall see (p. 24), the movement for a return to the Promised Land had the powerful backing of Orthodox religious leaders.

It is important to note at this stage that the Palestinian community has always contained a fair number of Christians, some of whom have been highly influential. Ibrahim Sus, for example, one of the Palestine Liberation Organization's (PLO) representatives in Paris, was a Christian. It is no great surprise, therefore, that it took so long for Palestinian anger towards the Israelis to acquire a religious hue. When it did though, it raised the conflict to new levels of bitterness, intolerance and violence.

In depth: the Jewish Diaspora

The Jewish people, identified by their distinguishing faith, originally appeared on the historical records in the region of Palestine. Between the eighth century BC and the second century AD, huge numbers of Jews were either driven from Palestine or voluntarily migrated elsewhere. As a result, for almost 2,000 years the Jews remained physically dispersed yet managed to retain an extraordinary religio-cultural cohesion. This paradox – unity despite disunity – is what has generally become known as the Jewish Diaspora.

Historically, the Diaspora began with the destruction of the northern Jewish kingdom in the eighth century BC and the dispersal of many of its citizens (see p. 5). Then came the Babylonian Captivity when the southern kingdom of Judah was conquered, the Jewish Temple in Jerusalem destroyed, and many Jews taken to exile in Babylon (in Mesopotamia).

By the first century AD, there were more Jews living outside Palestine than within. The contrast was even sharper following the brutal suppression of the anti-Roman revolts of 66–73 AD and 123–35 AD that involved the total destruction of the rebuilt Temple. Henceforward, the Jewish faith and way of life were maintained not by a central authority but by rabbis and law codified in the Mishna and Talmud (see p. 12).

Over the following centuries, Jewish communities were established around the Mediterranean and Middle East, then in Western and Eastern Europe and, eventually, in the United States of America. Even after years of immigration to Palestine and Israel in the twentieth and twenty-first centuries, the Jews of the Diaspora – those living outside the 'Promised Land' – remained a majority. In 2005, for example, Israel's Jewish population was outnumbered by the 5 million Jews living in the USA. A further 1 million lived in the former USSR and another 500,000 in France.

(Contd)

In Jewish teaching, the term 'Diaspora' has a variety of religious and philosophical connotations. The very idea of 'scattering', for instance, emphasizes the place from which the dispersal took place – i.e. Judea/Israel. Thus Orthodox Jews support the return of Jews to the modern land of Israel in preparation for the arrival of God's Messiah (see p. 12). Reform Jews, on the other hand, hold that the scattering of the Jews around the world was part of a divine mission to spread knowledge of the One God.

In depth: Jerusalem, holy city

Jerusalem, a city uniquely holy to three faiths, lies at the very heart of the Israeli–Palestinian conflict. As well as being dear to Christian hearts as the place of Jesus' death and resurrection, for Jews it is both holy and historically precious, while it is also the third holiest site in Islam.

The Jews did not found Jerusalem. However, at the end of the eleventh century BC, King David conquered the city and made it the political and religious capital of his kingdom. His successor, Solomon, built the first Temple on a platform known as Temple Mount. Strict Jews believe that the divine presence has never left this sacred spot. Although the first and second Temples have long since been destroyed, part of the Mount's ancient western retaining wall remains intact. Known as the Wailing Wall, it is paramount as the physical focal point for Jewish worship and prayer.

The Prophet Mohammed, who openly acknowledged the Jewish and Christian roots of his teaching, knew the spiritual importance of Jerusalem in the monotheistic world. Indeed, he bade his followers face Mecca when praying only after he had failed to attract Jews to his faith by ordaining that the direction should be towards Jerusalem. There is also a tradition that one night a winged horse named Lightning had carried Mohammed from Mecca to Jerusalem. Here, from the Sacred Rock that once marked the centre of Solomon's Temple, the Prophet had climbed a ladder of light to heaven. He noted the delights there, met Allah, then returned to Mecca the way he had come.

True or not, this story was sufficient to make Jerusalem a site worthy of Islamic pilgrimage. At the end of the seventh century, a magnificent, gold-capped shrine, known as the Dome of the Rock, was built over the place from which Mohammed was said to have made his ascent. A few years later, the impressive Al Aqsa Mosque was erected nearby.

For over 400 years, Ottoman and British control over Jerusalem saved it from excessive sectarian nationalist feuding. This changed in 1948. After Israel had declared itself an independent state, its forces seized West Jerusalem (see p. 67) and the city was made the capital of the new state. Nineteen years later, Israeli troops occupied the entire city. This event presented would-be peacemakers with a conundrum that none of them has yet managed to solve.

10 THINGS TO REMEMBER

1 *The roots of the modern Israel-Palestine conflict reach back to the early human settlements of the Fertile Crescent at the very dawn of history.*

2 *By 150* AD*, the Romans had annihilated the first Jewish state, scattering its population far and wide.*

3 *The dispersal of the Jews over the globe is known as the Jewish Diaspora.*

4 *Islam emerged in the first half of the seventh century* AD *and swiftly spread over a huge area through Arab military campaigns.*

5 *Christian attacks on the Holy Land in medieval times provide today's Islamists with a powerful image of aggressive Western imperialism in the Middle East.*

6 *Between the early sixteenth and twentieth centuries, the Holy Land was part of the Turkish Ottoman Empire.*

7 *The three leading monotheistic religions – Judaism, Christianity and Islam – share a common heritage as well as a reverence for the ancient city of Jerusalem.*

8 Jihad *(Islamic holy war) can be interpreted as a physical or spiritual struggle.*

9 *The two principal divisions within Islam are between Sunni (the majority) and Shia (the minority, based largely in Iran).*

10 *Until modern times, Jews and Muslims were usually notably tolerant of each other.*

2

Whose land? c. 1815 to 1918

In this chapter you will learn about:

- ***the development of nineteenth-century Palestine***
- ***the emergence of Zionism***
- ***Arab nationalism and the roots of Palestinian national awareness***
- ***diplomatic wranglings over Palestine during World War I.***

During the century or so that elapsed between the withdrawal of Napoleon and the ending of World War I, Palestine changed more swiftly and dramatically than at any other period in its previous history. Slowly at first but with gathering momentum, a thinly populated Middle Eastern backwater was transformed into a burgeoning, bustling and cosmopolitan land rarely off the front pages of the world's newspapers. Sadly, the news was not all good.

Although by 1918 the Ottoman Empire had collapsed, the people of Palestine were not in control of their own destiny. New masters, the British, were imposing their distinctive style of paternalistic colonial rule on the territory. More depressing in the long run, the swelling population of Jews and Arabs was becoming more divided almost by the day. Two forces had been at work, imperialism and nationalism, creating an inflammatory mix that would soon catch fire and burn for decades.

Nineteenth-century Palestine

REFORM AND REBELLION

It is estimated that the population of Palestine at the time of Napoleon's visit was probably no more than 250,000. Jerusalem, a shabby shadow of its former glory, housed around 8,750 souls, of whom some 4,000 were Muslim, 2,750 Christian and 2,000 Jewish. The other principal towns – Nablus, Hebron and Ramallah – were little more than large villages, and the Mediterranean ports, with the exception of Acre, were tired and inward-looking.

As noted (p. 11), the brief French occupation introduced Palestine to the wider world. More important was the occupation 40 years later by the forces of the independent viceroy of Egypt, Mehemet Ali, who was carving out an empire of his own within that of the Ottomans. Led by the viceroy's adopted son, Ibrahim Pasha, the Egyptian force not only took over Palestine but also set about introducing a series of administrative and economic reforms intended to make the province more efficient and profitable. Change was not welcome and the demands for taxation and conscripts provoked a fierce uprising, based in Nablus, which was crushed with blood-curdling ferocity.

The Egyptians' attempt to take over the entire Ottoman Empire was halted when a coalition of European powers intervened and the rule of the Ottoman sultan in Istanbul was restored. A lesson had been learned, however, and over the years that followed, the Ottomans pursued a number of policies similar to those introduced by the Egyptians. Town councils improved local administration and an attempt was made at more efficient tax collection. Land ownership had to be registered, making purchase easier. From 1867, to encourage investment, for the first time foreigners were allowed to buy land within the Ottoman Empire. In an effort to boost the standing of Russian Orthodoxy in the city, no less a person than the Tsar of Russia bought several Jerusalem properties.

ECONOMIC EXPANSION

Comparatively speaking, the economy boomed as measures to encourage cash crops rather than subsistence farming were introduced. Large estates took over unregistered land and prospered, especially those with enough capital to move from cereal crops into orange trees. By the end of the century, Palestinian oranges, soap and olive oil were being exported in large quantities to Europe. This in turn helped the ports. The population of Haifa, for example, rose from around 3,000 in 1830, to 6,000 by 1850 and 20,000 by the outbreak of World War I. Communications slowly improved to cope with demand. By 1914, railways linked the coastal towns to each other, to Jerusalem and to the line running from Damascus to Arabia.

At the same time, the population of Palestine was rising dramatically. From a mere 250,000 at the beginning of the nineteenth century, it had tripled by 1914. Much of this increase was due to the rising birth rate, improved public health and lower infant mortality. There were other factors at work in the sharp economic upturn – and this is where the rosy picture takes on a somewhat darker hue.

IMMIGRATION

As well as a flood of pilgrims, including the Emperor of Germany, European immigrants arrived from France, Russia and Germany. Some have termed the incoming wave of non-Muslims as an 'unarmed crusade'. Many Christians came for religious reasons, establishing and maintaining monasteries, schools, surgeries and missions. They came singly or in small family or other groups. The sultan expressly forbade the immigration of large, cohesive groups for fear they would disrupt existing social and administrative patterns. His ban, reissued several times, was easily avoided.

The sultan's prohibition was aimed at a specific type of immigrant, the European Jew. As we have seen, there had been Jews in Palestine since time immemorial. Despite the Diaspora and periodic persecution, a handful had remained in specific settlements, notably in Jerusalem and in the Galilee region. Their numbers had been growing. A census taken in 1844, for instance, revealed that they had become Jerusalem's largest religious group. Even so, they comprised no more than 15 per cent of Palestine's total population. In the years immediately before World War I, however, the situation was beginning to change noticeably.

The number of Palestinian Jews doubled between 1840 and 1870. In 1880 it had reached 24,000, by 1900 it was perhaps around 60,000, and some estimates claim that by 1914 it was as high as 100,000. At the same time, Jewish families were living away from traditional areas of settlement and engaging in a far wider range of occupations than had hitherto been the case. Understandably, tension between the Muslim and Jewish communities rose.

Zionism

AFTER THE DIASPORA

The Diaspora left Jews living in relatively isolated communities around the world. As a distinctive minority, they were an obvious target for racial hatred and were subjected to almost continual discrimination and ill-informed hostility from both Christians and Muslims. From time to time this flared into full-scale slaughter, as happened in Arabia in the seventh century, all over Germany at the time of the Crusades, and periodically throughout Europe and the Middle East thereafter.

Prejudice gained official support when the Roman Catholic Church condemned the Jewish people as the 'killers of Christ'. An example of the sort of wild accusation Jews had to put up with was the charge of 'blood libel' – using the blood of a slaughtered child for ritual purposes.

Insight

Blood libel against Jews can be traced back to the first century AD. It told (falsely) how Jews kidnapped Christian boys, tortured them to death and used their blood in black magic rituals.

In the nineteenth century, an unholy alliance of the political right, the Roman Catholics, and the Orthodox Church blamed them for conspiring to bring about the excesses of the French Revolution. In Russia, popular misconception held them responsible for the assassination of Tsar Alexander II in 1882, a misconception that led to fierce pogroms.

Insight

Pogrom, meaning a violent attack on a specific racial group, was originally used for the attacks on Jewish communities in Russia that began in Odessa around the early part of the nineteenth century.

For centuries, persecution probably made Jewish communities more determined to maintain their faith and way of life. Then in the first half of the nineteenth century, a new attitude began to stir Jewish communities, particularly those in Eastern Europe. Instead of accepting persecution, they could do something about it: not by meeting violence with violence but by moving themselves out of the firing line. The movement that emerged was known as Zionism.

INTELLECTUAL FOUNDATIONS

Zionism was a drive to restore the Jewish people to the land their distant ancestors had occupied in Biblical times. Zion was Mount Zion in Jerusalem, a symbol of the Jewish homeland since the sixth century BC. Its emergence owed much to three factors: nationalism, imperialism and a Jewish religious movement that believed that the Jews could redeem themselves and hasten the arrival of the Messiah if they returned to the Holy Land and prepared it for His arrival.

Nationalism had been around since the late Middle Ages but it was given fresh impetus when the French Revolutionary armies broke up existing empires and encouraged national self-determination. The development gathered momentum over the course of the century that followed, leading to the establishment of the Kingdom of Italy, a united Germany, and many smaller independent states like Belgium, Greece and Serbia. With such templates before them, Jewish intellectuals wondered why their people too should not have a state of their own. The trouble was, where and how?

This is where imperialism came in. Just as the Jews saw new nations emerging all around them, so too they saw new empires being created and old ones expanding. The principal motives for the acquisition of these empires were commercial and political. They were justified, however, on less materialistic grounds. Scrupulous imperialists tended to claim that as Europeans were more politically, technologically and perhaps even morally advanced than the peoples they governed, it was their duty – 'the white man's burden' – to civilize them. The less scrupulous preferred a crude paraphrase of Darwin's thesis (1859): 'the survival of the fittest'. This was certainly the attitude of some Zionists, whose attitude towards the native Palestinian Arabs was anything but complimentary. This is implicit in the extraordinary Zionist slogan: 'A land without people for a people without land.' No one disputed the second half of the catchphrase, but to dismiss the 615,000 Muslim Arabs and 70,000 Christians living in Palestine in 1914 as non-existent was racist arrogance.

In the minds of some Orthodox Jews, nationalistic and imperialist impulses mixed with the theological idea of redemption. No longer did they have to wait for God to send his Messiah and deliver the Jews and all others from wickedness – instead the Jews could prove their eagerness for such deliverance by returning to the Holy Land, where the Messiah would appear, and preparing it for him. Such thinking appeared as early as 1834 in a book by the Serbian Jew, Yehuda hai Alkalai, who called for Jewish colonies in Palestine. In the years that followed, the call was taken up and expanded upon by other Jewish writers. It led in 1882 to the foundation of the *Hovevei Zion* (Lovers of Zion) movement, begun by a group of Jewish exiles meeting in Constantinople. They called unequivocally for 'a home in our country' that had been given to them by God – a gift 'registered in the archives of history'. By 'our country', of course, they meant Palestine.

THE JEWISH STATE

Until the 1890s, Zionism was primarily a religious and economic movement. Theodore Herzl made it a political one. An Austrian Jew working as a journalist and playwright, Herzl covered France's anti-Semitic Dreyfus scandal of 1894–5 for his newspaper. The story convinced him that the 'Jewish problem' could be solved only by the creation of a Jewish national homeland. He set out his ideas in a small but powerful and highly influential book, *The Jewish State* (1896). Interestingly, he did not specifically plump for Palestine as the place where this state might be established. A sparsely populated area of Argentina was one option and later a region in East Africa was suggested. For obvious reasons, neither was acceptable to religious Zionists.

> ***If the present generation is still too obtuse, another, better, more advanced generation will come along. Those Jews who want a state of their own will have one, and deservedly so.***
>
> (From Herzl's Preface to *The Jewish State*, 1896.)

The year after the publication of Herzl's book, a new body, the Zionist Organization, held its first meeting in Basle, Switzerland. (In 1960, it changed its name to the World Zionist Organization.) The mood was positively pro-Palestine and a mission was sent out to explore the ground. Its reply encapsulates with poetic precision what would become the tragedy of that land: 'The bride is beautiful but she is married to another man.' In other words, the region was well-suited to settlement but was already inhabited. Such sentiments might well have been expressed by British pioneers upon reaching the land they were to call Rhodesia; just as it did not stop them going ahead with their settlement plans, neither did it stop the Zionists.

Seeking official backing for his dream, Herzl made several visits to the Ottoman sultan. At one stage, in what might appear a parody of archetypal Jewishness, he even offered to buy Palestine! Deeply affronted, the sultan said the territory was not his to sell. Herzl's requests for special status for Jewish immigrants also came to nothing. In fact, in 1900, the Ottoman government even banned Jewish settlements in Palestine.

Istanbul's hostility to extensive Jewish immigration into Palestine had little practical outcome partly due to conditions on the ground and partly because Herzl had more success getting backing from the major European powers. The German Kaiser, who developed a close relationship with Istanbul in the years before World War I, was attracted by the idea of a Jewish Palestine pledged to support Germany commercially and politically. The British government had doubts about Palestine as a Jewish homeland, but British Jewry was rich and influential and there was always the hope that a friendly Palestine would further secure Britain's position in the Middle East. Furthermore, after a vicious pogrom in 1903, in which dozens of Russian Jews were killed and wounded, the Russian government came to see Jewish emigration to Palestine as a useful way to lessen domestic tensions.

COLONIZATION

The steady trickle of Jewish immigration into Palestine in the earlier years of the nineteenth century swelled markedly from about 1880 onwards. The Jews recognize two waves, known as the First and Second Aliyah (going up): 1882–1903 and 1904–13. As we have seen, although the numbers were not huge, by 1914 Jews were an appreciable minority – perhaps one-seventh – of the Palestinian population. More significant than their numbers, however, was what they were doing.

With the help of super-rich individuals such as Baron Edmund de Rothschild, followed later by organizations such as the Jewish National Fund (1905) and the Palestine Land Development Fund (1908), Jewish settlers were able to establish institutions, set up businesses, buy the best land and use it to grow the most profitable crops. It was up to five years, for instance, before a newly planted orange grove bore commercial quantities of fruit; few Arab farmers could afford to wait that long. A Jewish agricultural school was set up in 1870, the same year as Jewish settlers first made their homes on the coastal plain. Other institutions and settlements followed: de Rothschild funded a whole new village in 1882, a Hebrew high school opened in Jaffa in 1906, Tel Aviv was founded on land bought from the Turks in 1909, and two years later the first Jewish hospital opened. By now Palestinian communities were expressing alarm at what was beginning to look like an attempt to create a state within a state.

Insight

Jewish settlers founded Tel Aviv on the sand dunes north of the ancient Mediterranean port of Jaffa. By 1914, it had expanded to cover more than 100 hectares.

CONFRONTATION

Confrontation between Jews and Arabs was not inevitable. Herzl expressed a wish that two substantially sized communities would be able to live together in harmony, although the realism of this vision has to be questioned. Early friction between immigrants and the indigenous population arose not out of racist or even religious hatred but because of simple misunderstandings over questions such as the precise boundaries of the land Jews had purchased. By 1914, although Jews owned only about two per cent of the land in Palestine, the pattern of their purchases was causing resentment.

Some Jewish immigrants had absorbed Zionist propaganda about their superiority to the local people and about the land being theirs by God-given right. Moreover, the new arrivals were often separatist. The original Palestinian Jews had been city dwellers, living largely within the communities of Gaza, Hebron, Jaffa, Jerusalem and elsewhere. The new arrivals planted exclusive, self-contained colonies such as Tel Aviv. By the end of World War I, there were 47 of such colonies.

One of the earliest manifestations of hostility towards Jewish immigration and land settlement was the choice of two anti-Jewish deputies to represent Jerusalem at the first Ottoman parliament, 1876–7. In 1886, Arab peasant farmers attacked a Jewish settlement after a squabble over land; the following year, a Jewish woman was killed as the result of a similar confrontation. By the 1890s, both Roman Catholic and Muslim leaders were petitioning Istanbul, asking the sultan to do something about the flood of Jewish immigrants that was distorting the traditional fabric of the country. There was another outbreak of Arab–Jewish violence in 1891. Tensions rose again with the upsurge in Arab nationalism that followed a change of regime in Istanbul in the period 1908–9.

Conflicting nationalisms

ARAB NATIONALISM

In the second half of the nineteenth century, as nationalism burned bright across Europe, its flames had stirred hearts in the Middle East, too. From the 1860s onwards, Arab intellectuals began to talk of an Arab nation. This romantic concept rested on three legs – two historical, one linguistic. The first was the shared past of the people who had spread Islam; the second the common heritage of an empire (the Caliphate) that at its height had been larger than that of the Romans; and the third a common language.

The Arab 'awakening' found its first voices in literary and scientific societies. One of its earliest focal points was the Syrian Protestant College of Beirut, later to become the American University of that city. The movement was given a pronounced fillip when, in 1908–9, an opposition group known as the Young Turks forced the sultan to accept constitutional rule and then to abdicate when he tried to backtrack. The Young Turks had acted in the name of nationalism, but because only 30 per cent of the sultan's subjects were Turks, the message relayed across the Arab world was not the same as that heard in Istanbul and Anatolia. To the intellectuals of Cairo, Damascus and Baghdad, nationalism meant rejection of Ottoman rule and the gathering of all Arab peoples into a huge Arab nation.

Or did it? Could a nation state of such diversity as the Arab-speaking world really be created on the basis of a common language and faith? Was it genuinely realistic to think of the citizens of Morocco, Syria and Arabia living as harmoniously together as those of, say, Provence, Brittany and Burgundy, or even Texas, New York and California? The truth was then, as it is today, that Arab nationalism was a chimera, a beautiful dream rather than a realistic possibility. Within the Arab-speaking world, other nationalisms were a far more realistic possibility.

PALESTINIANS?

Although few would deny the existence of Palestinian nationalism today, there is widespread disagreement over when it came into being. Roughly speaking, there are three schools of thought. Most Israelis maintain that before the 1960s the idea of a Palestinian nation had not existed and it came into being only as a reaction to the creation and expansion of Israel. Of course, such a position helps justify Jewish immigration into Palestine and the creation of the State of Israel. In establishing a country where one had not existed before, the argument runs, the Jews were doing little more than others, like the Americans, who had built nations in tribal lands.

It goes without saying that the majority of Palestinian historians deny this claim. The more hard-line among them insist that the Palestinian nation has existed since time immemorial, tracing its roots, like those of the Jews, to Biblical times. Such a position is difficult to accept: there may have been a land generally known as Palestine all that time, but territory and name alone do not make a nation. A great deal more realistic is a third view – that the Palestinian nation has emerged gradually over the last 200 years.

... a Palestinian national identity, like those of other modern nations, has been created – invented and elaborated – over the course of the last two centuries.

(Baruch Kimmerling and Joel S Migdal, *The Palestinian People, A History*, Harvard UP, 2003, p. xxvii.)

A suggested starting point is the 1834 revolt against the invading Egyptians (see p. 20). The movement united all sections of Palestinian society in a common cause for the first time, thereby creating the sort of shared heritage nationhood requires. Ottoman reforms and nineteenth-century economic development added to a vague sense of national cohesion. Far more influential was resentment at Jewish encroachment. Like the 1834 rebellion, the perceived threat to their traditional way of life led increasing numbers of educated Palestinians to think in terms of a Palestinian nation. This found concrete expression in Arabic newspapers intended for a specifically Palestinian readership. There was no Palestinian head of state, flag, anthem or even national government, but the soil had been prepared in which the desire for such things would grow.

The impact of war

TAKING SIDES

World War I changed Palestine for ever. The region's inhabitants had little or no direct interest in the causes of the conflict but were drawn into it because of their Turkish overlords. At the beginning of 1914, Turkey was not allied to any of the major powers. Recently, it had been turning away from its traditional friendship with Britain and drawing closer to Germany. German finance was behind the ongoing project for a Berlin to Baghdad railway, and German officers were helping to modernize the Turkish army. Both Berlin and Istanbul shared a mistrust of Russian imperial ambitions. As a consequence, following a secret treaty with Germany and a series of provocative blunders by the Allies, in early November 1914 Turkey joined the war against Britain, France and Russia.

The Turks had been finding it difficult enough holding together their shrinking empire in peacetime; the strain of war broke it completely. Over the next four years they faced an Anglo-French naval blockade of their coastlines, an Anglo-Indian force invading from southern Mesopotamia (Iraq), a brutal campaign with Russia in the Caucus region, allied occupation of the Gallipoli Peninsula, and a British invasion from Egypt closely linked to a British-assisted Arab revolt beginning in the Hejaz (Western Arabia). As far as Palestine was concerned, the last two were crucial.

VAGUE PROMISES

The Middle East was vital to Britain because of the region's strategic position on the route to British possessions in India and the Far East, and because its oil was used to power British warships and an increasing proportion of British industry. With huge numbers of British troops tied down on the Western Front, British diplomats looked around for allies in their campaign against the Turkish Empire. The Arabs, always resentful of Turkish overlordship and now nationalistic as well, were an obvious target.

Thus, in 1915–16, Sir Henry McMahon, the British Consul-General in Egypt, engaged in a lengthy correspondence with Hussein, the clever but enigmatic Grand Sharif or Emir (a sort of hereditary governor) of Mecca. As head of the Hashemites, a clan descended from the Prophet Mohammed, and guardian of the Muslim holy cities of Mecca and Medina, Hussein had as good a claim as anyone to speak for the Islamic Arab 'nation'. Since his allegiance to the Ottomans was known to be shaky, McMahon believed he could be persuaded to throw in his lot with the allies.

The Consul-General was right. Speaking for the British government, Sir Henry said it would support Arab independence and help the Arabs establish such states as they thought fit out of the territory in which they lived. Specifically, 'portions of Syria lying to the west of the districts of Damascus, Homs, Hama and Aleppo' were excluded from the agreement as Sir Henry felt that they 'cannot be said to be purely Arab' (Sir Henry McMahon, letter to the Sharif of Mecca, 24 October 1915). The correspondence was not accompanied by maps.

The Grand Sharif accepted the terms and, led by his son Faisal and assisted and perhaps even inspired by the able and eccentric self-publicist T.E. Lawrence ('Lawrence of Arabia', the Arabs rose up in the Hejaz and drove north to link up with British forces that had advanced into Palestine from Egypt. General Allenby was in Jerusalem by Christmas 1917 and had advanced north to Damascus and Aleppo by the end of the war.

Outside Arabia, full Arab independence did not follow. And even when it eventually did, Palestine was not included. Politicians and scholars returned to Sir Henry's letter. Had the diplomat been thinking of Palestine when he excluded certain regions from Arab rule? If so, either his geography was somewhat awry or the true meaning had been hidden in translation between English, a fairly specific language, and the more poetic Arabic. The Arabs felt betrayed.

Insight

Precise translation between English and Arabic, with its vast range of nuances (dozens of words for a horse, for example), is virtually impossible and has led to a range of diplomatic and commercial misunderstandings.

DOUBLE-DEALING

Six months after Sir Henry's promise to support Arab independence, the vigorous British diplomat Sir Mark Sykes negotiated a secret understanding with his French counterpart François Georges-Picot. Worried that Arab portions of the disintegrating Turkish Empire might come under Russian influence, the Sykes–Picot Agreement divided the Middle East into five parts. Britain and France were each to have an area they controlled directly, and another that lay within their 'sphere of influence'. The independent Arab states promised by McMahon were included, somewhat paradoxically, within these spheres of influence. Palestine, labelled 'international sphere' on the accompanying map, featured in neither.

To confuse the situation even further, on 2 November 1917, the British Foreign Secretary, Arthur James Balfour, declared that, 'His Majesty's Government viewed with favour the establishment in Palestine of a national home for the Jewish people.' All sorts of reasons have been put forward for this statement, including a crafty plan by the British government to bring the 'international zone' of the Sykes–Picot Agreement within its sphere of influence.

In the end, though, Balfour's motive was irrelevant. What mattered was that the world's foremost imperial power appeared to have given its blessing to Zionism. In so doing, although it had used 'home' instead of the more confrontational 'state', it had further reneged on its agreement with the Arabs. At the same time, it had raised the hopes and expectations of Jews living in Palestine or hoping to move there, and dealt a bitter blow to the Palestinian Arabs. Small wonder, therefore, that the 18-word sentence quoted above is often held up as British diplomacy's biggest single blunder of modern times.

10 THINGS TO REMEMBER

1 *Palestine experienced an economic boom in the 75 years before the outbreak of World War I.*

2 *The same period saw perhaps as many as 8,000 Jews emigrating to Palestine.*

3 *Nineteenth-century Jewish thinking was strongly influenced by 'Zionism', a drive for Jews to return to their Holy Land.*

4 *Zionism was linked to imperialism and nationalism.*

5 *Theodore Herzl's The Jewish State (1896) was a key text in the development of Zionism.*

6 *Jewish immigrants to Palestine received substantial backing from wealthy Jewish families in Europe and the USA.*

7 *By the twentieth century, Arab-Jewish relations in Palestine were becoming strained.*

8 *Arab nationalism emerged as a powerful movement in the later nineteenth century, linked with the emergence of Palestinian nationalism.*

9 *In 1915–16, the British Consul-General in Egypt, Sir Henry McMahon, accepted the idea of Arab independence – except for a vaguely defined area west of Syria.*

10 *Shortly after Britain and France had made a secret deal to carve up the Middle East between them, British Foreign Secretary Arthur Balfour gave his government's backing (the Balfour Declaration) for a Jewish 'national home' in Palestine.*

3

The mandate 1919 to 1945

In this chapter you will learn about:

- ***Palestine's emergence as an embryonic state after World War I***
- ***British government of the Palestinian 'mandate'***
- ***mounting Arab–Jewish–British mistrust and violence***
- ***attempts to solve the 'Palestine problem' before 1945.***

In the 37 years that separated the end of World War I from the end of World War II, Palestine changed from being a problematic district within the Turkish Empire to a disputed land discussed and argued over throughout the world. This was partly because, under British rule, the Arab–Jew tensions just becoming visible in 1914 developed into an armed conflict. The dangerous situation was greatly complicated by events in Europe, namely the systematic attempt by the Nazis to wipe out European Jewry. As a consequence, by late 1945, Palestine was close to being torn apart in a three-way battle between the British, the Arabs and the Jews.

Peace-making

LEGACY OF WAR

Palestine had a hard time during World War I. As an Ottoman territory, its overseas trade was disrupted by allied naval power. Poverty increased and all sectors of the population suffered from outbreaks of typhus and cholera. Fighting, notably the advance of

British and Arab forces across Palestine in 1917, caused inevitable hardship, loss and suffering. Many Jews who had retained their Russian citizenship in order to avoid conscription into the Ottoman Army were forcibly deported. The population of the entire territory fell by an estimated 160,000. It was with a degree of relief, therefore, that all those living in Palestine heard that Turkey had accepted defeat on 30 October 1918.

The relief was coupled with anxious anticipation. What would happen to their land? The only fact locals could be sure of was that they themselves would probably have little say in whatever was decided. Would their territory become an independent Arab state, as Grand Sharif Hussein said Britain had promised? If so, then how could this be reconciled with the Balfour Declaration of support for a Jewish 'homeland' in Palestine? And what about the Anglo-French Sykes–Picot Agreement to carve up ex-Ottoman territories in the Middle East between them, leaving Palestine as some sort of international protectorate? In the end, an attempt was made to implement all three policies – and the result, understandably, was an unholy mess.

Insight

Although Jews celebrate 2 November (the anniversary of the Balfour Declaration) as 'Balfour Day', two points are easily overlooked:

- *The Declaration spoke of a Jewish 'homeland', not a state.*
- *It stated categorically that in the establishment of this homeland 'nothing shall be done which may prejudice the civil and religious rights of existing non-Jewish communities in Palestine.'*

BRITAIN'S MANDATE

The several separate treaties that followed World War I, broadly known as the Versailles Settlement, were supposed to be based upon US President Wilson's principle of national self-determination. In practice, the principle raised as many difficulties as it solved. What did self-determination mean in Palestine, for instance? To find out,

Wilson asked the King–Crane Commission (1919) to investigate and report back to him. Not surprisingly, the Commission declared that the situation was extremely tricky: the Arabs, comprising 90 per cent of the population, wanted Palestine joined to the emerging Syria or set up as an independent entity, while the Zionist Jews pressed for it to become their homeland. Left in a quandary, Wilson accepted the status quo. He was not the first politician stymied by the Palestinian situation, nor by any means the last.

The status quo at the end of the war was that British troops occupied Palestine, making it a de facto addition to their empire. Their imperialist land-grabbing was given a fig leaf of respectability by the 'mandate' system. Backed by the newly created League of Nations, mandates were territories deemed suitable for democratic independence after a period of assistance and tutelage by an established Western democracy. That meant Britain and France. The latter took responsibility for Syria and Lebanon, Britain for Iraq and a large Palestine that extended across the River Jordan (see Figure 3.1). In fact, the Palestinian mandate involved the twin tasks of preparing the country for independence while also fulfilling the Balfour Declaration's promise of giving the Jews a homeland there.

The ill-thought-out Palestinian scheme ran into difficulties almost immediately. Not only did tension between Jews and Arabs rise dramatically as a fresh wave of Jewish immigrants descended on the country, but circumstances obliged the British to divide the country in two. In 1921, Prince Abdullah, Grand Sharif Hussein's second son, turned up with a small army in the Palestinian territory on the eastern bank of the River Jordan. Having been replaced by his elder brother as King of Iraq, he was on his way north to try his luck in Syria. He got no further than the tiny settlement of Aman. Here he received a British proposal that he become king of the mandate territory he occupied. Thus, in an extraordinarily cavalier piece of state-making, the British divided their Palestinian mandate. Territory to the west of the River Jordan remained as Palestine, while that on the other side of the river became the new mandate of Transjordan. Given independence after World War II, it emerged as the Hashemite Kingdom of Jordan.

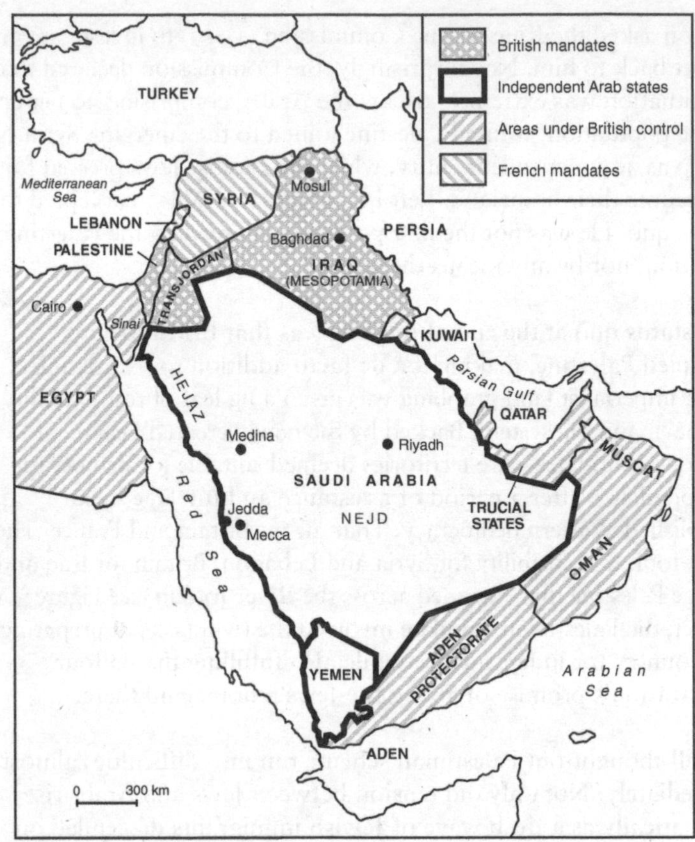

Figure 3.1 The Middle East mandates.

Insight

The Hashemite tribe trace their descent back to the prophet Mohammed and earlier. Divisions within the tribe between Hashemites and Umayyads gave rise to the original Sunni–Shia split.

GOING NOWHERE

British administrators carried out the logistical side of their mandated duties with laudable efficiency. Their efforts to improve life in Palestine attracted Arab immigrants as well as Jews. They modernized transport by expanding the rail network and building roads; they built schools and sewage treatment plants; laid water pipelines and increased the provision of electricity. Medical services improved too, leading to lower child mortality and an increase in the population. Palestine's relative stability and security during the 1920s and early 1930s allowed the expansion of industry and commerce that began before World War I to continue.

Material progress was not matched by any similar progress in the political sphere. Britain's mandate from the League of Nations had included neither a time limit nor specific targets for independent institutions. That was just as well, for no target would have been attainable. Arab opinion, as voiced by the unelected Palestinian National Congress, rejected the mandate as long as it incorporated the hated Balfour Declaration. The Jews refused to endorse an elected all-Palestine government for fear it would ride roughshod over the aims and aspirations of the Jewish minority.

As a consequence, despite many meetings and proposals and much talking, there was very little progress towards independence. The Arabs ran their own local affairs and the Jews ran theirs. Somewhere in the middle, spending a fortune on translating between three official languages (Arabic, Hebrew and English) but enjoying three days of holiday per week (the Muslim Friday, the Jewish Saturday and the Christian Sunday), the British bureaucracy attempted to hold the ring while dealing with issues like transport and immigration that required a mandate-wide policy.

Breakdown

1920s – UNEASY PEACE

Although during the early years of the mandate there was less violence in Palestine than in either Syria or Iraq, several factors were making some sort of future bloodletting highly likely.

The lack of a date or even preconditions for British occupation to end led to mounting hostility in both communities, but especially among the Arabs. Indeed, they were beginning to talk of 1920 as their 'Year of Catastrophe'. What right had foreigners, they asked, either to divide their land or force them to accept a state within a state?

The British government's appointment of Sir Herbert Samuel, a Jew and an openly enthusiastic Zionist, as Palestine's first all-powerful High Commissioner hardly displayed tactful even-handedness. Sceptical Arabs believed the British government was so inherently pro-Zionist that it intended to hang on to Palestine until sufficient Jewish immigrants had arrived to make them the majority of the population. Nor were Jewish Palestinians delighted with their British overlords. The more extreme among them, in particular, were infuriated by the decision to make Transjordan a separate mandate because the move reduced the chances of recreating the ancient Judean Kingdom of David that bestraddled the River Jordan (see p. 5).

Meanwhile, streams of Jewish immigrants continued to flood into Palestine. The Jewish population of the mandate probably doubled in the ten years after World War I. By 1922, they made up 11 per cent of an overall population that had risen to around 750,000. After an initial rush, the British, worried by the Arab reaction, imposed limits on immigration. Nevertheless, by 1928 Jews amounted to 16 per cent of Palestine's population.

More importantly, ten years after the end of World War I, Jews owned 4.2 per cent of Palestinian land. This may not sound much, but a good deal of it was in areas where the soil was fertile and suitable for agriculture. Such areas were comparatively rare before the introduction of large-scale irrigation. Land purchases were a regular source of friction, too. This was not because they were done illegally or by force but because, in the semi-feudal society of rural Palestine, land rights were often assumed rather than documented. Moreover, much land was bought from absentee

Arab landlords who had little knowledge of or interest in their tenants. Such sales led to Arab peasants being turned off land they and their ancestors had farmed for generations.

EMBRYONIC INSTITUTIONS

During the 1920s, the Jews rapidly established the embryonic apparatus of a distinctively Jewish state: a Jewish National Assembly, trade unions, schools, industrial enterprises, a university, and so forth. They even had their own fighting force, the Haganah – labelled a 'defence force' by Jewish historians and a 'terrorist organization' by Arab ones (see p. 61).

Unlike the immigrant Jews, the Palestinian Arabs did not benefit from starting with a clean slate when it came to organizing themselves and establishing institutions. The territory had been served by an official and semi-official administrative network for centuries but this did not always harmonize with British plans. The imperial power, for instance, set up a Palestinian Arab Congress that was empowered to choose a Palestinian Arab Executive. But when the Palestinian Arab Executive boycotted the mandate concept because it incorporated the Balfour Declaration, Anglo-Arab co-operation was severely shaken.

The complexity of the situation is reflected in the fact that a Supreme Muslim Council operated in parallel with the Palestinian Arab Executive. The Council was headed by Amin al-Husseini, Grand Mufti (expert on Muslim religious law) of Jerusalem. To make matters even more difficult, his position was hotly disputed after a very dubious election had been overruled by British fiat. He also suffered from traditional rivalry with the an-Nashasibi family. Husseini supported the Arab Executive, for example, while the Nashasibis preferred to operate through yet another rival organization, the National Defence Party. When ancient town–country, tribal and religious divisions are added to the mix, it is not difficult to see why the Palestinian Arabs failed to present a united front against the Jews and the British.

Insight

A Grand Mufti is the most senior Sunni law expert in a state. While Grand Muftis' opinions and recommendations are highly valued, normally they do not have law-making powers. Within their mandates, the British accepted the Grand Mufti of Jerusalem as pre-eminent.

EARLY VIOLENCE

In 1920, during fairly widespread anti-Jewish riots, Bedouin tribesmen attacked a Jewish settlement in Upper Galilee and killed six settlers. The following May, inter-community violence left almost 100 dead, equally distributed between Jews and Arabs, and several hundred injured. There was further fighting towards the end of the year. These events provoked two responses. First, the British temporarily limited immigration into Palestine – there was actually a net emigration from the mandate in 1927. Second, the Jewish community established the Haganah. Thereafter, the situation remained tense but calm until the end of the decade.

The uneasy post-war peace collapsed in 1929. Each side blamed the other. The Jews and most of the British criticized the Grand Mufti and a journalist named Arif al-Arif for stirring up anti-Jewish feeling among the Arab population. The Arabs said they were responding to an aggressive call by the Zionist extremist Ze'ev Jabotinsky for the massive increase in Jewish immigration necessary for the formation of an all-Jewish state in Palestine. Within Jerusalem, tension had been building over several months because of the erection of screens to separate Jewish men and women at the Wailing (Western) Wall of Temple Mount (see p. 15). The Wall was regarded as sacred by both Jews and Muslims and any form of furniture there (including screens) was supposedly banned by mandate law. When a Jewish boy was stabbed to death after kicking a football into an Arab garden, his funeral provoked demonstrations and eventually, in August 1929, a full-scale, bloody riot.

Fired-up Arab peasants armed with a variety of weapons descended on Jerusalem and, in the ensuing orgy of murder, rape and pillage, slaughtered 133 Jews. Before order was restored, 116 Arabs also lay dead, a few killed by Jewish vigilantes but most by the gunfire of the British security forces. Later, further Arabs died in a Jewish reprisal attack. Whatever slight hope there had been of Jews and Arabs living together in a single harmonious Palestine was all but gone; there was a grim inevitability about what followed.

Mission impossible

1930s

During the 1930s, the situation in Palestine became simultaneously more complex and more intractable. It became more complex as Palestinian Arabs felt increasingly threatened by growing Jewish immigration – a British census of 1931 revealed that the mandate's population was now over 1 million, of which 16.9 per cent was Jewish. The nature of this Zionist community was important, too. Particularly after the Nazis took power in Germany and connived at the repatriation of many German Jews to Palestine, Palestinian Jews were comparatively well educated, politically sophisticated, united in their objectives and, above all, internationally funded.

In comparison, after centuries of relative cultural, political and economic stagnation under Ottoman domination, the deeply fragmented Palestinian Arab community was only slowly losing its parochial, semi-feudal mentality. Although numerically superior, in almost all other respects it was anything but the dominant force.

A British committee report, blaming excessive Jewish immigration for the 1929 bloodshed, suggested that only another 50,000 Jews be allowed to enter Palestine. This target was soon overturned. 30,000 German Jews arrived in 1933, rising to 61,000 in 1935. By World War II, the Jewish community in Palestine numbered around 467,000, almost one-third of the total population. It owned around 6 per cent of the land and had established some 300 Zionist colonies.

The 1929 violence provoked a split among Palestinian Jews. The majority followed the more moderate ('Labour') leaders of the World Zionist Organization, Chaim Weizmann in London and David Ben-Gurion in Palestine. They sought a socialist Jewish state in Palestine separate from a Palestinian Arab one. The Haganah would be needed to defend this state, but force was not an integral part of it.

Jabotinsky's was the more extreme, minority view. He and his World Union of Zionist Revisionists had set up a militant security force of their own, the Irgun. Their policy, later known as the 'iron wall', was based on four principles. First, the Jews were the standard-bearers of a superior Western civilization into the Middle East. Second, Zion should comprise all Palestine on both banks of the Jordan ('Greater Israel'). Third, the Arabs would never voluntarily accept this. Fourth, the only answer, therefore, was force: Zionists had to carve out their state and secure it behind an iron wall. Only when the Arabs knew they could never win, would they accept the presence of the Jewish state in the Middle East. When we wonder why peace between Palestinians and Israelis is so elusive, we have only to look to this inflexible Revisionist doctrine to grasp at least part of the answer.

PALESTINIAN UPRISING

The later 1930s were dominated by a massive uprising of the Palestinian Arabs against the whole mandate apparatus. Although perhaps deliberately started by Grand Mufti Husseini, it soon acquired an instinctive, chaotic momentum of its own. Consequently, it has been likened to the 1834 revolt against the Egyptian Mamluks and to the more recent Intifada uprisings (see p. 192 and p. 240). Paradoxically, the revolt of 1936–9 played an important part in strengthening a sense of Palestinian nationalism while at the same time fragmenting that nation's social and political structure.

The uprising took place against a background of rising three-way – Arab–Jewish–British – violence. It was sparked by rumours of planned Jewish construction work around Jerusalem's Temple

Mount and the British killing in battle of a Syrian freedom fighter/ guerrilla named Sheikh Izz al-Din al-Qassam. Arab resistance took the form of a general strike, which left its own supporters deeply impoverished, a refusal to pay tax, and sporadic violent attacks against Zionist communities, the British and even Christian Arabs. By 1938–9, the revolt and the tough British response had so disrupted the Arab community that fighting between rival villages was as violent as that against their common enemies.

At first, Arab leadership was exercised by the traditional notable class, especially Grand Mufti Husseini. Already president of the Supreme Muslim Council, in 1936 he became president of a newly created Arab Higher Committee. His authority did not last beyond 1937, when, wanted by the British after the assassination of a British commissioner, he fled in disguise to Lebanon where the French put him under house arrest. His Higher Committee was forcibly dissolved along with other Arab political organizations. Rumours that the Arab revolt had received Nazi funding were given some credence when, during World War II, the Grand Mufti co-operated with the regimes of both Hitler and Mussolini.

By the end of the revolt, a new class of radicalized Palestinian Arabs had emerged. Its members were usually young men not related by blood or temperament to the community's traditional, Jerusalem-based ruling class. They were urban, wage-earning (if in work), aggressively violent and often employed Muslim terminology. The kafiya, later made famous by Yasser Arafat, was their badge of resistance and their loyalty was to the red, black and green of the Palestinian flag.

PARTITION

After a fairly low-key initial response, in 1937 the British set about quashing the revolt with determination. Martial law was imposed and the Palestine garrison increased to over 20,000 troops. Far more controversial and destructive of Anglo-Arab relations was the creation, in co-operation with Jewish volunteers, of a fighting unit called the Special Night Squads that attacked Arab villages suspected of harbouring rebels. Within four years, perhaps 10,000 Arabs were killed (albeit a fair proportion at the hands of other Arabs) and 15,000 wounded.

Jewish co-operation with the British was by no means guaranteed. The Revisionist faction, regarding British attempts at even-handedness as hostility, reacted to the hanging of an Irgun member in 1938 by blowing up a bus in Haifa, killing 74 passengers and bystanders. At the same time, the Irgun pressed on with its own private battles with the Palestinian Arabs, killing dozens while picking up comparatively few casualties itself.

Insight

It is frequently forgotten that the earliest examples of Middle East terrorism in modern times were committed not by Arabs but by Jews hostile to the government of the British mandate.

By now the chances of Arabs and Jews living together in a single Palestinian state, never great, had vanished. This was recognized by the British Royal Commission, usually known as the Peel Commission, which examined the Palestine situation over the winter of 1936–7. Its recommendations, published in July 1937, were headed by a new principle: partition. The British had already resorted to this in Ireland, where sectarian differences had seemed beyond reconciliation, and they were to do the same when separating Pakistan from India at the time of independence. Although superficially attractive as a way of solving a difficult problem, in fact partition was a way of avoiding that problem rather than solving it. Britain's mandate had been to create a single Palestine, not two. Partition would mean creating minority communities in either state or a near impossible, forced movement of peoples from one region to another.

The Peel Commission suggested a three-way split:

- *a Jewish state comprising about one third of the land of Palestine but with almost half the mandate's population of Arabs*

- *a larger Arab state*
- *a special zone controlled by the League of Nations (in effect, Britain) that included Jerusalem and its surrounding holy sites.*

Interestingly, a somewhat similar partition plan had been agreed 19 years earlier by Chaim Weizmann and Prince Faisal but it had been dropped after rejection by other Arab leaders. Acceptance then would have avoided an immense amount of blood and tears.

Ben-Gurion, the most influential Jewish leader, gave the latest British proposal a cautious welcome. It did, after all, offer his people a nation state of their own. The Revisionists, on the other hand, rejected it outright as a sell-out. Likewise, the Arab Higher Committee turned the proposal down flat. What right had a Western power, they asked, to descend on their land, allow hundreds of thousands of strangers to settle there and then, when the locals objected to the influx, give away a large chunk of territory to the newcomers so that they could have a state of their own? This far from illogical position, spiced with religious overtones, remains that of militant Palestinians to this day.

World War II

CHANGING COURSE

By 1938, as the British were struggling to regain control of the upland villages of eastern Palestine, it was becoming clear to the government in London that it would soon be involved in war on a vastly greater scale with the fascist regimes of Germany and Italy. In this situation, the last thing Britain wanted was a row with the Arab world that might provoke a cut in oil supplies and even some sort of fascist-Arab alliance based on Nazi promises of full Arab independence. (This was precisely the sort of deal Britain had struck to get Arab support during World War I!) Furthermore, there was the possible meeting of minds between Germans and Arabs over the Jewish 'problem'.

The international situation, coupled with yet another report from the mandate, led to a conference, a debate in Parliament and a White Paper that signalled further change in British policy. Partition was ditched. In its place, Britain proposed full independence for a united mandate in ten years' time, Jewish immigration limited to 15,000 a year for five years and thereafter only with Arab consent, and a limit on land sales. As might have been expected, this pleased no one. The majority of Jews were particularly disappointed at the way their dream of independence had been dashed.

WAR EFFORTS

Moderate Arabs and Jews agreed on one thing: the threat posed by the fascist Axis was worse than anything Britain could throw at them. On the outbreak of war, inter-community conflict died down and large numbers from both sides agreed to support Britain and its allies in their struggle. As many as 27,000 Jews and 25,000 Arabs (particularly in the famous Arab Legion) fought with the British Army. With funds pouring into the mandate to support the 280,000 allied service personnel based there, after 1941 the Palestinian economy roared into double-figure expansion. The Jewish sector did particularly well, developing its industry to meet allied war needs.

Insight

Formed to defend the newly created Transjordan mandate, the Arab Legion (officially the Arab Army) comprised Arab soldiers commanded by British officers. After notable success in World War II, the Legion fought against Israel in the war of 1948–9.

There were exceptions to this comparative harmony. One was the Grand Mufti (see p. 41). Revisionist Zionists, whose main instrument of guerrilla rebellion remained the Irgun, also maintained their hostility towards Britain. One notorious sect, the Stern Gang, actually tried to open negotiations with the Nazis. Their assassination of a Zionist-inclined British minister in Cairo in 1944 did not win them many friends, either. Indeed, by this date the Haganah and Irgun were in open conflict, the former handing over 1,000 of their Jewish rivals to the British.

Despite the British limit, large numbers of desperate Jewish immigrants continued to pour into Palestine from Nazi-threatened Europe. Perhaps as many as 40,000 managed to enter in 1940. Dreading an Arab backlash, Britain tried hard to maintain its quota system, often with tragic results. One incident in particular caught the world's attention. It involved the ancient and unseaworthy steamship *Struma*, which in December 1941 left the Romanian port of Constanza for Palestine with 769 Jewish refugees on board. The ship's engines gave out en route and she was towed into Istanbul where all but a handful of passengers were denied entry visas for Palestine. Towed back out to sea, the *Struma* drifted helplessly until sunk by a Russian torpedo with the loss of virtually everyone on board.

Another effect of the war was to draw the USA deeply into Middle Eastern politics for the first time. Like Britain, the USA needed Arab oil and poured money into Saudi Arabia to keep it stable and on side. Nevertheless, the pro-Arab stance of President F. D. Roosevelt ran contrary to the growing pro-Zionist sentiments of the US people at large. Following a visit of Ben-Gurion and Chaim Weizmann to the USA, a programme of support for the Zionist project (the Biltmore Programme) gained widespread backing, even from Congress and presidential election candidates.

INTO THE ABYSS

In the end, World War II did little more than put the Palestinian crisis on hold. If anything, the situation in 1945 was worse than it had been in 1939. As the full extent of the horrifying Nazi slaughter of some 6 million European Jews became known, a worldwide tide of support for Zionism ran strongly. Jews everywhere were more determined than ever to carve out a secure homeland for their people, whatever the cost. Rulers of neighbouring Arab states made the appropriate pro-Palestinian noises while watching the situation carefully to see what political opportunities it might offer. Britain, bankrupt and exhausted by almost six years of total war, had no stomach for further conflict in Palestine and wanted out.

Somewhere in the middle of this venomously complex equation were the Palestinian Arabs. Although most were better off than they had been, the majority were still poor. In the towns they were small shopkeepers or wage-earners. In the countryside they were landless or farmed small parcels of stony soil. They lacked unity and leadership. In short, they were totally unprepared for the storm gathering on the horizon.

In depth: Mohammed Amin al-Husseini (1893–1974), Grand Mufti of Jerusalem

Born into a respected, aristocratic Palestinian family, (Haj) Mohammed Amin al-Husseini was the most influential figure in Palestinian politics between the World Wars. His fervent Arab nationalism won him many supporters, but his links with the Nazis and their policies has left a stain on his reputation that Israeli propagandists were not slow to emphasize.

After dabbling in law at Cairo University and administration in Istanbul, al-Husseini made a pilgrimage to Mecca before joining the Ottoman Army as an artillery officer in 1914. He returned to Jerusalem on disability leave two years later, changed sides, and worked for the British. After the war, he campaigned for Palestine to be incorporated within a Greater Syria. When this idea collapsed, he adopted the cause of Palestinian nationalism and the expulsion of Jews from the mandate.

Sentenced to imprisonment by the British for stirring up racial hatred, al-Husseini took refuge abroad before being pardoned and appointed Grand Mufti of Jerusalem by High Commissioner Sir Herbert Samuel, in an extraordinary piece of imperial high-handedness. As he was also president of the Supreme Muslim

Council, with control over Sharia (Islamic) courts and the appointment of teachers and preachers, al-Husseini had become the most powerful Arab in the mandate. The striking gold-covering of Jerusalem's Dome of the Rock owes much to his fundraising at this time.

Jewish sources accused the Grand Mufti of provoking the 1929 massacre of Jews in Hebron but a British enquiry found no evidence for this. During the 1936 Arab Revolt, however, al-Husseini's anti-Semitic and anti-British inflammatory pronouncements were widely attested and he escaped arrest by fleeing to Syria and then Iraq. By this time he had established links with Hitler's Nazis, whose anti-Semitism he hoped to exploit for Palestinian ends. During World War II, he worked with pro-fascist elements in Iraq, mixed with Nazi leaders in Germany, and supposedly recruited Bosnian Muslims for the Waffen SS in Yugoslavia.

In 1945, the exiled Grand Mufti fled to Cairo via Switzerland and France. Greeted as a hero, he continued his ruthless campaign for the creation of an independent Arab Palestine. However, his power and influence rapidly dwindled after the Arab League bypassed him and his forces disintegrated during the 1948 war with Israel. By the time of his death, leadership of the Palestinian cause had passed to a distant cousin of his popularly known as Yasser Arafat.

In depth: Haganah and Irgun

The Haganah began as a small group of volunteer settlement guards known as the Guild of Watchmen. During the 1920s, the guild grew into a large but still illegal and relatively ill-coordinated collection of poorly armed defence units. Following the 1929 massacre (see pp. 42–3), the Haganah was developed into a serious force of several thousand, with organized training and its own weapons' workshops.

In 1931, Haganah's more right-wing elements set up the Irgun movement. During the 1936–9 Arab Revolt, the 10,000-strong

(Contd)

Haganah received semi-official recognition from the British, whom it helped in their struggle to hold down the Arab population. The training and experience gained at this time was to prove invaluable in Israel's 1948–9 War of Independence.

During World War II, the Haganah defied the British by continuing to facilitate illegal entry of Jewish refugees into Palestine. At the same time, it threw its weight behind the anti-fascist war effort and was eventually allowed to form a distinct Jewish Brigade of the British Army. From 1945–8, the Haganah switched to anti-British tactics of sabotage and terrorist-style bombings before being transformed into the Israeli Defence Force (IDF). By this time, two future prime ministers of Israel, Yitzhak Rabin and Ariel Sharon, as well as future Defence Minister Moshe Dayan, had all passed through its ranks.

The Haganah was closely associated with the socialist ethos of the majority of Jewish immigrants who arrived in Palestine during the first part of the twentieth century. This political stance, together with the Haganah's reluctance to use brute force, irritated hard-line Zionists who, in 1931, left to form the Irgun (or Etzel) group. Opposed to both socialism and restraint, Irgun's members included future Israeli Prime Minister Menachem Begin.

From the beginning, Irgun organized clandestine attacks on Arab targets, claiming over 250 'enemy' deaths by September 1939. Like the Haganah, Irgun also organized illegal immigration into Palestine. From 1940–3, Irgun joined Haganah in suspending anti-British activities, although these were continued by extremist splinter groups such as the Stern Gang. In 1948, Irgun resumed its attacks on the occupying power, the most notorious being the bombing of Jerusalem's King David Hotel (see p. 56). At the same time, its gunmen deliberately terrorized Arabs into leaving areas intended for incorporation into the State of Israel. Its best-known operations were the massacre of Deir Yassin and the attack on Jaffa.

10 THINGS TO REMEMBER

1 *After World War I, the League of Nations granted Britain a mandate to govern Palestine and prepare it for democratic independence.*

2 *In 1921, the British divided Palestine at the River Jordan into Palestine and Transjordan.*

3 *As Jewish immigrants continued to flood into Palestine, raising their proportion of the population to 11 per cent by 1922, the first inter-community violence broke out.*

4 *Hundreds were killed in the first large-scale Arab–Jewish confrontation, 1929.*

5 *Although the British imposed quotas on Jewish immigration, by 1939 the Jews comprised almost one third of Palestine's total population.*

6 *1936–9 saw a massive Arab revolt against the way the mandate was being run.*

7 *The British Peel Commission (1937) recommended that Palestine be partitioned to create an Arab state and a Jewish state.*

8 *In 1939, with war looming, the British announced independence for a united Palestine within 10 years.*

9 *Jewish and Arab units fought for the Allies in World War II and the economy of Palestine boomed.*

10 *By the end of World War II (1945), the Nazi Holocaust of European Jews had considerably strengthened Western support for the idea of a Jewish state in Palestine.*

4

Israel 1945 to 1949

In this chapter you will learn about:

- ***the situation in Palestine at the end of World War II***
- ***Britain's decision to hand over the 'Palestine problem' to the UN***
- ***unofficial war between Jews and Arabs, 1947–8***
- ***formation of the State of Israel and its war with Palestinians and other Arabs***
- ***the destruction of the embryonic Palestinian nation.***

The dying mandate

PALESTINE IN 1945

Almost as soon as World War II ended, Palestinian politics reverted to something close to its pre-war courses. Grand Mufti Husseini, the nominal leader of the Palestinian Arabs, gradually made his way back to the Arab world, calling for an independent Palestine and the destruction of the Jewish community there. As before, Muslim Arabs were deeply resentful of what they saw as a Western-backed attempt by the Jews to take over Arab land, and remained fearful of where this might lead.

Palestinian Jews of all persuasions had been quick to settle their wartime differences and were waiting impatiently to see precisely what Britain would do. Ernest Bevin, the Foreign Secretary in Britain's recently elected Labour government wondered, as had many of his predecessors in that office, whether there was any way of honouring the Balfour Declaration while still keeping in with the Arabs. He soon realized there was not.

Although the essence of the Palestine situation was the same as before the war – two peoples but only one land – several of the surrounding circumstances had changed significantly. Britain's imperial commitments were now more than it needed or could cope with, and it wanted to shed as many of them as possible. The League of Nations, by whose mandate Britain was still in Palestine, was defunct and about to be formally abolished. Palestine's neighbours were all either independent or about to become so. (Transjordan, the last, had to wait until 1948.) In March 1945, with British backing, Egypt organized an Arab League comprised of Syria, Saudi Arabia, Transjordan, Iraq, Lebanon, and Yemen. The League's primary purpose was to foster unity and co-operation among Arab peoples, and at first its activities were largely cultural, social and economic. Nevertheless, the League established a Higher Committee to lobby against Zionism and welcomed a spokesperson from the Palestinian people.

Two other factors profoundly influenced the Palestinian situation. One was the Nazi Holocaust, in which some 6 million European Jews had perished. This had had a double effect: raising a massive worldwide tide of sympathy for the Jewish people, and making the Jews themselves utterly determined that they would not allow anything even vaguely similar to occur ever again. Both militated in favour of the Jewish 'homeland' becoming a fully fledged state. Finally, there was the new global importance, power and influence of the United States of America. US input into the Palestine question was bound to be significant, although President Truman had to play a double game. For strategic and commercial reasons – essentially keeping out the Soviets and maintaining an uninterrupted supply of oil – the administration favoured a pro-Arab stance. American public opinion, however, was fiercely pro-Jewish. Truman had to tread carefully.

ATTACK ON BRITAIN

Foreign Secretary Bevin soon saw that allowing unlimited Jewish immigration into Palestine would only make Britain's task there ever harder, so he abandoned his party's traditional pro-Jewish stance and imposed a monthly ceiling of 1,500 Jewish immigrants. The move infuriated Palestine's Jewish community. While an estimated 250,000 Jews hung about in wretched camps around Europe waiting to be taken to the 'homeland', the Royal Navy was barring shipload after shipload of immigrants from entry. Some – including those on board the famous Exodus – were returned to Europe, others were interned in makeshift camps in Cyprus.

The Jewish community, headed by Jewish Agency President David Ben-Gurion, responded by organizing illicit immigration and waging a ferocious campaign against the British. Its aim was to make their presence in Palestine so unpleasant that they would withdraw and leave the Jews to set up a homeland on their own. The Haganah worked more or less closely with the Irgun and Lehi guerrilla organizations to target anything British. Railways were cut and bombs damaged airfields, bridges, oil refineries, radar installations, police stations and a host of other symbols of imperial occupation.

The two most dramatic attacks were the dynamiting of Acre jail to free prisoners and the bombing of the British security headquarters in the King David Hotel, Jerusalem (22 July 1946). The 91 people killed included British, Jews and Arabs. By the end of 1946, Jewish violence had claimed 373 lives, 300 of whom were civilians. When, later in the century, Jews found themselves the targets of similar outrages perpetrated by Arabs, the cruel irony of the situation was plain to all. Back in 1945–6, though, Arab violence was largely confined to attacks on fellow Arabs who sold land to the Jews.

Enter the UN

VAIN PROPOSALS

By the end of 1945, President Truman was seeking popular approval in the USA by asking Britain to accept at least 150,000 more Jewish immigrants into Palestine. Although the imposition of martial law and other strict security measures were failing to halt the Jewish terror campaign, Britain refused to allow more immigrants until the Haganah called a ceasefire. It would not. Deadlock ensued. When an Anglo-American committee of investigation also called for the immigration limit to be raised, the British government again refused. Believing that too many immigrants were coming in already, the Arab community called a strike.

Another set of Anglo-American proposals, this time suggesting a federal Palestine based on provinces, was rejected by Jews and Arabs. By now the Grand Mufti was back in Egypt and trying, with other members of his family, to put together some sort of unity among the fragmented Palestinian Arabs through an Arab Higher Executive. He met with little success. Finally, worn down by Jewish guerrilla violence, international condemnation and the intransigence of both sides, Britain invited the newly established United Nations to investigate the Palestinian problem and come up with a solution.

The United Nations Special Committee on Palestine (UNSCOP) produced majority and minority reports in September 1947. The former proposed a partition of Palestine not unlike that put forward by the Peel Commission: separate Jewish and Arab states, joined in an economic union, with Jerusalem and its environs under international control. The latter resurrected the federation idea. The USA, the USSR and the Jewish Agency accepted the partition plan; the Palestinians, the Arab League and Britain rejected it. Shortly afterwards, the British government announced that, whatever happened, it was pulling out of Palestine in six months' time. In November, after intensive lobbying from the

USA, the partition plan was put before the UN General Assembly where 33 nations voted in favour, and ten against. Tragically, UN intervention had polarized the position in Palestine rather than placated it. The vote was for war.

Insight

While there were several reasons why Britain decided to hand over the Palestinian problem to the UN, an unwillingness to alienate the USA – a key ally and strongly pro-Zionist – was certainly high on Whitehall's list.

TWO STATES AND NONE

Ben-Gurion and the majority of the Jewish leadership in Palestine did not believe for one second that the UNSCOP majority plan was the last word on the subject. They accepted it because it offered them a UN-sanctioned state as a launching pad for further expansion. The plan was just as unacceptable to the Arabs as the other suggested partitions had been, because it took away, without consent, land that was rightfully and legally theirs.

The situation was this: In 1947 the Jews owned some seven per cent of the land of Palestine, including much of the best farmland. They had bought it in Ottoman times, picked it up after the Ottoman withdrawal or purchased it from Arabs, many of whom had been absentee landlords, between the wars. The Jewish population was around 600,000, the Arab population about 1.2 million. Yet the UNSCOP proposal was for the new Jewish state ('Israel') to have 56.5 per cent of the land of Palestine and the Arab state a mere 43.5 per cent. Some 80 per cent of the land of the new Jewish state would be Arab-owned (rather than Israeli-owned), including over 85 per cent of the Arabs' orange groves.

Jerusalem was another sticking point. The UN committee decided that as neither Jew nor Muslim would surrender control over so holy a city, it should be placed under permanent international trusteeship. A quick glance at the map (see Figure 4.1) shows why such a proposal appeared to favour Muslims over Jews.

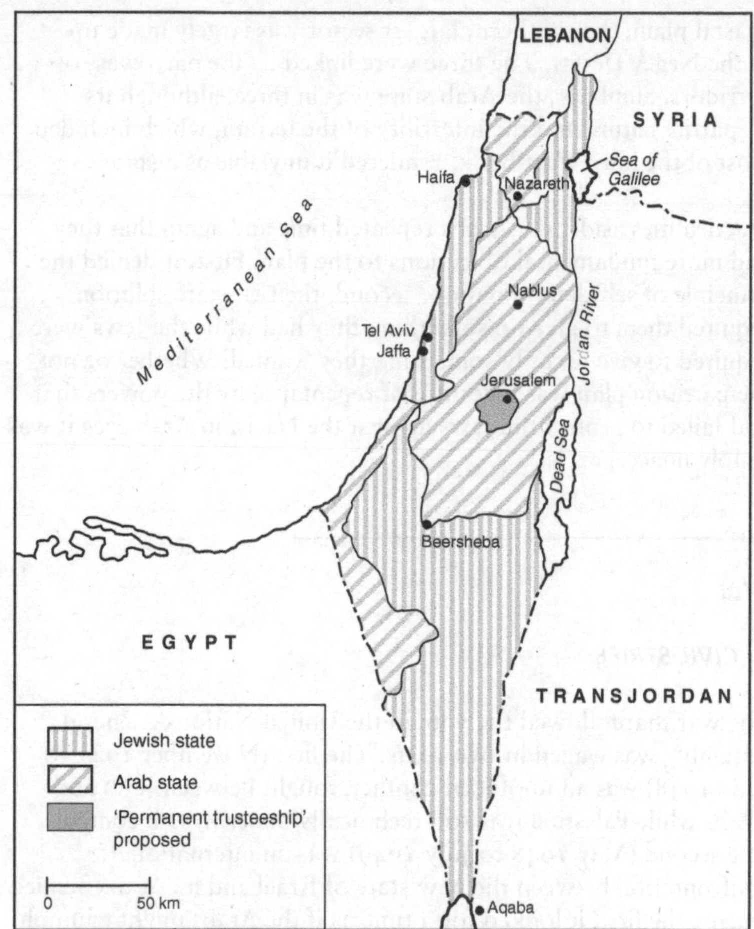

Figure 4.1 The UN's proposed two-state solution, 1947.

The city was envisaged as an enclave within the Arab state. In other words, in order to visit the Wailing Wall and other holy sites, Jews would have to pass through or over hostile territory.

The same map reveals another flaw with the UNSCOP plan: the frontiers. The proposed Jewish state was in three scarcely linked blocks. The northernmost, around the Sea of Galilee, had good access to fresh water; the central part contained most of the fertile coastal plain; the southern, largest sector was largely made up of the Negev Desert. The three were linked by the narrowest of corridors. Similarly, the Arab state was in three, although its tri-partite nature and the infertility of the terrain, which included most of the hilly West Bank, rendered it unviable as a state.

Practicalities aside, the Arabs repeated time and again that they had more fundamental objections to the plan. First, it denied the principle of self-determination; second, the two-state solution required them to give up something they had while the Jews were required to give up only something they wanted. Whether or not the partition plan was a gesture of repentance by the powers that had failed to protect the Jews against the Nazis, in Arab eyes it was simply unacceptable.

War

CIVIL STRIFE

The war that followed the vote in the United Nations' General Assembly was waged in two parts. The first (November 1947 to May 1948) was an unofficial conflict, fought between Jews and Arabs while Palestine was still technically under British control. The second (May 1948 to July 1949) was an international confrontation between the new state of Israel and its Arab enemies. During the first, it looked for a time as if the Arabs might triumph; the second saw the State of Israel emerge as a fixture on the world map and the embryonic nation of Palestinian Arabs scattered and all but destroyed. Small wonder, then, that the Jews remember the struggle as the War of Independence while to Palestinian Arabs it is simply *Al Nakba*, the Disaster.

Having fixed 15 May 1948 as the date when its forces would be withdrawn from Palestine, Britain was prepared to do no more than protect its own interests in order to keep casualties and economic loss to a minimum. Into the vacuum thus created stepped Jewish and Arab militias. The Zionist campaign was predominantly masterminded by the Jewish Agency, headed by Ben-Gurion, which controlled the disciplined and relatively experienced Haganah forces numbering at least 40,000. The Irgun, Stern Gang and other guerrilla groups worked more or less together with the official forces.

The internal and external Arab forces were poorly co-ordinated but, initially at least, relatively numerous and determined. The Arab League paid for an Arab Liberation Army and gave command to Fawzi al-Din al-Qa'wuqji, a charismatic but militarily suspect veteran of the 1936 Arab Revolt. Although he eventually commanded about 6,000 men, he had little respect for local Arab fighters, refused their requests for assistance and even co-operated with the Haganah against fellow Arabs. Meanwhile, the Grand Mufti had moved to Lebanon to be nearer the action and had given his heroic nephew, Abdul Qadir al-Husseini, command of a volunteer Holy War Army. Some 2,000 Muslim Brotherhood volunteers also moved into Palestine from Egypt. These forces were supplemented by local village guards and other warbands assembled to defend lives and property against Jewish depredations.

Insight

The red-haired, blue-eyed outlaw Fawzi al-Din al-Qa'wuqji was another Arab leader who did his cause no good by co-operating with the Nazis during World War II. His chequered past and incompetence as a field commander reflected the Arabs' failure to coalesce behind wise and determined generals.

PLAN D

The fighting was sporadic but bitter and both sides perpetrated horrific war crimes. The Jews' weakest point was Jerusalem, where thousands of co-religionists were besieged by al-Husseini's men. Elsewhere the Haganah and Irgun implemented a policy of 'aggressive defence', clearing Arabs from areas allocated to the

State of Israel. This ruthless and often cruel process has since come to be called 'ethnic cleansing'. Starting along the coastal plain and later moving north, the tactic was either to force Arab families to pack up their belongings and leave or to scare them into doing so by perpetrating some atrocity and then deliberately exaggerating its scale. As the deaths and casualties on either side rose into the thousands, neither a UN arms embargo nor repeated calls for a truce from the USA managed to stop the bloodshed.

Insight

This paragraph is, I admit, contentious. There is little consensus over the reasons why so many Palestinians became refugees during the 1948–9 war. Interpretations vary from Arab scaremongering to deliberate Israeli ethnic cleansing.

By the late spring of 1948, the poorly equipped Jewish forces were under serious pressure. At this stage Ben-Gurion decided to launch Plan D, a strategy that had been devised for when the British eventually pulled out. It involved not only seizing territory assigned to Israel by the UN but also moving into areas allocated to the Arab state. The first target was to open up a corridor through Arab lands to Jerusalem.

It was during this campaign that Jewish guerrilla forces sacked the Arab village of Deir Yassin, which had made a non-belligerency pact with local Jews. After the withdrawal of Palestinian Arab irregulars from the area, the Irgun under Menachem Begin and the Lehi under Yitzhak Shamir moved in and slaughtered large numbers of men, women and children. Original reports spoke of over 250 killed, although modern research has suggested that the true figure was less than half that number.

At the time, it was in the interests of both sides to exaggerate the scale of the outrage: Jews did so in order to terrify other Arab villagers into fleeing lest they be the next victims, and Arabs did so in order to persuade the world that they were innocent victims of Jewish barbarity. The importance of the Deir Yassin massacre, therefore, was not so much in what happened – there were similar tit-for-tat outrages going on all over Palestine – as in its effect as propaganda.

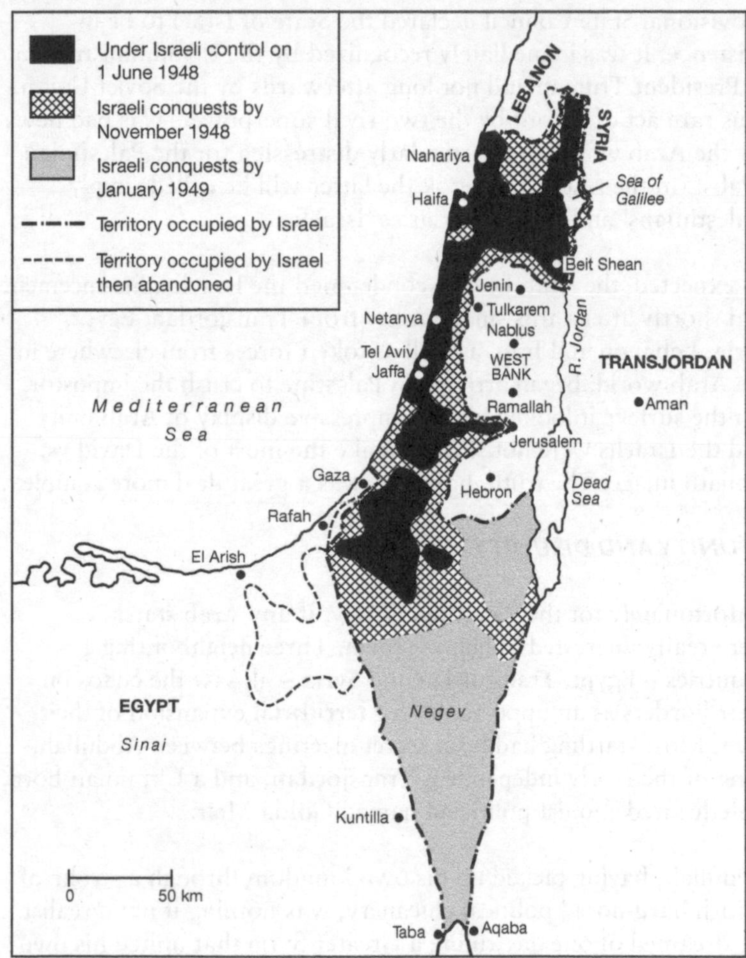

Figure 4.2 Expanding Israel, 1948–9.

By the end of April 1948, just as Ben-Gurion and his provisional government in Tel Aviv had planned, perhaps 200,000 Arabs had fled their homes in areas coveted by the Jews (see Figure 4.2).

ISRAEL AND WAR

The British finally pulled out of Palestine on 15 May 1948. The previous day, at 16:00 hours local time, Ben-Gurion's Zionist

Provisional State Council declared the State of Israel to be in existence. It was immediately recognized by the US administration of President Truman and not long afterwards by the Soviet Union. This rare act of accord by the two rival superpowers was bad news for the Arab world and particularly distressing for the Palestinian Arabs. (In the rest of this book the latter will be called simply 'Palestinians' and their adversaries 'Israelis'.)

As expected, the Arab League condemned the Israeli announcement and shortly afterwards small armies from Transjordan, Egypt, Syria, Lebanon and Iraq, as well as token forces from elsewhere in the Arab world, began arriving in Palestine to crush the impostor. On the surface it looked like an impressive display of Arab unity and the Israelis were not slow to make the most of the David vs. Goliath image. The truth, however, was a great deal more complex.

UNITY AND DISUNITY

Unfortunately for the Palestinians, few, if any Arab states were really interested in helping them. Three neighbouring countries – Egypt, Transjordan and Syria – all saw the chaos on their borders as an opportunity for territorial expansion of their own. Most startling had been secret meetings between Abdullah, King of the newly independent Transjordan, and a Ukrainian-born, US-educated Zionist politician named Golda Meir.

Abdullah, having picked up his own kingdom through a stroke of British hard-nosed political chicanery, was nothing if not a realist. He dreamed of one day ruling a Greater Syria that united his own state with the Syrian one to the north and Palestinian territory to the west of the Jordan River. The last thing he wanted was a flourishing Arab Palestine and he shared the Israelis' detestation of Grand Mufti al-Husseini. Consequently, he had no problem reaching an agreement with the equally realistic Mrs Meir, which was that in the event of full-scale war between Israel and the Palestinians, he should take over Palestinian territory on the West Bank of the Jordan and leave the Israelis to grab what they could of the rest. The status of Jerusalem was left open.

In an effort to tie the hands of a monarch they did not trust, the other warring Arab states appointed Transjordan's King Abdullah Commander-in-Chief of the Arab forces. The military title was meaningless. The King produced no overall strategic plan and his allies refused him permission to ascertain precisely the state of their forces. These were not as sizeable as might have been expected, either. In mid-1948 it is estimated that the non-Palestinian Arabs managed to put about 23,000 troops into the field. The better-trained Israel Defence Force (IDF), created by forcing the experienced Haganah, Irgun and smaller groups to amalgamate, then stood at around 35,000. This eventually rose to over 96,000, at least double that of the increased Arab armies. Particularly after the rearmament of the summer of 1948 (when weapons and ammunition of all kinds came in from Soviet-backed Czechoslovakia, France and private US sponsors), the IDF was better armed than the Arabs. It even secretly acquired three US Flying Fortress bombers, with which it was able to attack Cairo.

Despite cultural differences between Jews originating from Europe (Ashkenazim) and those from Eastern lands (Sephardim), all Israelis knew that they were fighting for their very existence. This gave them a ruthless determination, sometimes known as the 'Holocaust syndrome'. Israelis had seen what had happened to the meek and conforming Jews who had trusted others – they had been exterminated. The 'fighting Jew' would never let this happen. Their toughness might make them feared – hated even – but it would keep them safe.

To the first generation of Israelis, the end justified the means – even if it meant attacking their own unarmed trucks in order to provoke further fighting with Egypt; even if it meant the Haganah troops of future Prime Minister Yitzhak Rabin killing Irgun fighters who had rejected a unified command (another future prime minister, Menachem Begin, survived the attack); even if it meant extremist assassins commanded by yet another future prime minister, Yitzhak Shamir, killing the UN mediator because he seemed too pro-Arab; even if it meant Moche Dayan's forces terrorizing Arab villages outside Israel so that their inhabitants would learn to live in fear of their neighbours. All of these acts of desperate cruelty actually happened. Understandable but nevertheless abhorrent, they built the wall of hatred and mistrust that has yet to be broken.

Faced with steely Israeli unity, the motley Arab forces stood little chance. Apart from Egypt, their states were largely new creations. Most were politically unstable (the Egyptian prime minister was assassinated in 1949 and the country had nine further changes of government over the next three years) and unable to cope with the strains of full-scale, long-distance warfare. Moreover, although some troops might have been inspired by feelings of Arab or Muslim unity, their leaders were not. The Grand Mufti, Palestine's nominal leader, did not get on with the Arab League. The aim of the Egyptians was to seize as much land as possible on the Sinai side of the Suez Canal. The Syrians wanted the fertile land in the Golan Heights and around the Sea of Galilee. The Saudis sent one paltry battalion; the Lebanese and Iraqis were there largely because it was politically less trouble than not being there. As we have seen, Commander-in-Chief Abdullah wanted only a limited campaign in order to take Palestinian land on the West Bank.

Insight

A common faith and language and hazy memories of former glories may help foster a sense of nationhood, but they are not in themselves sufficient to overcome personal, political, tribal and regional differences – as Arab nationalists discovered.

Palestine destroyed

PHASE 1

During the first phase of the international war, which lasted until a UN-brokered truce on 11 June 1948, neither side gained the upper hand. Indeed, the Israelis found themselves hard-pressed on all fronts. They suffered from a lack of suitable aircraft, making do by rebuilding and adapting old World War II Messerschmitts, Spitfires and spotter aircraft. Without either heavy armour or artillery at this stage, they were at a distinct disadvantage when confronting the better-equipped Egyptians in the south. In the streets and outlying districts of Jerusalem, they also met a better-organized and armed fighting force in the British-trained Transjordanian Arab Legion.

The truce was arranged by Count Bernadotte, a UN official from Sweden. By agreeing to the month-long break in the fighting, the Arab forces lost the initiative and with it their chance of bringing the Israelis to their knees. The interval enabled the Ben-Gurion government and its high command to reorganize, re-train and reinforce. When the truce was broken on 8 July, the Israelis were able to go on the offensive to devastating effect.

PHASE 2

In the second phase, interrupted by a second truce between 18 July and 15 October, the war dragged on into 1949. In reality, by the previous autumn the Arab forces had lost the stomach for a fight and the conflict had become largely an Israeli mopping up operation. The acts of terror continued, one being the Israeli assassination of Count Bernadotte because he was thought to favour the Arabs. It was a tragic, unnecessary end for a man who had personally been responsible for saving many Jews from the Nazi Holocaust.

Far too late, in September 1948 the Grand Mufti and his Arab Higher Committee announced the formation of a Government of All Palestine with the Mufti as president, Jerusalem as its capital and Gaza as its seat of government. The empty gesture raised little enthusiasm and evoked even less worldwide response. Abdullah emphasized the point by setting up a larger rival Palestinian Congress in Aman. Meanwhile, Israeli forces crossed the Negev Desert to Eilat, advanced into southern Lebanon, took the western half of Jerusalem and were only prevented by the intervention of the RAF from occupying Sinai. By the spring of 1949, the Israelis possessed over three-quarters of the territory that the UN had allocated to the state of Palestine. The only exceptions were an Egyptian-held coastal strip around Gaza and the West Bank, which was now in Transjordanian hands.

Israel agreed truces with Egypt in February 1949, with Lebanon in March, Transjordan in April and Syria in July. Jerusalem was divided between an Israeli west and a Transjordanian east with a demilitarized zone between them. A similar zone ran between Israel and Syria in the north. Over time the truces matured into more durable armistices with every state except Iraq. No proper peace treaties were signed, however, implying that the fighting was by no means over. All that the war of 1948–9 had achieved, in fact, was the morphing of the 'Palestine question' into the equally insoluble 'Israeli–Palestinian conflict'.

In depth: David Ben-Gurion (1886–1973)

Arriving in Palestine in 1906, David Ben-Gurion (born David Gruen) went on to mastermind the formation of the State of Israel and become the country's first prime minister. For his many achievements he is revered in Israel as the 'Father of the Nation'.

During his youth in Russian-occupied Poland, the young Ben-Gurion became aware of European anti-Semitism and the exciting dreams of the early Zionists. Palestine was the obvious destination for a young man fired by Zionist enthusiasm, and before World War I he worked there as an agricultural labourer. In 1915, the Ottoman authorities threw him out on account of his cocktail of socialist and Zionist views. He travelled to the USA, where he campaigned vigorously for the Zionist cause before joining the British Army's Arab Legion. Resettled in Palestine after the war, he devoted his considerable talents to the creation of an independent Jewish state out of the British mandate. To this end he founded and led the Histadrut, a union of Jewish workers in Palestine, and the socialist Israeli Workers' Party (Mapai), which he also headed. By 1935, he was the dominant figure in the international Zionist Executive and Palestine's Jewish Agency.

Originally hostile to Palestinian Arabs as the principal stumbling block on the path towards a Jewish state, from 1940 onwards Ben-Gurion was suspicious of the Arab-friendly British. After the end of World War II, while publicly condemning the extremes of groups like the Irgun, he pursued a policy of 'fighting Zionism' that led to Britain handing over the future of Palestine to the UN and the eventual foundation of Israel in May 1948. Taking the posts of prime minister and minister of defence, he insisted that all Jewish fighting forces amalgamate into the IDF. That done, he masterminded the campaign that saw Israel assimilate most of the land the UN had allocated to an Arab state.

After the War of Independence, the extraordinarily hard-working and enthusiastic Ben-Gurion continued his double role as prime minister and defence minister to 1953 and again from 1955 to 1963. His policies were straightforward and direct: strengthen Israel through immigration, irrigation, education, industrial development and, above all, hard manual work; and come down heavily on any Arab state that threatened the country's security. On retirement – hastened by suspicion of clandestine anti-Western operations in Egypt – he devoted his time to writing and research. He was recognized by the influential *Time* magazine as one of the leading figures of the twentieth century; Israel's major airport is named in his honour.

In depth: Al Nakba

Israelis like Prime Minister Golda Meir, wanting to justify what happened in 1948–9, claimed that a Palestinian nation had never existed before the later twentieth century. Until then, there had simply been Arabs living in an administrative district known as Palestine, without distinctive national religious, social, cultural or historical traditions.

Most historians now disagree with this thesis. A sense of Palestinian nationhood had been evolving since the early nineteenth century, originally in opposition to outside intervention. The British mandate,

(Contd)

reintroducing the ancient concept of Palestine as a distinct entity and offering it future independence, considerably boosted nationalist sentiment. It was further enhanced by the 1936 Arab Revolt against the British and by the wishes of the Jews to break up Palestine or even fashion it as a Zionist state. Lack of leadership and a fragmented social set up prevented the Palestinians from realizing their ideal before *Al Nakba*, the Disaster, of 1948–9 set it back half a century and more.

The war that led to the creation of Israel saw the destruction of 360 Arab villages and 14 Arab towns. About 70 per cent of Palestinians (those people who might have expected to live in a UN-fashioned Palestinian Arab state) had become refugees. Some were forcibly evicted from their homes, others left because they feared what would happen to them if they did not. After the war, around 165,000 remained as a second-class minority within Israel. The number forced to become refugees was disputed. The Israelis said 520,000, the British between 600,000 and 760,000, and in 1949 the United Nations registered 726,000.

Whichever figure is correct, the scale of the exodus was staggering. A whole society was dispersed: men, women and children, healthy and infirm, rich and poor. Some families herded before them livestock they had been able to rescue. Others managed to get away with just a few household possessions, dragging them in carts or squeezing them into buses and lorries as they headed for the safety of the border and life in a makeshift camp. Over 200,000 crammed into the Gaza Strip, more than 300,000 ended up in the West Bank, perhaps 100,000 made it to Lebanon, another 100,000 to Syria and around the same number to Transjordan.

Scattered, temporarily housed in tents and rough shelters, without running water and proper sanitation, deprived of schools and medical facilities, the Palestinian nation came of age. It was an understandably bitter and angry people, too, and one that would not – could not – forget. In time, therefore, their Disaster became the whole world's.

10 THINGS TO REMEMBER

1. *As soon as World War II ended, the Jewish community in Palestine launched a ferocious campaign against the occupying British – beside whom they had been fighting only months before.*

2. *In September 1947, a UN committee – UNSCOP – produced a report recommending that Palestine be partitioned into two states bound in an economic union.*

3. *Fighting between Jews and Arabs for control of post-mandate Palestine broke out in November 1947.*

4. *During the conflict of 1947–49, perhaps 700,000 Palestinians became refugees. The circumstances under which this occurred are hotly disputed.*

5. *At 16:00 hours on 14 May 1948, the Palestinian Jews declared the State of Israel to be in existence.*

6. *Arab support for the Palestinian cause was strong on rhetoric but weak on practical assistance. Israel's neighbours were more interested in grabbing what they could for themselves.*

7. *Although promoting a 'David v Goliath' image to the world, in fact after the first few months of fighting the Israeli forces were in almost every way superior to those of their enemies.*

8. *In pursuing their 'War of Independence' with ruthless ferocity, the Israelis committed a number of atrocities, including the assassination of UN mediator Count Bernadotte.*

9. *The UN-brokered ceasefire of 11 June–18 July 1948 enabled the hard-pressed Israelis to regroup and reorganize.*

10. *When Israel agreed truces with the Arab states in 1949, it was in possession of all Palestine except the Gaza Strip and the West Bank.*

5

Battle lines 1949 to early 1950s

In this chapter you will learn about:

- *the new State of Israel*
- *the fate of the Palestinians after the war of 1948–9*
- *the impact of the war on the Middle East and beyond.*

To most Jewish people living in the Middle East and elsewhere, the war of 1948–9 had been an outstanding success, almost a miracle. True, losses had been high. With 6,000 killed and 30,000 wounded – 4.6 per cent of its population – Israel's first war would be its costliest. But the outcome had been remarkable: the birth, survival and widespread acceptance of the State of Israel. The 'homeland' was no longer a dream, an aspiration or even a target – it was a living, tangible reality. Tragically, though, partly because of the way the state had been forged and partly because of the way it conducted itself during its first years of existence, this was by no means the end of the story. Rather, it was merely the close of a chapter – and those that followed were sadder, more harrowing and infinitely more complicated.

The winners...

ISRAEL

Having absorbed 77 per cent of the UN's proposed Palestinian state, Israel was some 21 per cent larger than the country envisaged by the 1948 partition plan (see p. 57). Unlike that state, the new Israel had defendable frontiers – though not as defendable as some in the military would have liked. The population comprised 717,700 Jews (with Ashkenazim outnumbering Sephardim 6:1) and 165,000 Arabs (almost one fifth of whom were Christian).

Strict Zionists claimed that Israel was not a new country but simply the restoration of a very old one. That belief, together with British influence and the need for flexibility, persuaded the Israeli governing elite not to draw up a written constitution. Instead, the country's parliamentary system evolved through legislation, practice and executive orders. The system established in the late 1940s, outlined below, remains largely the same today.

Insight

One reason why Israel has no written constitution is the lack of accord between liberals and the ultra-orthodox over what its basic principles might be. The latter's call for a constitution based on Jewish teaching – the Torah – would have made Israel a religious state, like modern-day Saudi Arabia or Iran.

The cabinet, invariably a coalition, was the lynch pin of Israeli government. The country's central democratic body was the Knesset, a 120-seat representative assembly. Normally elected every four years on a proportional basis, it ensured reasonably fair representation for Israel's Jewish and Arab populations, each of which was politically and religiously extremely diverse. All adult citizens had the vote and Hebrew and Arabic were recognized as official languages. Proportional representation produced a multiplicity of parties. The largest, Mapai (Labour – see pp. 127–8), provided Israel with its first (David Ben-Gurion) and second (Moshe Sharett) prime ministers. Further left was the Mapam Party, while Herut inherited the right-wing mantle of the Irgun. The Knesset elected Chaim Weizmann to the largely honorary position of president.

Experience had taught the leaders of the Jewish community to temper Zionistic idealism with practical pragmatism. Thus, as there was no written constitution, so there was no Bill of Rights.

The independent judicial system operated through municipal, religious and military courts inherited from the mandate. The law derived from Ottoman and British traditions, adapted by religion, precedent and legislation.

As one might expect in a country born in war, the military played a far larger part in Israeli life than in many Western states. Military service was compulsory for all non-Arabs and in matters of budget, planning, transport and foreign policy, the needs of the IDF and the security services generally had priority.

BEN-GURION

David Ben-Gurion dominated Israeli politics for the first 15 years of the country's existence. As prime minister for all but two years during that period, he determined key policies that decided how the country saw itself, how it presented itself to the outside world and, most importantly, its relations with the people upon whom it had stolen such a decisive march – the Palestinians.

The key to Ben-Gurion's thinking was that Israel, surrounded by enemies and harbouring potentially dangerous minorities within, could not afford to relax its guard for one moment. Everything had to be geared to maintaining what had been won and, where possible, to strengthening it. Domestically, his policy may be divided into the following strands:

- *Minimizing the internal Arab threat by relocating some of Israel's Arabs away from the borders and keeping others under military rule*
- *Developing economic self-sufficiency*
- *Building up the country's resources, especially its agriculture through irrigation*
- *Encouraging as many Jews as possible from the worldwide community to return to the homeland.*

The 1950 Law of Return, which granted citizenship to all immigrant Jews, was a key instrument in doubling Israel's population by 1952. Some of the new immigrants came from

Europe but a high proportion were refugees from Arab lands where, after the war of 1948, they found themselves shunned and even persecuted. As one might expect, immigration on such a vast scale produced problems. There was a serious shortage of housing (see below) and defining Jewishness was sometimes a tricky business. Moreover, most Sephardim had been raised very differently from their European counterparts. They were usually less well educated and their attitudes were urban and socially conservative. In business, politics and administration, they found themselves occupying a sort of intermediate position between the Ashkenazim and Arabs, leading to political tensions.

Housing was a thorny issue, too. When the Knesset allowed the state to appropriate abandoned Palestinian property, thousands of empty houses were given to immigrants. Even so, there were not enough to go around. Sprawling shanty towns of makeshift shelters spread out around major cities and in 1951 there were still 100,000 Israelis living in tents. Most of these were recent Sephardim immigrants.

Self-sufficiency did not come easily. Israel had to cope with an Arab boycott (see pp. 93–4) and at least one major irrigation scheme met with serious political objections (see p. 85). Even so, the armistice line of 1949 (see p. 67) was soon known as the 'Green Line' because the fertility on the Israeli side contrasted so starkly with the barren waste opposite. The economy also benefited from the substantial donations made to individuals and institutions by overseas Jewish groups, especially US ones. By 1952, Israel was also in receipt of hefty overseas aid. The most controversial donations came from West Germany: the right-wing Herut Party violently condemned them as 'blood money'.

... and the losers

PALESTINE

The war of 1948–9 erased the name 'Palestine' from maps printed outside Arab lands. The lion's share of what had been Palestine had been swallowed up by Israel. Around 40 per cent of the land it had absorbed (or stolen, depending on one's viewpoint) had only months previously been Arab-owned. In the north, a demilitarized zone separated Israel from Syria, which coveted half the Sea of Galilee and land nearby. As agreed with Israel before the war, Transjordan had occupied the adjacent part of Palestine known as the West Bank. A year after his armistice with Israel, King Abdullah held a dubious consultation in the West Bank before annexing it formally to his renamed Kingdom of Jordan. The move was accepted by Britain and the USA, but rejected by Israel and all Arab states except Iraq. The city of Jerusalem remained divided between Israel and Jordan.

In the south-west, Palestine had been carved up by Israel and Egypt, the latter taking the Gaza Strip. The Egyptians also cast covetous eyes over the neighbouring Negev Desert (see Figure 4.2 on p. 63). An Egyptian-backed attempt by Mufti Husseini (whose reputation stood even lower after the 1948–9 debacle) to form a sort of mini-Palestine in Gaza, came to nothing: the exiled and ageing cleric remained the putative ruler of a state that simply did not exist.

PALESTINIAN DIASPORA

What of the Palestinian people themselves? Broadly speaking, they may be divided into three. Those left within Israel, those who had fled or emigrated to more distant lands, and those for whom home was now a refugee camp in the Gaza Strip, the West Bank, Jordan, Syria or Lebanon.

Many of the relatively small middle classes of Palestinians – the teachers, doctors, better-off businessmen – managed to get away from the frontier areas and start new lives in cities elsewhere in the Arab world or even further afield. Kuwait became the largest community, hosting some 400,000 Palestinians by 1990. Quite large numbers found their way to the USA, where the Palestinian diaspora grew to over 100,000. These better-educated and generally wealthier refugees were not always popular or well-treated in their new homes (hard-working immigrants rarely are) but at least they had a future. They had a past, too, which not all were prepared to forget: it was from middle-class exiles that a new Palestinian leadership would eventually emerge.

Insight

While working in the Arab world, I was surprised at the hostility towards Palestinians shown by some of their fellow Arabs. Such sentiments were in stark contrast to the pronouncements of their leaders.

ISRAEL'S PALESTINIANS

Around ten per cent of all Palestinian Arabs remained behind and eventually became citizens of Israel where they made up some 15 per cent of the population. Clustered in Galilee and between Jerusalem and the coast, theirs was a difficult existence on the margin of two communities. This is witnessed by the names by which they were known, the 'Arab citizens of Israel', 'Palestinian Israelis' and 'Israeli Arabs'.

For at least 20 years, Israel's Palestinians remained a shocked, leaderless, depressed and isolated minority. Families had become separated by the Green Line, which they might not cross. Their communities were subjected to military control, limiting the ability to assemble or travel without permission. During the fighting of 1948–9, many thousands had abandoned their original homesteads in search of safety and in most cases they were unable to return. Thus they became refugees within their own country. Even harder to bear, they were regarded with suspicion, even as traitors, by Arabs living elsewhere.

The position of Israel's Palestinians on the political margins is illustrated by the fact that only the Israeli Communist party accepted both Arab and Jewish members. No Arab became a member of the ruling coalition. Exemption from the draft meant they missed out on the privileges afforded to veterans. To political and social exclusion was added economic discrimination. Arabs were not allowed to form co-operatives and their settlements had less adequate water and electricity supplies than their Jewish neighbours. Not afforded sufficient building land, the crowded dwellings erected for their swelling population were often put up illegally and therefore under continual threat of demolition.

Hard though life was for Israel's Palestinians, their suffering was relative. Their standard of living might have been lower than that of most Israelis but it was still way above that of the refugees. The same can be said of the education they received. As a consequence, the third generation of Israeli Palestinians, while maintaining a distinct Arab identity, began to identify more closely with the state into which they had been born than with the land beyond the Green Line.

THE CAMPS

Palestinian refugees marooned beyond Israel's frontiers were gathered together by relief and other agencies and settled in vast tented camps: four on the East Bank of the River Jordan, 19 on the West Bank; 15 in Lebanon; eight crammed into the Gaza Strip; nine in Syria (see Figure 5.1). Over time, some of the original, temporary camps were emptied and their occupants moved on. Syria's Lattakia camp is a good example. Housing Palestinians originally from Jaffa and villages of northern Palestine, it was founded in 1955–6 on the edge of the Mediterranean town whose name it bears. Its occupants earned what they could from fishing, casual labour in the port and tourism.

Depending on their point of view, outsiders saw the camps as a ring of either shame or dangerous hatred around the newly fledged Israel. Almost 60 years later, with some exceptions and additions, they were still there: hotbeds of hatred, bitterness, prejudice, hopelessness and fantastic dreams – a nation in waiting. Over time it was this sense of being in limbo that the refugees found most debilitating. In just a few months, they had fallen from being founder members of a new country to being merely stateless 'Arab refugees', at best pitied, at worst derided as unwanted intruders.

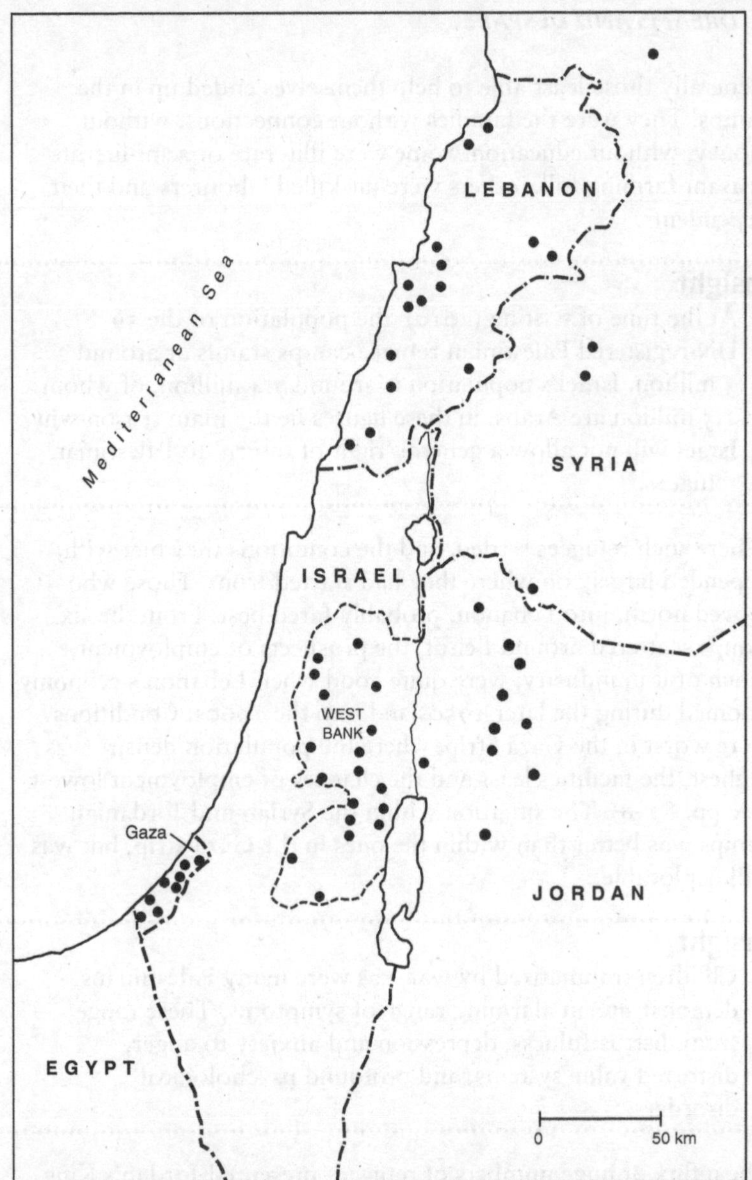

Figure 5.1 The main Palestinian refugee camps 1950.

Generally those least able to help themselves ended up in the camps. They were the families without connections, without money, without education. Some were illiterate or semi-literate peasant farming folk, others were unskilled labourers and their dependents.

Insight

At the time of writing (2010), the population of the 59 UN-registered Palestinian refugee camps stands at around 5 million. Israel's population is around 7.4 million, of whom 1.5 million are Arabs: in these figures lie the main reason why Israel will not allow a general 'right of return' to Palestinian refugees.

Where such refugees settled, and the conditions they met with, depended largely on where they had started from. Those who moved north, into Lebanon, probably fared best. From the six camps scattered around Beirut, the prospects of employment, much of it in industry, were quite good when Lebanon's economy boomed during the later 1950s and into the 1960s. Conditions were worst in the Gaza Strip, where the population density was highest, the facilities least and the chances of employment lowest (see pp. 87–8). The situation within the Syrian and Jordanian camps was better than within the ones in the Gaza strip, but was still deplorable.

Insight

Children traumatized by war – as were many Palestinians – demonstrate an alarming range of symptoms. These range from distrustfulness, depression and anxiety to anger, distorted value systems, and profound psychological disorders.

The influx of huge numbers of refugees presented Jordan's King Abdullah with a problem. His native Jordanians were suddenly outnumbered by immigrants in the ratio 2:1, not something he had foreseen when making his pact with Israel (see pp. 64–5). The newcomers were generally better educated too, for although the mandate schools had not been wonderful, they were better than anything the King had provided for his subjects.

Abdullah responded by claiming to be the true leader of the Palestinians. This was in a sense true because he hoped to rule a Pan-Arab country that included his own state (incorporating the West Bank), Syria, Lebanon and perhaps even Iraq. The majority of the refugees inside Jordan were given Jordanian citizenship and their education was designed to raise them as Jordanians rather than Palestinians. To support this programme of Jordanization, Palestinian nationalist organizations and media were banned, as were all political parties. Although 25 per cent of Jordan's East Bank population lived in the camps, they provided not one member of the country's consultative parliament in the period 1950–65.

THE 'LOST GARDEN OF PALESTINE'

On the West Bank, attempts at Jordanization were less successful. The population here had risen from 400,000 to 700,000; the new arrivals being distributed fairly equally between towns, villages and camps. The strain on local services was immense and there was constant feuding between the original inhabitants and the refugees. The situation, like that in Gaza, was made worse by lack of leadership. The better off and educated Palestinians with marketable skills had not remained with the traumatized masses. The leadership drain did not stop, either: between 1950 and 1954, a further 100,000 West Bankers emigrated from the forlorn hillsides.

Dismayed and dispirited by their own weakness, for a time Palestinians took hope in Nasser's talk of reviving Arab nationalism (see p. 104) – the Arab nation would unite, drive out the imperialists and Zionists, and the people of Palestine would be free to return home. But nothing happened. Nasser, quite logically, put his own people's interests before others. When it came to executive decisions, so too did other regional heads of state. For all of them, 'Palestine for the Palestinians' was good rhetoric but bad policy.

Where did that leave the Palestinians, a people with no state and no leader? It left them with memories that merged with their dreams. Determined to cling on to their heritage, they assiduously preserved the names and customs of their former life. The homeland from which they were excluded became the 'Lost Garden of Palestine' to which one day, somehow they would return. Slowly, the men chatting in the streets of Nablus and the refugee women gathering in the markets or outside the tents began to realize a vital lesson. No one – not the Americans, not the Russians and not even their Arab brothers and sisters – was going to put themselves out to help the Palestinians. In the end, if they were to get back what they had lost, they had to do it themselves. To achieve their goal they had to be just as ruthless, just as single-minded as the Zionists had been.

Impact of war

CONFLICTING NATIONALISMS

Instability had been a hallmark of the Middle East since the collapse of the Ottoman Empire and the subsequent attempt to set up nation states in the region. After World War II, three developments undermined regional stability still further. The first we have already examined: the 1948–9 conflict and the emergence of the non-Arab, non-Muslim State of Israel. The second was a conflict of nationalisms, and the third the Cold War.

Arabs had been talking of 'Arab nationalism' for over a century. Although it had proved a useful stick with which to beat a common enemy – the Ottomans, British, French or Jews – it had rarely produced much in the way of co-operation. This was obvious after the appearance of Israel and the failure of the Arab forces to work together to crush the new state. Part of the problem was that most

Arab countries were themselves new, insecure creations. In trying to forge feelings of national unity, their rulers had to overcome the rival pull of tribalism and regionalism. In these circumstances, calls for Pan-Arabism or Islamic unity were useful only when serving national rather than trans-national ends.

THE COLD WAR

The Cold War was the long period of superpower confrontation in which the Soviet Union, the champion of communism, stood toe-to-toe with the USA, the champion of democratic capitalism. It is generally said to have begun with Winston Churchill's famous statement, delivered at Fulton, Missouri, in March 1946, that an 'iron curtain' had fallen across Europe. The rivalry between the two sides of the curtain – communist East and capitalist West – fed wars, coups and terrorism all over the globe.

Two issues brought the Cold War to the Middle East. One was the falling of a second iron curtain across the Palestine region, dividing Jews from Arabs. Although both the USA and the USSR had initially been favourable towards Israel, it was perhaps inevitable that before long they would try to use the regional stand-off to increase their local influence. The second issue was oil. The Middle East's share of world oil production was rising daily and was already crucial to the USA.

The USSR generally had to play second fiddle to the USA in the region. Its strongest cards were a traditional hostility to imperialism, a willingness to provide arms (often through an intermediary such as Czechoslovakia) and the popular appeal of socialism and communism in a region where wealth and privilege were often concentrated in a few hands. However, the Soviet Union was officially an atheist state with a history of persecuting its own Muslims. Nor did it have a tradition of involvement in the Middle East. Consequently, the Soviets found it difficult to take the initiative in a part of the world where Britain and, increasingly, the USA were well established. Both of these powers knew, however, that the communists needed only half an invitation to move in.

Presidents Truman (1945–53) and Eisenhower (1953–61) were obliged to play a tricky balancing act: backing democratic Israel, which was strongly supported by the American people as well as certain powerful business and financial interests, while at the same time keeping in with the Arabs, particularly those of the oil-producing states. This resulted in the international politics of the Middle East becoming a contest of bluff and counter-bluff, deceit and counter-deceit that not even the players themselves were able to control.

SYRIA

When, under international pressure, the French withdrew from Syria in 1946, they left it with a shiny new democratic and republican constitution. Nevertheless, given the country's complicated religious, social and economic diversity, stability was unlikely. For the US State Department the tipping point came with the failure of Syria's corrupt Sunni government to triumph in the war with Israel. There was now a possibility, the USA believed, that this vital link in the oil pipeline route from the Gulf to the Mediterranean would fall to the communists.

To pre-empt such an event, in March 1949, the CIA engineered a coup by Colonel Husni al Zaim. The plan did not achieve the desired results. Zaim soon fell and Syria entered upon a prolonged period of instability marked by several further coups. The corruption and chaos bred a new movement in Syrian politics: the Arab Socialist Renaissance (or Baath) Party. Fiercely anti-Western, its manifesto claimed all boundaries between Arab peoples to be merely imperialist devices.

Not surprisingly, Baathist sentiment was intractably hostile to Israel. The demilitarized zone between the two countries was already a source of friction. In 1953, tension in the region rose further when Syria strongly objected to Israel drawing irrigation water from the River Jordan as it flowed through the demilitarized zone. With no progress on turning the 1949 armistice into a permanent settlement, there was every chance that at some future date Israel and Syria would find themselves at war again.

LEBANON

Parliamentary democracy fared slightly better in Lebanon. The delicately balanced Muslim–Christian constitutional arrangement survived the war with Israel, prompting the leadership to declare that Lebanon was not really an Arab country and had never wanted to go to war in the first place. A Syrian-backed coup attempt was foiled. Thereafter, despite an assassinated prime minister, a president removed by a general strike and the destabilizing presence of large numbers of Palestinian refugees, Lebanon's Western-inclined political system survived more or less intact.

JORDAN

King Abdullah of Jordan – condemned by his fellow Arabs as 'the dog who sold Palestine to the Zionists' – was the neighbour Ben-Gurion's government found it easiest to deal with. Both were realists. Given this trait in his personality, it is surprising that Abdullah risked visiting the Al-Aqsa mosque in Jordanian-occupied Jerusalem. Here, on 20 July 1951, a Palestinian assassin shot him dead, claiming the King had betrayed the Palestinians and the entire Arab nation.

Two years later, Abdullah's schizophrenic son was declared unfit to rule. The crown passed to his 18-year-old son, Hussein, who had been beside his grandfather at the time of his death and had himself narrowly escaped being killed. The crown was scarcely less dangerous. With turbulent Palestinians inside his borders and ambitious Israelis just the other side, the young, English-educated King would need every one of the political skills he had inherited from his grandfather if he were to survive.

IRAQ

Defeat of its small force by the Israelis did not bring about an immediate change of regime in Iraq, the only combatant country not to agree an armistice after the 1948–9 war. Regent Abdullah, helped by rising oil revenues and the behind-the-scenes power of the army, maintained a ragged version of democracy during the minority of King Faisal II. The overthrow of two prime ministers by popular uprisings and a period of martial law were not good omens, however, and a lot of hopes were pinned on the young Faisal. When he came of age in 1953, the anticipated reforms and crackdown on corruption failed to materialize. As would soon become apparent, the King's lack of charisma and political instinct (handicaps at the best of times) in post-war Iraq were fatal.

EGYPT

The shaky constitutional monarchy that Britain had handed down to Egypt was disastrously undermined by the extraordinary figure of King Farouk, a bloated playboy monarch who dabbled in politics with dangerous ineptitude. His corrupt and inefficient government handled the conflict with Israel badly. It even scored a spectacular own goal when, in the middle of the war, an attempt to suppress the increasingly popular Muslim Brotherhood led to the assassination of the prime minister and the subsequent killing of the Brotherhood's leader by government agents.

As well as disliking their own government and wanting revenge on Israel, Egyptians also harboured a strong dislike of the continued British presence in their country. Dating from a pre-war treaty, in the Suez Canal Zone Britain maintained and defended ten airfields and two naval dockyards. By the early 1950s, guerrilla attacks on these positions had become commonplace, provoking fierce retaliatory raids by the British. Egypt, the most populous and potentially most influential state in the Middle East, was ripe for revolution.

Farouk's fantasy reign ended with a near bloodless coup in July 1952. It was conducted, perhaps with CIA help, by a group of army personnel calling themselves the Free Officers. They were led by Colonel Gamal Abdul Nasser, a 32-year-old veteran of the Israeli war. For the time being, Nasser allowed attention to be focused on the higher-ranking General Mohammed Naguib, who became president of the Republic of Egypt.

Chaired by Nasser, a Revolutionary Command Council banned political parties, disbanded parliament and began reforming the country's grossly unequal system of landholding. Despite the new regime's undemocratic and socialist inclinations and its talk of uniting all Arabs into a single nation, several Western governments, including the USA, gave it a qualified welcome. Israel was more sceptical, however, and it was not long before the USA was coming round to a similar point of view.

In depth: Gaza Strip

Gaza had been the poorest district in the Palestinian mandate. The fighting of 1948–9 left the eastern section, the Negev, in Israeli hands and a tiny western section, the Gaza Strip, under Egyptian control. Almost overnight, this wretched parcel of land, some 45 kilometres long and eight kilometres wide, became one the most densely populated and poorest areas in the world.

Around 80 per cent of Gaza's population lived in eight refugee camps hastily organized by the United Nations. Water was always scarce and electricity, where available, was unreliable. The sanitation often beggared belief. In these conditions, without sufficient arable land or irrigation, the traditional agricultural economy of orange groves and grain collapsed. There was no industry to replace it. The people of Gaza, whose average income was estimated to be around US$80 a year (£50), were almost totally dependent upon handouts of food and money from relief agencies. Only in the later 1950s, as trade opened up with Eastern Europe and better-off Egyptians used Gazan smugglers to bypass Nasser's high tax regime, did the Strip's economy pick up somewhat.

The Gaza refugees lived in a political limbo. Unlike the West Bank, where Palestinian Arabs were offered Jordanian citizenship, Gazans were not invited to become Egyptians. Like those it replaced,

(Contd)

the Nasser government feared an influx of poverty-stricken, revenge-seeking Palestinians and made it very difficult for Gazans even to visit Egypt. The only exceptions were small numbers of students gaining places at Egyptian universities. Within Gaza, political and other potentially inflammatory organizations were not permitted and the bands of *feyadeen* (meaning 'those prepared to sacrifice themselves') sent on raids into Israel were under strict Egyptian control (see p. 94).

Unwanted, stateless, poverty-stricken and traumatized, the Palestinians of the overcrowded Gaza Strip developed a unique camp society of their own. It was a curious mix of cold realism, despair and romantic yearning for a lost Palestinian paradise. Traditional tribal and extended family structures competed with new ones based around gangs and successful small-scale entrepreneurs. The soaring birth rate made the overpopulation rapidly worse. Where possible, those with skills moved out. They left behind a society shorn of educated leaders, where bickering and petty rivalries marred everyday life, and where cross-border and internecine violence was never far away.

The children and grandchildren raised in these hopeless circumstances are those who periodically burst upon our TV screens: given their tragic, desperate heritage, it is no wonder their lives are so torn by bloodshed and strife.

In depth: UNRWA

During the ethnic cleansing of Palestinians from Israel in 1948–9, streams of desperate, destitute refugees fled abroad. Some found their way into villages and towns, but the majority – several hundred thousand men, women and children – had nowhere to stay. Initially they sheltered as best they could, using such materials as they had brought with them or found – literally – lying around. Their suffering was immense and hundreds died.

Local individuals and services laboured selflessly to help. Before long they were being assisted by larger international agencies such as the Red Cross and Red Crescent. However, the scale of the problem demanded something special. Consequently, in December 1949, the United Nations General Assembly voted to set up UNRWA, the United Nations Relief and Works Agency for Palestine Refugees in the Near East. It began work the following May.

The first task of the Agency was to see that those in its care were given adequate shelter. At first this was mainly tents. By the mid-1950s, these were gradually being replaced by more substantial shelters of block and corrugated iron, large numbers of which remain in service today. Food and water were brought in daily. Communal standpipes and drains eventually followed, and shops and regular distribution centres were established. The larger roads were paved. Where possible the work was done, and still is, by members of the camps themselves. Payment was often in food.

In 1950, the medical situation was dire, with high infant mortality, widespread malnutrition and frequent deaths from communicable diseases like malaria, gastroenteritis and TB. Years of special diets, immunization and health education eventually brought the situation under control. Even then, adequate sanitation was still scarce.

UNRWA's education plan was its great triumph, providing the refugees with the most comprehensive primary education system in the Middle East. Girls, in particular, benefited. The programme's aim was to enable refugee children to find jobs and so end their families' cycle of deprivation. Sometimes this happened but despite UNRWA's efforts there are twice as many Palestinian refugees today as there were in 1950. Critics say that UNRWA is largely to blame for this. Its relief, they argue, has acted like a drug. By giving immediate respite without tackling the root causes of the malaise, it had produced a dependency culture that is difficult to throw off.

10 THINGS TO REMEMBER

1. *Around 4.6 per cent of Israel's population was killed or wounded in the fighting of 1947–9.*

2. *Of Israel's original population of around 880,000, almost one fifth were Arabs.*

3. *Israel's parliamentary system, never enshrined in a written constitution, incorporated a proportional voting system that produced coalition governments headed by multi-party cabinets.*

4. *Helped by massive foreign aid (most controversially from Germany), Israel's economy expanded rapidly over the first ten years of the country's existence.*

5. *The armistice line between Israel and its neighbours became known as the Green Line because of the western side's comparative fertility.*

6. *The 10 per cent of Palestinians remaining within Israel found themselves mistrusted and treated as second-class citizens.*

7. *Better-off Palestinian refugees with transferable skills did not have too much difficulty making new lives for themselves and their families overseas.*

8. *The poorer and less well-educated bulk of the original population of Palestine were herded into UN-managed refugee camps around Israel's borders.*

9. *The East–West Cold War that developed after World War II exacerbated national instability and international tensions across the Middle East.*

10. *The democratic systems of government left by the colonial powers in Syria, Iraq and Egypt all failed to survive for long in the post-war world.*

6

The second round and its aftermath 1949 to c. 1964

In this chapter you will learn about:

- ***border incidents between Palestinians and Israelis***
- ***the Anglo–French–Israeli alliance and the Suez war, 1956***
- ***Israel after the Suez war***
- ***growing instability in the Arab world.***

Israel and its neighbours

SECURITY BEFORE PEACE

In 1948, as Israel was beginning its international war, the rest of the world was starting to recover from its second global conflict in 30 years. This had been caused partly by a failure of the victors of World War I. After defeating Germany and her allies, Britain and France had acted without either generosity or understanding. The legacy of humiliation and bitterness thus created had helped prepare the ground for Nazism and the outbreak in 1939 of a new and even more terrible European war. It is tragically ironic that this lesson – the need for magnanimity in victory – was lost on those who had suffered most as a consequence, the Jews.

Having won a startling and comprehensive victory by the middle of 1949, Israel failed to cement its position by reaching an accommodation with those it had overcome. Prime Minister Ben-Gurion's position was straightforward: after the embarrassing defeat of 1948–9, no Arab government would accept peaceful co-existence with Israel. The new state therefore was obliged to adopt a policy of 'aggressive defence' – responding to any threat, however small, with overwhelming retaliation and, if necessary, launching pre-emptive strikes. The policy persists to the present day, as those familiar with the news from Israel and Palestine will recognize.

Ben-Gurion also insisted that there was absolutely no question that Palestinian refugees, whatever their reasons for leaving, could be allowed back into Israel. Although, by joining the United Nations in 1949, Israel had theoretically accepted a UN resolution insisting on the right of Palestinian return, Ben-Gurion had no intention of ever complying. He saw the refugees as an Arab problem, not an Israeli one: permitting their return would simply admit a gigantic and probably fatal fifth column (see insight box p. 80, top).

SECURITY FIRST

To an outsider Ben-Gurion's stance might seem extreme, almost paranoid. That would be to ignore what he and like-minded Zionists saw as the bitter lessons of history. They argued that for almost 2,000 years, in much of the Middle East and Europe, the Jews had been a despised and persecuted race. This had culminated in the Nazis' deliberate attempt to wipe them out. Yet thanks to their remarkable resilience, intelligence, determination and, some believed, the protecting hand of God, they had survived and remained true to the ancient Jewish heritage.

Now at last, the hawks' argument ran, the Jews had a country of their own, a safe and secure haven where they would be free from persecution. It would be wicked folly to do anything, anything at all, that might threaten this new-found security. As the Arabs found at the barren Lausanne Peace Conference (1949), if there was to be lasting peace between Israel and her neighbours, it would be on Israel's terms. Until that time, it would wait, impervious behind its military superiority, and continue to respond to any threat, real or perceived, with merciless force.

Not all Israelis signed up to the grim Ben-Gurion doctrine. Foremost among those who took a less hawkish line was the urbane, Ukrainian-born Moshe Sharett. One of the founders of Tel Aviv, the intellectual Sharett served as Israel's foreign minister in 1948–56. He played a key role in the armistices of 1949, in getting Israel accepted by the UN and in establishing his country's diplomatic network of embassies and consulates. Although accepting the prime importance of security, he believed that in the long term it could come only by reaching some permanent agreement with Israel's neighbours. This might at some future stage involve a land-for-peace deal.

Insight

Having lived in an Arab village as a boy, learning to read and write Arabic fluently, and then serving in the Ottoman army during World War I, Foreign Minister Moshe Sharett probably had more insight into Muslim and Arab ways than a good many of his Jewish contemporaries.

The two positions – Ben-Gurion and Sharett, hawk and dove – have remained at the heart of Israeli politics from the moment of independence to the present day. Both are understandable. Yet neither addresses the view held by hundreds of thousands of Palestinians: that Israel was a state created on their stolen land.

INCURSION AND RETALIATION

The hostile pronouncements of Israel's Arab neighbours were not matched by significant military action. Evidence suggests that for several years Arab governments did not encourage commando-style raids on Israel. Their most successful measure was an economic boycott that included not just Israeli goods but those of companies trading with Israel. As oil wealth and population growth made the Middle East an increasingly important market for Western manufacturers, so the boycott came to bite deeper. A company like Land Rover, for example, because it traded with Israel, found itself excluded from the extremely lucrative Middle Eastern 4 × 4 market.

Only ten per cent of cross-border infiltrations into Israel during 1950–5 were by military bands and they instigated only 25 major incidents. The bulk of the early border troubles were heart-breaking cases of desperate Palestinians sneaking back to collect possessions, harvest crops or even just set eyes on the homesteads they had lost. Sometimes the incursions were simply Bedouin tribesmen wandering across unmarked borders. Whatever the intruders' motives, the IDF responded with ferocity. Borders were mined and suspects shot on sight. The bodies of those slain were booby trapped to kill relatives coming to collect them. Over six years, perhaps as many as 5,000 Palestinians were slain, most innocent civilians.

FEDAYEEN

Minor aggressive infiltration into Israel began in 1950. From then until 1956, the number of Israelis killed annually by Arab raiders rose from 19 to 54, and the wounded from 31 to 129. The first semi-military incursions were small-scale sorties by independent groups of Palestinian *fedayeen*. In 1953, with Egyptian backing, young Palestinians started launching regular, planned attacks on Israeli civilians. To counteract such activities and, if possible, wipe out these 'terrorists', the IDF set up Unit 101 under the ruthless Major Ariel Sharon. Opinion is divided over Unit 101's action. Critics say it provoked Palestinian anger and increased the chances of further attacks; defenders credit it with keeping Israel safer than it would otherwise have been. No one denies that its tactics were extremely fierce.

Within weeks of its creation, the non-uniformed Unit 101 was responsible for two incidents that the Palestinians were swift to label massacres. The first occurred when Israeli forces, supposedly targeting an Egyptian *fedayeen* co-ordinator, were discovered inside the al-Bureij refugee camp in the Gaza Strip and fought their way out. Some 50 Palestinian civilians died. Two months later, Unit 101 responded to the *fedayeen* killing of an Israeli woman and her two children by destroying the Jordanian village of Qibya. Between 53 and 69 Palestinians were killed in the operation. Half of those who died were women and children.

Ben-Gurion lied that the atrocity had been carried out by local Jewish settlers provoked by Arab attacks. Few believed him and the USA withheld aid worth $75 million. More significant for the future, the al-Bureij and Qibya attacks entered Palestinian folklore, inspiring future generations to maintain the armed struggle against what was perceived as an evil enemy.

Suez

NASSER'S HONEYMOON

The removal of the Egyptian monarchy by the Free Officers received a cautious welcome in the USA (see pp. 86–7). Britain and Israel reserved judgement. Their fears were somewhat allayed when the Officers, despite a pledge to end colonialism, said they would not take sides in the East–West Cold War. The position was wisely pragmatic. Nasser, who assumed the presidency in 1954, needed all the economic and military aid he could lay his hands on. His stance was rewarded when the USA and Britain offered $270 million to help Egypt build a high dam at Aswan to control the waters of the Nile.

Anglo-Egyptian talks on other matters went well, too. Britain agreed to give Sudan full independence and to withdraw from its bases in the Suez Canal zone by 1956, retaining the right to return if the zone were attacked by a third party. The deals brought howls of protest from the Muslim Brotherhood, Islamic fundamentalists who wanted union between Egypt and Sudan and Britain's immediate withdrawal from all Egyptian soil. When the

Brotherhood sponsored an attempt on Nasser's life, he outlawed the movement and rounded up as many of its leaders as he could.

THE BAGHDAD PACT

Meanwhile, with US backing, Britain was attempting to put together a NATO-style anti-communist alliance in the Middle East. Emerging in 1954, it was known as the Baghdad Pact. The first states to agree to work together against 'Soviet expansionism' were Turkey and Iraq, joined later by Britain, Iran and Pakistan. The key to the Pact's success, however, was getting Egypt on side.

To Britain's intense irritation, Nasser would have none of it. The Pact, he warned, was a 'festering crime' and an insult to the Arab nation. Egypt would not join. Moreover, he put pressure on Jordan not to sign up. It's important to remember that because of its size, population and history, Egypt was already the most influential Middle Eastern state. Nasser's flamboyant pronouncements on Arab unity and ending Western interference in the region enhanced this position.

ARMS FOR SALE

Size, population and rhetoric were all very well but, as Arabs recognized only too clearly after 1948–9, they needed to be supported by military force. Here Nasser had a problem. There was no difficulty with personnel – what he lacked were modern armaments in the form of tanks, artillery and aircraft. Britain and the USA had provided him with some but their policy of balancing Israel's forces with those of its enemies meant he had far fewer than he wanted. Early in 1955, Israel proved his point for him. Responding to the killing of an Israeli cyclist by an Egyptian intelligence-gathering mission, the IDF launched a massive raid on Gaza that left 38 Egyptian soldiers dead.

Within weeks, prompted by a meeting with officials from communist China, Nasser had gone behind the USA's back and struck a deal with the Soviet Union. In return for US$300 million worth of cotton, the Soviets, using Czechoslovakia as an intermediary, would re-arm Egypt with 100 self-propelled guns, 200 armoured personnel carriers, 300 tanks, 200 MIG-15 fighters and 50 bombers. Such a formidable battery of firepower would make Nasser a real force in the region and seriously threaten Israel's ability to defend itself in any future conflict.

The Soviets were not concerned that arming Egypt might harm Israel, as their brief friendship with the Jewish homeland had already faded. By the mid-1950s they were much more interested in Syria, where their influence was growing markedly. Meanwhile, the Syrians' relations with Israel had deteriorated to the point of heavy border fighting.

NASSER, ISRAEL AND THEIR ALLIES

Egypt, the USSR's latest Middle East protégé, was also going through a difficult time in its relations with Israel. Even before the bloody Gaza raid (above), the Israeli secret services had been exposed as an international menace when an attempt to implicate Egypt in anti-Western terrorism – the Lavon affair – was badly bungled. In September 1955, Nasser raised the temperature several degrees by closing the Strait of Tiran, cutting access to the Red Sea from Israel's southern port of Eilat. Less than a year later, he made an even more dramatic gesture: he nationalized the Suez Canal.

Insight

Britain's commercial interest in the Suez Canal dated back to November 1875 when, acting on behalf of the British government, Prime Minister Benjamin Disraeli had bought nearly half the shares in the Suez Canal Company from the ruler of Egypt. He did so with £4 million borrowed from the Jewish Banking house, Rothschild.

The Canal was a vital international waterway. In the pre-supertanker age, two-thirds of Europe's oil, including one-third of Britain's, passed through it. It also provided Britain and France, major shareholders, with useful revenue. Nasser's offer of compensation was unacceptable because of the one-sided way he had acted and because neither of the European powers wanted such a key strategic link in the hands of someone they did not trust. Talks aimed at reaching a compromise got nowhere, nor did efforts by the French, British and Israeli secret services to eliminate Nasser.

Franco-Israeli co-operation was already an established fact. Paris detested Nasser for the support he was giving to the FLN independence fighters in the French colony of Algeria. France had supplied Israel with the technology to build a nuclear power plant, and therefore possibly a nuclear bomb. The French had also become Israel's major arms supplier, providing sophisticated Mystère jets and tanks in larger quantities than was announced officially. It was no great surprise, therefore, to find Israel and France plotting together against Egypt.

A combined Anglo-Israeli operation was much more of a surprise. It was, after all, only eight years since Jewish gangs had been killing British soldiers and civil servants in the mandate territory, and Britain's traditional friendships were with their ex-colonies and protectorates in the Arab world. Nevertheless, Nasser's opposition to the Baghdad Pact and high-handed action regarding the Canal had so angered Prime Minister Anthony Eden that he was prepared to risk his career to bring down the man he now termed 'the Muslim Mussolini'.

The secret plan was as simple as it was crude. Using recent *fedayeen* incursions as an excuse, the IDF would drive across the Sinai towards the Suez Canal. Britain and France, pretending to act as mediators, would demand that Egypt and Israel withdraw their forces from the war zone. When Nasser refused to remove Egyptian troops from Egyptian territory – as he surely would – the Europeans would invade, Nasser would fall… and all would be well with the world once more.

THE SUEZ CAMPAIGN

The first part of the coalition plan went like clockwork. Israel's one-eyed (literally) Chief of Staff, Moshe Dayan, eager to get to grips with Egypt before their Soviet rearmament was complete, swept into Gaza and the Sinai on 29 October 1956. Within a week the IDF was at the Canal. When Nasser rejected the Anglo-French ultimatum, European fighter-bombers smashed Egyptian military installations and destroyed almost all its air force's new hardware. The Canal was blocked accidentally by a bombed ship and deliberately by concrete-filled Egyptian hulks. British and French marine and airborne troops landed nearby – and there the stop-Nasser campaign fell apart.

To begin with, it had been poorly planned. Neither Britain nor France had consulted with potential supporters, nor had they got the media on side with careful briefing. The time that elapsed between the air bombardment and invasion had been too long, allowing public opinion to turn against the venture before it had properly begun. A blocked Suez Canal necessitated fuel rationing in Britain, which was already close to bankruptcy. The situation worsened when Syria, hearing that Iraq had given the attack a tentative welcome, cut the pipeline that conveyed Iraqi oil to the Mediterranean.

Far more serious than all this was the response of the superpowers. The Soviets threatened missile attacks on Israel, France and Britain unless the fighting stopped immediately. US President Eisenhower was not only furious at his allies' lack of consultation, but he was simultaneously in the middle of conducting an election campaign on a peace manifesto and trying to handle the crisis caused by the Soviet invasion of Hungary. He absolutely refused to toe the anti-Egyptian line. Israel dared not go against so powerful a paymaster, while Britain had neither the heart nor strength to countermand the leader of the West. Therefore, when the USA took the matter to the UN and an immediate ceasefire was demanded, Israel and Britain obliged. This forced France to do the same.

Anglo-French forces were home by Christmas 1956. The Israelis lingered longer, refusing to give back their conquests until they had received assurances about open seaways, *fedayeen* raids and a UN peace-keeping force (UNEF) in Sinai. When these were given, they too went home. That left Nasser, the man who had outfaced two major imperial powers and kept Sinai and his nationalized Canal, the undisputed hero of the Arab world.

Israel after Suez

ILL AT EASE

The Suez War changed for ever the way Israel was seen abroad. Despite its small size, it was now perceived in the West as an important power rather than simply a collection of valiant homesteaders. Outbreaks of violent behaviour had damaged its reputation, too. In April 1956, an artillery bombardment of Gaza City had left 59 dead. Just before the fighting broke out, at Kafr Qasim, 47 Israeli Palestinian agricultural workers were unnecessarily shot and killed for being out after a curfew about which they had not been told. It was estimated that during the war a further 1,000 Palestinians died, many of them civilians.

Israel was also less at ease with itself. Ben-Gurion, the elderly godfather of the state who by now could do no wrong in his people's eyes, remained prime minister until his resignation in 1963. The Suez setback had ended any lingering hopes he may once have had of Israel living at peace with its neighbours within secure frontiers. He considered further conquest unwise, however, urging instead that Israel remain ready to meet any threat the Arabs might pose. This involved massive military spending, which by the 1960s accounted for one-third of the country's Gross National Product (GNP).

PROSPERITY AND CHANGE

Israel's economy continued to grow, the GNP doubling between 1952 and 1965. However, by 1963 inflation stood at 18 per cent and the trade deficit at over US$500 million a year. Solvency was possible only with massive help from overseas. This came from the USA, where first Democratic Senate leader L. B. Johnson and then Democratic President J. F. Kennedy looked more favourably on Israel than

Eisenhower had done. The other major donor was West Germany, whose reparation payments met a quarter of Israel's budget.

Israeli society was changing too. Fresh waves of immigration and a high birth rate drove up the population to around 2.2 million by 1961. Not long after this, the Sephardi element outnumbered Ashkenazi for the first time. The distribution of power did not change, however, with Ashkenazim (the 'First Israel') dominating almost all important positions in politics, the military, academia and employment. The result was resentment from the Sephardim (the 'Second Israel') that in 1959 led to riots in the slum Wadi Salib suburb of Haifa.

Such incidents, coupled with the continued third-class status of Israeli Arabs and the dreadful misery experienced by their fellow Palestinians in the camps, led to painful heart-searching among more liberal-minded Israelis. Was there a possibility, some wondered, that the people who throughout history had suffered more than others from racial discrimination were now themselves guilty of the same injustice? Might the Ashkenazim treatment of the Sephardim and the Jews' treatment of the Arabs be almost a form of apartheid?

Insight

Those who criticize Israel are frequently condemned as anti-Semitic racists; at the same time, Israel itself is often pilloried as a racist state. As a consequence, in the present climate, the terms 'racist' and 'racism' are probably best avoided with reference to the Israel–Palestine situation.

The 11-year peace

ISRAEL AND THE WORLD

The Suez campaign bought Israel 11 years of peace and only a slightly shorter period free from cross-border *fedayeen* attacks.

For the Palestinians who hoped of one day establishing their own state, it was a time of increasing hopelessness and desperation. Israel was untouchable, powerfully backed by France, Germany and, increasingly, the USA. The USSR was prepared to make the appropriate anti-Israeli noises to attract Arab opinion but to take no action. The same, it seemed, applied to President Nasser.

With several Arab states moving to the left (see p. 104), the Western-backed Israel found itself isolated from the affections of much of the Third World. It used two tactics to get round this. The first was to act as a conduit for clandestine US support for anti-Soviet regimes, such as those in Uganda and Ethiopia. The second was to befriend states, like Iran and Turkey, that were hostile to Egypt. On occasion Israeli agents were even believed to have warned Nasser's enemies of assassination plots.

Dwight Eisenhower was US president until 1961, during which time he maintained his policy of not showing undue favour towards Israel over its Arab neighbours. In 1957, for example, in the 'Eisenhower Doctrine' he declared the USA willing to support any Middle Eastern state exposed to the 'possibility of communist aggression'. During the two years the policy was current, the USA strongly backed Jordan and Lebanon, states that had fought to prevent the emergence of Israel in 1948–9.

Eisenhower was less than impressed when his spy planes revealed that Israel's industrial complex at Dimona was not a textile factory, as advertised, but a secret plant using French technology for the development of a nuclear weapon. President J. F. Kennedy (1961–3), on the other hand, was prepared to value Israel as a key piece in his Cold War jigsaw. The Hawk surface-to-air missiles he sent to Israel, for example, were that country's first official arms provision from the USA.

PALESTINIANS SIDELINED

President Nasser's pro-Palestinian stance went no further than setting up a Voice of Palestine radio station, a Palestinian newspaper and getting the first Arab summit to create the Palestine Liberation Organization (PLO, 1964) and, two years later, the Palestine Liberation Army (PLA). Nasser selected Ahmad Shukayri to lead the PLO. The blustering lawyer from Acre did so with some proficiency, exerting his supremacy over the elderly but still active Haj Amin al-Husseini (see pp. 50–1). Nevertheless, Shukayri, the PLO and the PLA were all creatures of the Arab states that had set them up. It was their masters' will they were obliged to follow, not that of the Palestinian people.

The PLO had been established as a response to Israel's completion of the National Water Carrier scheme, a canal (Beit Netopha) that took water from Lake Tiberias to the Negev Desert. Understandably, the development infuriated Syria and, on several occasions, disputes between the two countries over the use of water from the River Jordan flared into serious border conflicts. In 1963, Syria had actually called for all-out war with Israel; Nasser refused to go along with the idea.

Insight

The importance of water in the conflict between Israel and its neighbours cannot be exaggerated. In making the Beit Netopha (described by Arafat as an 'imperialist event') its first target, Fatah were well aware that they were striking at the country's main artery.

Meanwhile, a far more significant event in the history of Israeli–Palestinian relations had taken place. Despairing of ever getting their Arab brethren to take meaningful action on their behalf, in 1959 a group of Palestinian exiles living in Kuwait had formed a nationalist organization of their own (see pp. 105 and 125). Its name was Fatah and among its leaders was a man who more than any other would determine the nature of the Palestinian struggle: Yasser Arafat.

TIMES OF TROUBLES

The years that followed the Suez War saw growing political turmoil in the Arab world. This revolved around three basic issues: East–West alignment in the Cold War, Arab nationalism (were the Arabs one nation or many?) and the regional leadership of Egypt's President Nasser. These coincided in 1958 when, to the surprise of many, Egypt and Syria joined together to form the United Arab Republic (UAR).

Officially non-aligned in the Cold War, the UAR designated Egypt the 'Southern Province' and Syria the 'Northern Province'. The military were under Egyptian command and Nasser was the head of state. It was heralded, somewhat optimistically, as the first step towards full Arab unity. The move delighted most Palestinians, who believed that their best hope of being restored to their homeland lay in all Arabs uniting in a single state. Such hopes were soon dashed. The UAR collapsed in a couple of years when the Syrians decided they wanted to be a bit more than just a province.

Playing his political cards well, Nasser replaced US funding for the Aswan Dam with loans from the Soviet Union, which also lent money to extend Egypt's programme of nationalization. Further indications of the progress of the left in the Middle East came when the Iraqi monarchy was overthrown in a socialist-inclined army coup. Seriously worried that events in Iraq might spark coups in Jordan and Lebanon – both more or less pro-Western and reasonably favourably inclined towards Israel – the USA sent troops into Lebanon and British paratroops went to shore up the authority of the young King Hussein of Jordan.

The interventions had the desired effect, although Hussein's position remained precarious. In 1960, for example, his prime minister was assassinated by Palestinians whom the King believed had Syrian backing. Only US pressure persuaded Hussein not to take matters into his own hands and invade his northern neighbour. More coups in Syria and Iraq saw the Baath Party come to power in both states. These were followed in 1963 by further talk of Arab unification, this time with the aim of bringing Iraq, Syria and Egypt together in a left-leaning federation similar to the defunct UAR. Once again Palestinian hopes were raised, only to be dashed when the talks broke down.

In conclusion, although the Suez War had not been followed by another international conflict, in 1963 the situation in the Middle East remained dangerously volatile. The Palestinians, exiled or under occupation, were bitter and frustrated. Iraq, Syria and Egypt had still not made peace with Israel, and their governments, many highly unstable, were prone to histrionic outbursts against the Jewish state. Jordan was less hostile but in no position to act unilaterally. In such circumstances, further armed confrontation was a distinct possibility. The only reasonable certainty was that, as on the two previous occasions, it was unlikely to solve anything.

In depth: Fatah

Founded in Kuwait in the late 1950s, Fatah's name, which means 'conquest', was a reverse acronym, in Arabic, of the Palestinian National Liberation Movement. Its founders, Yasser Arafat prominent among them, had become fed up with the failure of their fellow Arabs to help the Palestinians. Consequently, at first Fatah rejected the Palestine Liberation Organization (PLO) as just another empty gesture by the Arab states.

Fatah's claim was that by force of arms the Israelis had created a state that had no right to exist. Its aim was to destroy this state and replace it with a single, secular Arab–Jewish Palestine. Its platform, therefore, was both destructive and constructive. Unfortunately for its image, it was the former that attracted the most attention. However justified its cause, Fatah's violent tactics alienated a broad spectrum of world opinion. Attacks, bombings and hijackings carried out in the name of Fatah or one of its factions became a fact of life in the late 1960s and early 1970s (see pp. 109–14 and pp. 136–46). The weaponry and explosives were communist-supplied and Syria was identified as the state most likely to shelter Fatah's fighters. The movement was less well received elsewhere in the Arab world. Its leadership was forcibly expelled from Jordan in 1970–1 and from Lebanon ten years later (see pp. 138 and 180).

(Contd)

Arafat led the Fatah-dominated PLO from 1968, and during his lifetime the two organizations were often indistinguishable. From 1982 to 1993, for instance, while Arafat was taking refuge in Tunis, the Fatah and PLO leadership and administration were there with him. The Oslo Accords, which required the Palestinian leadership to renounce terrorism and led to the formation of the Palestinian Authority, obliged Fatah to consider more constructive policies and strategies (see pp. 216–21). It did not find the change easy for three reasons. First, it was essentially a guerrilla organization, attracting warrior types with little interest in administration and peaceful politics. Second, it was basically inefficient, even corrupt, and faction-ridden, unsuited to the task of government. Finally, Fatah was very much the creation of one man, Yasser Arafat. His energy and charisma held it together. When he died in 2004, Fatah found itself in trouble.

The Fatah veteran Mahmoud Abbas (see p. 256) was elected president of the Palestinian Authority in 2005, but in the 2006 elections to the Palestinian parliament, Fatah was trounced by the better-organized, more focused Hamas. There followed a period of trauma and strife marked by in-fighting, sometimes violent, between Fatah and Hamas, and between different factions within Fatah itself (see Chapter 14).

In depth: President Gamal Abdul Nasser (1918–70)

Born the son of a village postmaster near Alexandria, Nasser showed a strong interest in politics from an early age. He graduated as an infantry officer in 1938 and was posted to the Sudan. Here his anti-colonial sentiments led him to plan an anti-British coup with Axis agents. Fortunately for him, the idea never got off the ground.

After World War II, Nasser worked at the Military Academy where he helped form the Free Officers Association, the group that engineered the 1952 coup (see pp. 86–7). Two years later, already the commanding figure on the all-powerful Revolutionary Command Council, he became head of state. He was made president in 1956 and held the position until his death. His offer of resignation after the humiliating 1967 war was rejected by popular acclaim (see pp. 116–21).

A number of developments helped secure Nasser's place in Egyptians' affections. He took much credit for the long-needed agricultural reform instituted after the fall of Farouk. His brave reaction to a (possibly staged) assassination attempt in 1954 gave him heroic status. British withdrawal from the Suez Canal zone, and the subsequent failure of Israel, France and Britain to hold on to the gains they had made in the 1956 war, enhanced Nasser's prestige still further and made him the darling of anti-imperialists everywhere.

Over the next 13 years, a series of misjudgements and policy failures ensured that Nasser's legacy was at best mixed, although his popular status remained undiminished. To maintain his position, he made Egypt a police state. This drew him into conflict with Muslim extremists, liberal democrats and the judiciary. Closer relations with the Soviet Union brought welcome funding, particularly for the Aswan Dam (completed 1970), but took the Egyptian economy down the path of inefficient nationalization and state control.

Nasser's political and military errors were even more harmful. The plan for a United Arab Republic got no further than a temporary and half-hearted union with Syria (see p. 104). Egypt's armed intervention in Yemen was a military and economic disaster. Worse still was the posturing that provoked Israel into launching the Six-Day War of 1967, with consequential humiliation, loss of life and destruction of Egypt's military (see p. 121). Finally, more than perhaps any other Arab leader, Nasser was prepared to use the Palestinian issue as a rallying cry while doing nothing practical to help the exiles. This merely fed Palestinian extremism and made any settlement of the Israeli–Palestinian situation even harder to achieve.

10 THINGS TO REMEMBER

1 *From the outset, Israeli political opinion was sharply divided between those (doves) who wished for a compromise peace deal with the country's Arab neighbours, and those (hawks) who believed that peace could come only when the Arab world accepted Israel's existence unreservedly.*

2 *During the period 1950–5, some 5,000 Palestinians were slain while entering Israel illegally. Most were innocent civilians.*

3 *Israel's non-uniformed Unit 101, commanded by Ariel Sharon, conducted counter-Palestinian operations of extreme ruthlessness.*

4 *In September 1955, President Nasser of Egypt unilaterally nationalized the Suez Canal.*

5 *In the autumn of 1956, Egypt was attacked by a combined Israel, British and French force (Suez Crisis).*

6 *Threatened by the USSR and under heavy pressure from the USA, the humiliated invaders handed back the Egyptian territory they had taken and withdrew.*

7 *Israel, a major military power by the early 1960s, was spending one-third of its GNP on its armed forces.*

8 *Although their existence was never officially confirmed or denied, by 1970 Israel was reckoned to have possessed nuclear weapons manufactured using French technology provided in the 1950s.*

9 *In 1964, an Arab summit gave official support to the Palestinian cause by setting up the Palestine Liberation Organization (PLO).*

10 *More significant in the longer term was the emergence in the 1960s of Yasser Arafat's Fatah movement, dedicated to an armed struggle to restore Palestine to the Palestinians.*

7

The Six-Day War 1965 to 1967

In this chapter you will learn about:

- ***Palestinians in the mid-1960s***
- ***the build-up to war, 1963–7***
- ***the Six-Day War, 1967***
- ***the aftermath of the Six-Day War.***

Palestinian dead end

PAN-ARABISM

As we saw in the last chapter, the Suez War did nothing to help the Palestinian cause. Those Palestinians living within Israel – whom the authorities registered as Arabs, never as Palestinians – remained largely at the lower end of the economic spectrum and outside the political process. The only party that would accept them was the Israeli Communist Party, known as Maki, and under its auspices they were able to express limited anti-Zionist Pan-Arab sentiments. This was hardly political power or influence, and not until the 1990s were the votes of Arab members of the Knesset used to sustain a government (Rabin's: see p. 208).

Outside Israel, the Palestinians of the Gaza Strip had returned to Egyptian governorship after a brief period of Israeli military rule during the Suez debacle. Life in the overcrowded enclave remained as forlorn as before. Developments on the Jordanian-controlled West Bank were somewhat more interesting. Here, despite the best efforts of the royal government to integrate them into Jordan, the Palestinians obstinately retained their separateness. The well-intentioned work of UNRWA in the camps helped maintain the occupants' refugee status. Elsewhere, despite the official suppression of all expressions of Palestinian nationalism, the more numerous, better-educated and generally more prosperous immigrants remained unwilling to shed their separate identity.

After the establishment of Israel, as noted above, most politically minded Palestinians had looked to Pan-Arabism as their most likely saviour, arguing that there was no way Israel would be able to resist the demands of a single, mighty Arab state. Consequently, the majority had given Pan-Arabism priority over their own, Palestinian activism. The collapse of the Egypt–Syria–Iraq unification talks in 1963 shook this standpoint severely and the heavy Arab defeat in the Six-Day War would finish it off completely. Before then, however, a replacement had already emerged.

Insight

It is interesting how swiftly Pan-Arabism faded almost entirely from the Middle East agenda. Briefly all the rage in the 1960s, the secular, socialist movement was replaced by Muslim unity and a diversity of separate nationalisms.

FATAH

At the time of its formation, Fatah was just one of numerous Palestinian nationalist groups. Under the energetic leadership of Yasser Arafat, ably backed by the superior organizational skills of Khalid al-Hassan and Khalil al-Wazir (aka Abu Jihad), it found a distinctive voice based upon three principles:

- *The Palestinians alone are responsible for their own fate.*
- *The liberation of Palestine takes priority over Arab unity.*
- *The only effective tactic to achieve the desired goal is armed struggle.*

If these seem somewhat naïve, we should remember that at this time revolution was in the air the world over. From Greece to China, Algeria to Kenya, Cuba and Vietnam, armed struggle was the watchword. Fatah saw itself as not just anti-Israeli but part of a global struggle against all forms of Western imperialism. For several years, therefore, Arafat had found himself swimming against the prevailing Pan-Arabist tide. Indeed, he might even have sunk had not President Nasser persuaded his fellow Arab heads of state to establish the PLO.

ASSIFA

The formation of the PLO and the Palestine Liberation Army (PLA) seriously worried the Fatah leadership. Both were clearly an attempt to bring the various Palestinian groups under centralized control and prevent them from provoking Israel into war before the surrounding Arab states – united or not – were confident of victory. Arafat boycotted the first PLO convention, held in East Jerusalem, which drew up a Palestine National Covenant condemning Israel as an illegal, colonialist and racist state. Attracted by the publicity and the prospect of joining a Palestinian army, Fatah supporters deserted for the PLA. To save their movement, Arafat and his colleagues urgently needed to do something to divert the spotlight of publicity away from the PLO and draw it onto themselves.

What happened next is a remarkable example of the unpredictability of events. Early in 1965, amid a flurry of advance publicity and attempts by the Arab authorities to prevent it happening, a Fatah battle group named Assifa (the Storm) sneaked into Israel from Lebanon and planted an explosive charge on the National Water Carrier canal. To give the saboteurs time to get away, they set the detonator's timer for an extra-long delay – so long, in fact, that Israeli security forces found the device and defused it before it could go off. That should have been the end of that: total failure for Fatah. Instead, the Israelis gave the attack huge publicity in an attempt to show the world the sort of ruthless 'terrorists' they were up against. This had the unexpected effect of making

Fatah overnight heroes in Palestinian eyes, and Arafat, who had been briefly arrested in Syria during the debacle, was suddenly a figure of international importance.

At last, after 15 years of waiting, the exiled Palestinians had a figure around whom they could rally, a fighter, a man prepared to die for the Palestinian cause. Nasser and other Arab leaders took fright and denied Assifa's existence, saying it was a creation of Western intelligence and the National Water Carrier incident had been dreamed up to push the Arabs into a war they did not want. It was too late. Shukayri and his PLO had been eclipsed and thousands of young Palestinians flocked to join Assifa, which became Fatah's official military wing.

Over the next 18 months, Fatah launched a further 100 attacks into Israel, killing 11 and wounding 62. When Israel precipitated the Six-Day War, it listed the cross-border raids as a major provocation. Later, after the Israeli victory had confirmed the failure of Pan-Arabism, Arafat's Fatah was more than ready to replace it as the focus of Palestinian hopes.

The path to war

HAWKS AND DOVES

During the mid-1960s, opinions on both sides were divided over the advisability of another major Arab–Israeli conflict. Within Israel, Prime Minister Eshkol, who had replaced Ben-Gurion in 1963, was until the last minute wary of a war that would be costly, possibly even disastrous, and which was not strictly necessary for security purposes.

Other Israelis, including the ex-guerrilla fighters Menachem Begin and Moshe Dayan, a founder of the Haganah and chief of staff during the Suez War, were openly hawkish. Their message was simple: only by responding ferociously to Arab threats could Israel's security be guaranteed. Besides, the country could be more easily defended if its frontiers were expanded to include the water-rich Golan Heights on the border with Syria, the West Bank and the Sinai as far as the Suez Canal. Eshkol brought Begin and Dayan into his cabinet just before the outbreak of hostilities.

The Palestinians, with the Fatah faction to the fore, certainly wanted war. It was, after all, their only chance of getting their land back. The Lebanese and Jordanian leadership, on the other hand, were against further conflict. Syria, which experienced yet another change of regime in 1966, had earlier called for war over Israel's exploitation of Lake Galilee. The new government was strongly pro-Palestinian, too. However, it could fight only if supported by other Arab nations. Iraq, where a Sunni regime based on the clans around the northern town of Tikrit was establishing itself, was in a similar position.

The key player in all this was Egypt's President Nasser. He talked aggression. At an Arab summit in September 1965, for example, he agreed a three-year plan to build up Arab armies for a fresh assault on Israel. The next year he backed the formation of the PLA with the same intention. He spoke of the very existence of Israel being an 'aggression'. Yet in private he dreaded a war that he knew very well would probably end in humiliating defeat. In short, he was trapped. Leadership of the Arab world demanded striking rhetoric and gestures. Viewed from inside Israel, such behaviour was extremely worrying and played into the hands of the hawks. The end result was a war Nasser did not want.

Insight

The Palestine Liberation Army, largely the dream child of President Nasser, was never much more than a showpiece. Controlled by non-Palestinian regimes, in the 1990s the greater part of it was assimilated into the National Guard of the newly formed Palestine National Authority (see p. 216).

CROSS-BORDER CONFLICTS

As early as 1963, the UN had been called in to settle a dispute between Israel and Syria over the former's use of the waters of the upper Jordan and Lake Galilee. Two years later, there was more fierce fighting as the Israelis smashed Syrian dams intended to divert the headwaters of the River Jordan. There were clashes again in early 1967 when an Israeli tractor ploughing land within the demilitarized zone was fired upon and an artillery duel began. Syrian Soviet-built MIGs and Israeli French-built Mirages soon appeared overhead, a dogfight took place and four MIGs were downed. Two more were shot down within sight of the Syrian capital, Damascus, which the Israeli planes then buzzed. It was provocative action by any standard.

Meanwhile, Fatah and other groups had been stepping up provocation of their own. As early as 1965, their cross-border raids had drawn fierce Israeli reprisals. The following year, despite efforts by King Hussein to prevent attacks on Israel from Jordan because he was worried about their consequences and about his ability to control the guerrillas, members of Fatah, the PLA and the Arab Nationalist Movement (ANM, another militant group) raided Israel several times from southern Lebanon.

In November 1966, there were attacks in Jerusalem and Hebron; in the latter an Israeli military vehicle was destroyed, with three soldiers killed and a further four injured. The IDF's response was unprecedented. In broad daylight, protected by aircraft, a large force of tanks descended on the West Bank village of Samu. Reports vary, but perhaps 5,000 villagers lost their homes, their clinic, school and mosque. Several were killed and injured. Jordanian forces rushing to investigate were ambushed and more than 50 were killed and wounded. A Royal Jordanian Air Force plane was shot down.

The Samu raid had long-lasting consequences. In the rioting that followed, Hussein was almost overthrown for his failure to protect the Palestinians under his care. He was personally angered by the raid, too, which had taken place on his birthday and caused the death of a friend. Of all Israel's neighbours, Jordan had hitherto been the one it felt closest to. This was true no longer. The raid angered world opinion and led to calls for revenge in Arab states that wondered where the Israelis would strike next.

FALSE REPORT

For several years the Arab–Israeli conflict had been closely tied into the Cold War. As mentioned, for some time Israel had been in receipt of French weapons, the Mirage fighters that buzzed Damascus, for example. In 1965, following a mutual recognition agreement, the IDF was given West German armaments, too. In the same year, Democrat US President Johnson showed his willingness to maintain Kennedy's pro-Israeli policy by delivering a consignment of 210 US tanks and 48 Skyhawk bombers to his number one Middle-Eastern ally. The Soviets, already on quite good terms with Nasser, got on even better with the new regime in Syria. Their next move was to improve relations between the two states, which had been at a somewhat low ebb since the failure of the United Arab Republic in 1961. The result was a Soviet-brokered Egypt–Syria defence pact, which Nasser agreed to in November 1966 in the hope of steering the more aggressive Syria away from open conflict with Israel. The plan backfired, with appalling consequences for both Egypt and Syria.

At this point, shortly after the artillery and air battle on the Israeli–Syrian border, Anwar Sadat, the senior Egyptian aide in Moscow, was handed some alarming information from Soviet intelligence. Israeli forces were massing on the border with Syria. Their intention was clear: invasion. The information was false, and to this day no one is really sure why it was issued. Explanations range from the influence of alcohol (not as fanciful as it might seem in Russia) to a wish to precipitate a war in order to embarrass the Americans. Although he soon ascertained for himself that the Israelis were not preparing an attack, Nasser felt obliged to act in order to keep in with his Soviet paymasters and to avoid losing face among his fellow Arabs. So that Egyptian forces would be free to attack Israel from the south if it invaded Syria, Nasser asked Secretary-General U Thant to withdraw the UN observers (UNEF) from a section of Egypt's Sinai border with Israel.

WAR

Alarmed, U Thant talked to the Israelis and Egyptians and eventually decided to call Nasser's bluff by pulling UNEF back from all its positions in Sinai, Gaza and Sharm al-Sheikh (at the entrance to the Strait of Tiran). Contrary to the Secretary-General's expectations, Nasser made the grand gesture of occupying Sharm al-Sheikh and shortly afterwards closing the Strait of Tiran to Israeli ships and those of other nations carrying military supplies to Eilat. To Israel such action was tantamount to a declaration of war, particularly as Nasser accompanied it with another round of flamboyant anti-Israeli speechifying. Intended to make Arab hearts swell with pride rather than with the spirit of war, the aggressive rhetoric was just the excuse for combat that Israel's hawks had wanted.

For a couple of weeks, as the two sides eyed each other up with mounting suspicion, there was a flurry of diplomatic activity. The Soviets warned of dire consequences if Egypt were attacked. The Americans, reluctantly, stood by their ally while at the same time urging restraint. King Hussein, forced to come off the fence, flew to Cairo and made a defensive pact with Nasser. Other Arab nations made appropriate noises of solidarity. In Israel the mood was edgy. Frightened by Nasser's clumsy manoeuvring and expecting to be attacked at any moment, the Jewish population rallied behind their government. Behind the scenes the war cabinet planned a devastating 'anticipatory counter-offensive' – doublespeak for an attack.

The Six-Day War

UNEQUAL CONTEST?

As in 1948, it is easy by simply looking at the map (Figure 7.1) to see the 1967 War as another David vs. Goliath contest in which the little boy overcame the bullying giant. Certainly the combined populations of Israel's Arab neighbours vastly outnumbered that of Israel and, correspondingly, the potential number of troops they could have put into the field was also much greater. But that, and the fact that geography might enable them to attack Israel on several fronts at the same time, was where their advantage ended.

Israel was a state built by war. Defence, including aggressive defence, had always been its top priority. Each war it fought was, literally, a struggle for survival – military defeat might well mean the end of the Zionist dream. To avoid this, its defence forces were highly trained and extremely efficient. The pilots that began the assault early on the morning of Monday 5 June, for instance, had practised their attacks so often that they were able to fly in complete radio silence. Israel's tanks, artillery and aircraft were superior to those of their enemy and the Israelis knew how to use them more effectively. Above all, they had the supreme advantage of surprise, launching the war when and how they chose.

In contrast, Israel's Arab enemies – essentially Egypt, Jordan, Syria and Iraq, although others sent token contingents and provided some funding – were ill-coordinated, often poorly trained and were furnished with equipment, much of it made by the Soviet Union and its allies, that frequently proved less effective than that produced by the competitive capitalist armaments industries of France, Germany and the USA. Jordan, having made a defence pact with Egypt only at the very last minute, was a reluctant combatant. Fearing a repetition of 1948–9 and 1956, Nasser did not want war either. Iraq had no border with Israel, while the new regime in Syria had only a tenuous hold on the affections of its people. A more inauspicious set of circumstances would be hard to imagine.

AIR STRIKE

Moshe Dayan and his commanders knew that a swift, decisive strike was essential. If the war dragged on beyond a week or two, there was a very real chance that either the Soviets would become involved in some way or the USA would come down heavily on Israel to prevent escalation. A quick victory necessitated blitzkrieg tactics as employed by the German armies in 1940.

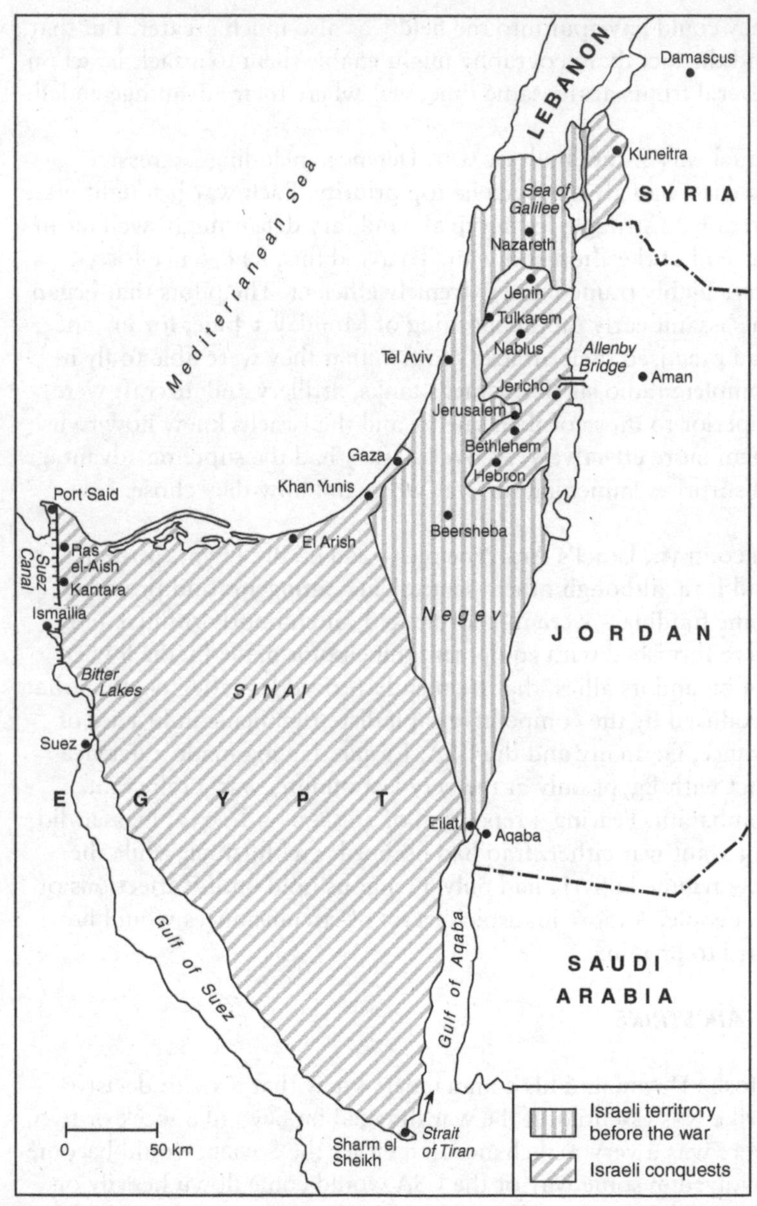

Figure 7.1 The 1967 war.

Unlike Korea and Vietnam (the two theatres of major conflict since 1945) the terrain beyond Israel's borders was ideally suited to a war of rapid movement – upon one condition: control of the air. Just as the Germans in 1940 would not risk exposing their forces upon the open sea between Britain and France before they had control of the air space above, so the Israelis could not risk exposing their armour and artillery in the open desert without first winning mastery of the skies. Again, the parallel with the Battle of Britain (1940) is instructive. The Luftwaffe came closest to victory not when it tackled the RAF in the air but when it struck at its airfields and planes on the ground. Indeed, had Goering persevered with his attack on British airfields and not diverted his aircraft to attacking London, he might well have won control of the skies and enabled the German armies to invade Britain. This vital lesson was not lost on the Israelis.

At 7.45 a.m. on Monday 5 June 1967, the Israelis put into operation a plan they had been hatching for five years. It began with a devastating attack by almost the entire Israeli air force on Egypt's air bases, radar sites and communications installations. The strike was unannounced and followed no declaration of war. The Israelis later lied that it had been provoked by large numbers of Egyptian troops moving towards Israel's southern border. A little over two hours and 500 sorties later, 309 of Egypt's 340 serviceable aircraft had been destroyed, including all its long-range bombers. With total control of the air and Egypt's communications in complete disorder, Israel was now able to drive across Sinai to the Suez Canal and south to link up with a naval force that had taken Sharm al-Sheikh. Thousands of Egyptian troops lost their lives in a merciless rain of high explosives and napalm. Beside their often unrecognizable bodies, the bleak desert was strewn with the burned-out hulks of around 700 tanks and countless guns, trucks and other debris of Israel's ruthless advance.

Unaware of what was going on to the south – Nasser actually told King Hussein on the phone that the Israeli air force had suffered heavy losses – planes from Jordan, Syria and Iraq made a few hesitant darts at Israeli targets. Within hours, these air forces had suffered the same fate as Egypt's. Jordan's was wiped out completely, Syria's reduced to one-third of its original strength and Iraq's irreparably damaged. By nightfall at the end of the first day, victory was already Israel's.

EXPANSION

Over the next five days, the amount of land under Israeli control tripled and the USA and the Soviet Union came close to armed confrontation. Nasser, his reputation in tatters, accepted the ceasefire supposed to come into effect around midnight on 7 June. Jordan's King Hussein had offered a cessation of hostilities the moment he learned of the loss of his air force. Despite US pressure, the Israeli cabinet rejected this offer. Their minimum target was East Jerusalem, with its old Jewish quarter and holy sites. While warplanes mercilessly harried the poorly coordinated Jordanian and Palestinian soldiers from the air, the IDF advanced steadily through the streets of Jerusalem and more quickly across the hills of the West Bank to the River Jordan. When they had reached all their objectives, they accepted the ceasefire. King Hussein followed suit, thereby also ending Iraq's ability to influence the conflict.

Since the destruction of its air force, Syria had done little but shell Israel across the border. Such inactivity was a good example of the Arab nations' failure to coordinate their military efforts. A Syrian offensive into northern Israel while Israeli troops were occupied elsewhere would probably not have altered the outcome of the war, but it would have made Israel's triumph considerably more difficult. As it was, the Israelis were able to leave the Syrian front until their hands were free. By then, the continuation of the war was getting difficult.

The ceasefire of Wednesday 7 June, supposed to cover all fronts, had been accepted by Syria as well as Israel. It was with consternation and annoyance, therefore, that the following day President Johnson heard that the Israelis were blitzing Syrian positions on the Golan Heights overlooking northern Israel. This action was particularly dangerous because of Syria's alliance with the Soviet Union. Johnson, who already had his hands full with the Vietnam war, insisted that Israel abandon its action immediately and abide by the ceasefire.

At this point one of the most controversial acts of the war occurred. The USA was monitoring Israeli communications via a clearly marked intelligence-gathering vessel, *USS Liberty*, that was patrolling off the coast of Gaza. Saying they believed this ship was Egyptian, Israeli planes and torpedo boats attacked it repeatedly. Although it did not sink, 205 of its crew were killed or wounded and its communications systems were smashed. Many Americans now believe the attack was deliberate, masterminded by Dayan himself. On the other hand, the Israelis still insist, as they have done all along, that the attack was a ghastly mistake. Deeply embarrassed, Johnson hushed the incident up. Temporarily freed from US oversight, the Israeli high command was able to launch the final part of its battle plan, the assault on the hills that fed the River Jordan.

The IDF attacked on the morning of Friday 9 June, claiming it was responding to provocative Syrian shelling. Although they resisted bravely, the Syrians were driven back until it was thought the Israelis might push on to Damascus itself. The recently opened hotline between Moscow and Washington glowed red as Soviet Premier Alexei Kosygin threatened dire retribution unless the attack on his ally was stopped. President Johnson, unwilling to be seen to bend to Soviet threats, ordered the US Sixth Fleet to hold a course that brought it into the path of a large fleet of Soviet warships. An even greater disaster was averted only when the Israelis, now in full possession of the Golan Heights, ceased hostilities on the evening of Saturday 10 June.

The war had lasted just five-and-a-half days.

After the war

THE COST

The casualties reflected the fighting. The Israelis lost only 779 soldiers and little equipment. The Arab casualties were around 20 times higher. Perhaps 11,500 Egyptians died with over twice that number wounded. Jordan lost about 6,500, including many Palestinians, and suffered approximately the same number of wounded as Egypt. Around 2,500 Syrians died and 5,000 were wounded. Iraqi casualties were negligible. The Arabs' loss of equipment was catastrophic, especially the destruction of virtually all their air forces. The combatant Egyptian land forces lost some 80 per cent of their equipment. The Jordanian and Syrian armies suffered equally severely.

In under six days of fighting, the IDF had captured the entire West Bank, Gaza, Sinai (closing the Suez Canal again) and the Golan Heights. This almost tripled the amount of territory under its control. It did not increase the size of Israel itself by much because, of the land it had captured, only East Jerusalem and a few surrounding areas were officially assimilated. The rest was simply occupied. Contrary to international law and convention but in accord with its long-standing declared intention, Jerusalem was made Israel's capital city. To make way for Israeli development, scores of Palestinian homes were bulldozed and hundreds of families made homeless. For 'strategic' reasons, other Arab villages were flattened elsewhere in the West Bank.

Insight

Although Jerusalem became Israel's official capital, foreign embassies remained in Tel Aviv or elsewhere. Only the USA, Greece and Italy have consulates in Jerusalem.

There were two reasons for Israel's unwillingness formally to incorporate all the captured territory. First, by keeping the West Bank and the Gaza Strip as zones of military occupation that might be returned, the possibility of a future 'peace for land' deal was left open. Second, if all conquered land had been absorbed into Israel, its large Palestinian populations would have become Israeli citizens and therefore entitled to vote. Given Israel's proportional electoral system, they would have had enough influence in the Knesset to destabilize the state. On the other hand, to have made them Israeli citizens without the right to vote would have been clear apartheid.

ROLE REVERSAL

As in the previous armed confrontations between Israel and the Arab world, it was the Palestinians who suffered most. The war created an estimated 323,000 new refugees, the majority from the West Bank, over 100,000 from the Golan Heights and 38,000 from Sinai. There were reports of Israeli police and army units actively encouraging Palestinians to flee, wrongly warning them that their houses were about to be shelled and shepherding them across the murky waters of the Jordan. By the end of 1967, over 1 million men, women and children who regarded themselves as Palestinians were living outside the land they knew as Palestine but which most of the rest of the world called Israel.

However, the 1967 War had helped the Palestinian cause by bringing together around 1 million Israeli, Gaza, Golan and West Bank Palestinians under the same administration. Although communications and travel were always difficult, the ironic consequence of Israeli military success was a greater sense of Palestinian cohesion and unity. This was fostered by Arafat's Fatah and the PLO, which it soon came to dominate. The war had finally revealed Pan-Arabism to be no more than a chimera born of a romantic reading of history. In its place Palestinians espoused Arafat's new, uncompromisingly aggressive and nationalistic leadership. Its unashamed acceptance of violence, within the Middle East and way beyond, would shock the entire world.

Israel had shocked the world, too. The war confirmed that it was a regional power, and one that even the West could not assume would automatically tread the moral high ground. No longer a mere survivor, it had shown itself to be a ruthless conqueror and a cruel master. In contrast, very gradually, and often despite their bloodthirsty actions, it was the turn of the Palestinians to attract significant international sympathy and attention. In short, they would change from being simply the sorry victims of war to a specific 'issue' that needed international attention.

RESOLUTION 242

There was much talk before, during and after the 1967 War about resolving the Arab–Israeli problem peacefully. Very roughly, Prime Minister Eshkol, King Hussein and President Nasser represented schools of thought that believed in a possible compromise involving the return of captured land in exchange for guarantees of peace. Hardliners on both sides – the Syrians and Menachem Begin, for instance – would have none of it. Begin and his right-wing Zionist ilk were in favour of gradually colonizing and absorbing all conquered territory into Israel. Syria opposed any talk of peace with Israel and managed to get this incorporated in a 'three-noes' resolution – no recognition, no negotiation, no peace – at an Arab summit in September 1967.

Meanwhile, the UN Security Council was searching for a peace formula of its own. The result was the British-worded compromise Resolution 242 of November 1967. This spoke of the illegality of conquest by force of arms, called for a 'just settlement of the refugee problem' and demanded that Israel return 'territories occupied' in exchange for peace. The word 'territories' was chosen, without a preceding 'all' or 'the', as deliberately ambiguous. Versions in other languages – French and Russian, for example – were more specific. The Israelis took the original text to mean 'some territories' while the Arabs believed it meant 'all'. It was three years before Israel accepted the Resolution, which became the basis of its future peace treaties with Arab states. Among the Arab governments, Syria was bitterly hostile to the Resolution.

Insight

Spot the difference? Here is the key clause of Resolution 242 in English, with no article before 'territories':

Withdrawal of Israel armed forces from territories occupied in the recent conflict;

And the same clause in French, sometimes said to be a mistranslation because the second 'des' might mean 'from the':

Retrait des forces armées israéliennes des territoires occupés lors du récent conflit;

As English and French are official UN languages, both are of equal validity.

The Palestinian leadership, as represented by Arafat, rejected Resolution 242 out of hand. The reference to the 'refugee problem' they condemned as feeble and insulting. And the concept of peace for land was to them preposterous. As in their eyes nearly all Israel was stolen territory, they argued that it was morally reprehensible to talk of returning some of these conquests in exchange for peace and recognition of the others. To do so would mean accepting that ultimately might was right, contradicting the Resolution's statement on conquest.

In many ways, therefore, the 1967 War and its aftermath fundamentally altered the Israel–Palestine situation. A formula now existed that eventually enabled Israel and all but one of its neighbours to make peace. In the end, a number of Palestinians would come round to the land for peace position, too. But that was still a very long way off, and the compromise would never be agreed by all. The way ahead remained long, bitter and bloody.

In depth: Yasser Arafat (1929–2004)

No figure in the Israeli–Palestinian conflict was more controversial than the man popularly known as Yasser Arafat. From his uncertain progeny and birthplace to his death from an undiagnosed blood disorder, the first chairman of the PLO and first president of the PNA lived a life of charismatic complexity. Born to middle-class Palestinian parents in Cairo (or Gaza or Jerusalem, depending on which version of his autobiography one chooses to follow), Arafat trained as an engineer. He was also attracted to politics and signed up to fight for the Arab cause against Israel in 1948–9. He flirted with the Muslim Brotherhood and served in the Egyptian army before

(Contd)

going to work in the British protectorate of Kuwait. Here, with a group of Palestinian exiles, he helped set up Fatah in about 1959.

Fatah was slow to get off the ground and did not launch its first guerrilla attacks on Israel until 1965. Arafat soon became well known for his determination and bravery, as well as for his quick temper and equivocation. Fatah's reputation climbed rapidly after the Six-Day War and in 1969 Arafat was elected chairman of the recently founded PLO.

The PLO was by this time based in Jordan, where it came into conflict with the government of King Hussein. The rivalry came to a head in 1970 when, following a mini civil war, the PLO was forcibly expelled from the Hashemite kingdom. Arafat and his supporters fled to Lebanon where once again they set about creating a Palestinian state in exile. Guerrilla warfare, seen by most as naked terrorism (a good example being the attack on the Munich Olympics) raised the profile of Arafat, Fatah and the PLO to the point where, in 1974, he was invited to address the UN General Assembly.

Eight years later, the Israeli army invaded Lebanon and Arafat was once again obliged to flee, this time to Tunisia. Here he and the PLO continued to launch *fedayeen* attacks, but found themselves increasingly out of touch with what was happening on the ground among their fellow Palestinians. Undaunted, Arafat recaptured the initiative in 1988 by renouncing terrorism and proclaiming the entire area of the British mandate to be the independent state of Palestine. Despite the blunder of backing Saddam Hussein in 1990–1, Arafat was gradually accepted as a genuine seeker after peace. Complex negotiations led to the Oslo Accords of 1993 and the formation of the Palestinian National Authority, of which he was elected president in 1996.

From this time onwards, Arafat appeared to lose control of events, descending into a confusion of contradictions and possibly lies. It appears that he re-espoused violence as a way of counteracting the Islamist threat. As a result, he was virtually imprisoned by the Israelis in a rubble-strewn compound in Ramallah from where he was finally airlifted to Paris to die.

In depth: the Israel Labour Party (also Mapai and the Alignment)

Israel's proportional electoral system produces a far more fluid party structure than is found in most other democracies. Discipline is weak and parties emerge and dissolve quite regularly. This makes generalization a tricky business, never more so than when dealing with the left-wing social democrat grouping that here is generally simplified as 'Labour'. In fact, we are talking about at least three parties: Mapai (1930–1965), Alignment (1965–1992) and Labour (1992 onwards).

Mapai, a Hebrew acronym for the Land of Israel Workers' Party, emerged during the mandate era as a socialist-Zionist coalition led by David Ben-Gurion. As the guiding force behind victory in the War of Independence (1948–9), it was rewarded with 35.7 per cent of the popular vote in the state's first elections. With 46 of the Knesset's seats, it formed the core of the coalition government and remained the dominant force in Israeli politics until merging with Labour Unity to form the Labour Alignment.

Technically speaking, Alignment was really a combined list of candidates for electoral purposes rather than a true party, so it is customary to talk of Labour remaining in power through the Six-Day War and the October 1973 War until losing control of the Knesset in 1977.

Since its inception, Labour had made security its number one issue (as it was in all Israeli politics) and its economic and social policies were not all that different from those of similar centre-leaning parties. By the 1980s, after the initial setback of the October War

(Contd)

and the shock of subsequent electoral defeat, Labour was generally more willing than its main rival, Likud, to seek some form of permanent settlement with the Palestinians. It was Yitzhak Rabin, a Labour prime minister, who signed the Oslo Accords and another, Ehud Barak, who tried to take the process further in the late 1990s.

Having joined Sharon's Unity Government in 2001, Labour left it in 2003. However, it went on to support Sharon's unilateral Disengagement Strategy of 2004–5 and, after coming second to Kadima in the elections of March 2006, joined Olmert's coalition. As minister of defence, Labour leader Amir Peretz was heavily criticized for the handling of the 2006 War with Hezbollah.

10 THINGS TO REMEMBER

1. *Before the 1967 war, most Palestinians' believed the best chance of defeating Israel lay with Pan-Arabism, a concerted effort by all Arab states acting together.*
2. *In 1965, Fatah shot to international prominence when it carried out an unsuccessful raid on Israel's National Water Carrier.*
3. *By the mid-1960s, there were voices inside Israel and in the Arab world calling for all-out war as a way of settling issues between them once and for all.*
4. *Israel responded to the slightest provocation with ferocity, shooting down Syrian jets and destroying the West Bank village of Samu (1966).*
5. *War became likely in 1967 when Egypt received false reports from the USSR that Israeli troops were massing on the border with Syria.*
6. *Better equipped and better trained than their adversaries, on 7 June 1967 the Israelis began the Six-Day War with devastating air raids that destroyed practically all their enemies' air forces.*
7. *During five-and-a-half days of fighting, the IDF defeated the land forces of Egypt, Jordan, Syria and Iraq, ranged against them.*
8. *The Six-Day War brought Sinai, the West Bank, Gaza and the Golan Heights under Israeli control, tripling the area of land they controlled.*
9. *An additional 332,000 Palestinian refugees were created by the 1967 war.*
10. *The UN Security Council's resolution 242 (November 1967) instigated the 'land for peace' formula that has been at the heart of all serious subsequent Israel–Palestine peace initiatives.*

8

Arafat and the PLO 1968 to 1973

In this chapter you will learn about:

- ***Israel after the 1967 War***
- ***how the Palestinian*** *fedayeen* ***attracted the world's attention***
- ***ongoing conflict between Israel and its Arab neighbours after 1967***
- ***the October War, 1973.***

Where now?

A DIVIDED NATION

Israel did not find it easy to come to terms with its position and status after the 1967 War. The communist Rakah Party, which with the support of most Arab voters had won three Knesset seats in 1965, called for immediate withdrawal from what the Israelis called the 'administered territories' of the West Bank and Gaza. Interestingly, this position was also that of ex-Prime Minister Ben-Gurion, who believed the conquered land would become a millstone round Israel's neck.

Perhaps a majority of Israelis thought and even hoped, however vaguely, that one day, when peace had been made with surrounding Arab states, the occupied land would be handed back either to those who lived there or to its previous rulers. A third group, the Zionist right, condemned such thinking as tantamount to treachery. Some of them argued that the 1967 frontiers, stretching to the physical boundaries of the Golan Heights, the River Jordan and the Suez Canal, would always be essential for Israel's future security.

More extreme in their views were Orthodox and Ultra-Orthodox Jews, many of whom regarded the 1967 triumph as a God-given opportunity for the Jewish people to return to the land given to them by the Almighty in Biblical times. Now the land was under Israeli control, it was their duty to settle it. In June 1968, by sneaking into a hotel in the West Bank city of Hebron disguised as Swedish tourists, a determined group of Jewish families outwitted Eshkol's uncertain government and established the first Jewish settlement in the Occupied Territories. Many, many more were to follow. The settlement issue split Israel's Labour movement from the Zionists, thereby breaking up the partnership that had masterminded the formation of the state. From this time forwards, a settlement of the Israeli–Palestinian situation became infinitely more difficult.

Insight

Many bodies, including the International Court of Justice, declare that Israeli settlements in the Occupied Territories are illegal. The counter-argument holds that as Gaza and the West Bank were taken 'in self-defence', the normal ruling on building on captured land is invalid. As Israel struck first in the 1967 war, was it really self-defence?

CARROT...

Israel's policy towards the Arab land it was occupying has been described as a classic case of 'carrot and stick'. The 'carrot' arose out of an understanding that it was much easier to manage an occupation if those affected were content. To this end, the people of Gaza and of the West Bank were given a high degree of self-government. The 1970s saw two rounds of municipal elections. The first returned largely conservative, Jordan-orientated candidates, but the second saw gains for the PLO. Education and most local affairs were left in Palestinian hands, and in 1972 the first Palestinian University, Bir Zeit, opened. There were two more by the end of the decade.

Economically, the Palestinians under Israeli occupation fared much better than they had under Egyptian and Jordanian rule. Again, the West Bank, a more viable entity than the Gaza Strip, gained most. The frontier with Israel was kept open, as was that with Jordan. This enabled goods to pass relatively freely and 'West Bankers' (as they tended to identify themselves at this stage, rather than as 'Palestinians') flocked in their thousands to work in Israel. Movement was helped by the network of roads the Israelis constructed for military purposes. By 1973, one-third of the West Bank workforce was employed in Israel – albeit in what were generally low-paid jobs – mostly in agriculture. Electrification spread and health care improved. Many benefited from the money sent back from better-paid family members who had left to work abroad, especially in the Gulf.

Of course, there remained tensions and the occasional violent flare-ups between the West Bank's original inhabitants and the refugees. There was always the presence of the Israeli military and police, too, sometimes just patrolling but also engaging in harassment or heavy-handed retribution for deeds committed by the *fedayeen*. On the whole though (and this is not saying very much), the 15 years after the 1967 War were some of the least stressful experienced by the nationless Palestinians.

...AND STICK

As before the 1967 War, Israel continued its policy of counteracting the activities of the Palestinian *fedayeen* with overwhelming and often ruthless force. This, coupled with the drawn-out military activity in the south, put a huge strain on the economy. The ongoing Arab boycott of any nation that traded with Israel was to some extent alleviated by the addition of Palestinian consumers who became the second largest external market for Israeli produce. Even so, Israel grew ever more dependent upon US aid.

Israel's security forces used a range of tactics when dealing with real or suspected *fedayeen* attacks. These escalated dramatically during the later 1960s. In 1969–70 alone, for example, Israel reported some 560 incidents on its border with Lebanon. Curfews were imposed, institutions closed and suspects held without trial. Sterner measures included the bulldozing of houses and retaliatory or pre-emptive raids into neighbouring states.

Several incidents attracted a great deal of attention. The first, in March 1968, saw a powerful Israeli strike force cross into Jordan about 16 kilometres north of the Dead Sea and make for the sizeable village of Karama (often spelt 'Karamah'). The Jordanian Army, the PLA and Fatah, which had set up a base in the village, managed to ambush the invaders and inflict quite heavy casualties on them before superior Israeli firepower, co-ordination and training became overwhelming. Although they lost over 170 men, the Palestinians and Jordanians hailed the temporary rebuff to the IDF, the killing of 28 of its soldiers and the destruction of some of its equipment, as a victory. The Israelis were no longer invincible, they crowed, and recruitment to the various Palestinian armed factions increased sharply. Undaunted, the IDF continued to push Palestinians from the Jordan Valley, driving up to 100,000 from their homes.

Insight

The 27 Israeli settlements in the Jordan Valley are among the most contentious in the entire West Bank. Started shortly after the 1967 war, they form a barrier between Jordan and the rest of the Occupied Territories. Although Israel sees them as essential to its security, they render a viable Palestinian state on the West Bank virtually impossible.

In terms of simply putting an end to attacks on Israel, the most successful operation was conducted by Ariel Sharon in Gaza in 1971. Entering the Strip with colossal force, he organized the destruction of houses and other buildings, the shooting (if they resisted) or arrest of numerous *fedayeen*, the detention of many suspects in specially built camps in Sinai, and the closure of the organs of Palestinian self-government. Attacks on Israel from Gaza were stopped for many years, but a legacy of suspicion and hatred was established that lasted even longer.

Longer-range Israeli strikes included two in 1973. The first hit Palestinian camps in southern Lebanon, killing around 40; the second targeted the Fatah headquarters in Beirut, killing three of the movement's leaders. The Israeli security services also waged a worldwide campaign of assassination of *fedayeen* leaders. Bombs – letter or less discrete types – were the favoured weapon and several prominent Palestinians were slain in this way.

SELF-RELIANCE

The Six-Day War brought to an end any realistic idea of Israel's neighbours 'liberating' the Palestinians. It was now obvious that, in the short-to-medium term at least, the Arab states were simply not militarily strong enough to tackle Israel. Activist Palestinians, therefore, had little choice but to accept what Yasser Arafat had been saying all along: there was no point in waiting for someone else to restore their land for them; they had to do it themselves. It was a similar mindset to that of the Jewish leaders who had established Israel in 1948.

The defeat of the Arabs, including the PLA, made Shukayri's position as head of the PLO untenable. Within two years, Fatah dominated the organization and Arafat was its leader and head of its executive committee. His style of leadership was charismatic but controversial: his energy, his determination, his bravery were never in doubt, and no one did more to bring the plight of the Palestinians before the international audience, but his political and administrative skills were often called into question. Some say the ramshackle, inefficient and corrupt nature of the PLO's structure and the constant divisions within the broader Palestinian movement were not his business. He was the figurehead, the inspiration, but never the manager. Critics, on the other hand, accuse him of inflexibility, organizational incompetence and political ham-fistedness. It will probably be a long time before anything like an historical consensus materializes.

Under Arafat's leadership, the post-1967 Palestinian movement evolved towards three policies. One was the proposed replacement of Israel and the Occupied Territories with a single state that harked back to the days of the British mandate: a secular, multi-racial and democratic Palestine in which Jew and Arab could live side by side. It was an attractive idea but one that had been impractical in the 1930s, let alone after 20 years of bloody conflict.

The second strand was building up the idea of a Palestinian nation in Gaza and the West Bank. There were also efforts at creating a separate Palestinian identity in Jordan and Lebanon, with disastrous results (see pp. 138 and 169). Nation-building, helped by elected organs of local government, was further developed by Fatah-prompted trade unions, schools, clinics, training centres and a range of other institutions and movements, including the Boy Scouts. One of the more difficult tasks was the settling of differences between the original West Bankers – those whose families had lived there before 1948 – and the refugee settlers in camps and elsewhere who had arrived subsequently and put pressure on the region's scanty resources.

Palestinian nation-building was equally vigorous outside the Occupied Territories. After the 1967 war, Fatah moved its headquarters to Jordan. With his organization now having joined the PLO, in 1969 Arafat was chosen as PLO chairman. Over time the two organizations, Fatah and the PLO, became inextricably intertwined. By 1970, their presence in Jordan had become so prominent and powerful that it threatened the government of King Hussein. In the armed conflict that followed, the PLO was driven out (see 'Black September' pp. 138–9).

From Jordan, the PLO leadership and administrative apparatus moved to Lebanon where it proceeded to establish what was virtually a state within a state. Lebanon's 235,000 Palestinians, many within cramped camps, paid Palestinian taxes, listened to Palestinian radio, were tried in Palestinian courts, went to schools where the curriculum was specifically Palestinian, and were treated in Palestinian clinics and hospitals. By the mid-1970s, the PLO employed an estimated 8,000 of its own civil servants. Not surprisingly, this situation severely destabilized Lebanon – already a highly insecure state – and was a major reason why it plunged into a horrific civil war (see Chapter 10).

'EXTERNAL OPERATIONS'

The third prong of Palestinian policy was armed action against any target that might, however vaguely, be Israeli or pro-Israeli. The operational *fedayeen* and their sympathizers referred to the assaults as 'external operations'. To Israel and the West, they were simply terrorism.

At this point the story of Palestinian resistance becomes almost unbelievably complicated. The reason is that beneath the PLO umbrella there appeared an impossibly large number of *fedayeen* groups: in 1970 there were perhaps 30 operating in Jordan alone. Some were independent; most were backed by an Arab state or a communist power, primarily the USSR and China. Many were infiltrated by the Israelis, the CIA or both. There were groups founded for a single mission and others with perhaps no more than two or three members. There was little or no co-ordination between them. Small wonder, then, that after an attack it was quite common for more than one group to claim responsibility.

The largest *fedayeen* organization was Arafat's Fatah, operating mainly out of Syria, Lebanon and Jordan (until 1970). Relatively small before the Six-Day War, its reputation was greatly enhanced by the Battle of Karama (see p. 133). Its best-known operation outside the Middle East, said to have been organized because Arafat was jealous of the high-profile actions of other groups, especially the Popular Front for the Liberation of Palestine (PFLP, see below), took place at the 1972 Munich Olympics. In a poorly planned and executed operation, Palestinian 'Black September' (see p. 138) *fedayeen* tried to take hostage the Israeli athletic team. In the subsequent chaos and bloodshed, 11 Israeli athletes, five *fedayeen* and a German policeman were killed. The IDF responded with heavy bombing of Fatah positions in Southern Lebanon and Syria, leaving between 200 and 300 dead. Around half of those who died were civilians. Neither side came out of the episode with their reputation enhanced.

Insight

As with all terrorist operations, the usefulness of the Munich attack to the Palestinian cause is open to debate. While arousing the hatred of millions, it certainly brought the perpetrators' cause enormous publicity and prompted politicians the world over to consider how the Israeli–Palestinian problem might be solved.

The PFLP, founded by the Marxist George Habash in 1968, had its roots among the students of the American University of Beirut. It combined its campaign against Israel ('that lap dog of capitalist imperialists') with an assault on the capitalist world in general. The following year saw the emergence of the Democratic Front for the Liberation of Palestine (DFLP), whose stance was even further left than that of the PFLP. Of the two the PFLP, which specialized in hijacking aircraft, attracted the most attention.

The world beyond the Middle East became directly involved in the Israel–Palestine confrontation in July 1968, when the PFLP hijacked an El Al (the Israeli airline) airliner en route to Rome from Algeria. The passengers were allowed to go free after the release of Palestinian prisoners. Following an attack by the same group on another El Al plane in December, Israeli commandos retaliated by destroying 13 Arab aircraft at Beirut airport. The violence escalated in 1969, with further hijackings, one of an American TWA airliner, and bomb attacks in Jerusalem and London. *Fedayeen* strikes, bombings and hijackings continued over the next few years, many provoking ferocious Israeli reprisals. None of this brought the Israeli–Palestinian problem any nearer to a solution; if anything, they had the opposite effect. Nevertheless, whatever the morality of the violence, it had managed to keep the situation in the Promised Land on the front pages.

'BLACK SEPTEMBER'

The most dramatic development among militant Palestinians took place in Jordan. Here, as in Egypt and most of the other Arab states, the *fedayeen* were regarded with suspicion because of their independent, anarchic ways, extreme tactics and links to the far left. Jordan's King Hussein did not approve, either, of their absolute refusal even to contemplate acknowledging Israel's existence. More immediately, he objected to the lawless behaviour of the PLO and its associates within the Hashemite kingdom. Many behaved as if they were above Jordanian law, terrorizing the locals with theft, extortion, beatings and even murder and rape. To the PFLP, the King was no more than a puppet of the West and clashes between his troops and the *fedayeen* were frequent and bloody.

Things came to a head in 1970. In the first half of the year, Hussein made two moves to solve the problem. First, with tacit Israeli support, he stepped up attacks on the *fedayeen*; second, he offered Yasser Arafat the post of prime minister within a Jordanian government. Shocked and a bit nonplussed by the idea of secure respectability, the PLO leader said no. Finally, after two further attempts on the King's life, the gloves came off.

In September, following a PFLP hijacking of four Western airliners, three of which were destroyed at Aman airport, Hussein declared martial law, clamped down on freedom of expression and sent in the army to tackle the militant Palestinians. Arafat responded by calling for the King to be deposed and urging his fellow Palestinians to lead the revolution. The pattern of subsequent events, in which Jordan descended into a brief civil war, was extremely complex. Estimates of the numbers killed vary hugely, from 1,500 to 30,000. The true figure was probably at the lower end – perhaps around 3,000. Iraq sent support for Hussein while Syria backed the Palestinians. Only the threat of USA–Israeli intervention prevented Syrian forces from participating openly in the Jordanian mayhem.

By the end of a month the *fedayeen* would remember as 'Black September', forces loyal to King Hussein had got the upper hand and large numbers of Palestinian fighters had fled the country. Their chosen refuge was Lebanon, most making their way there via Syria while a few risked passing through Israeli-occupied territory. Hussein survived and lived long enough to see his country at peace with Israel. The 'Palestinian problem', however, had merely been moved on – as the Lebanese would shortly discover to their cost (see Chapter 10).

Between the wars

THE WAR OF ATTRITION

If the Israelis thought their overwhelming victory in the Six-Day War would bring about a cessation of hostilities, they were wrong. As we have seen, *fedayeen* attacks escalated after 1967. Nor was Nasser, who had been deeply humiliated by his military's failures, content to let things rest. Not surprisingly, therefore, US Secretary of State William Rogers' early attempts at brokering a post-war peace deal came to nothing. Back on the front line along the Suez Canal, things were hotting up. By June 1968, the Egyptians were quite regularly bombarding Israeli positions along the Bar Lev, a massive defensive line they had constructed beside the Canal. The Israelis responded with shelling and air raids. By the following year the conflict, now even more ferocious, was becoming known as the War of Attrition.

Rogers arranged a ceasefire in July 1970, by which time the War of Attrition had taken a heavy toll. Israel had lost about 1,000 soldiers and the Egyptians many more. The fighting, which had included unwise Israeli air raids far beyond the battle zone, had caused 1.5 million Egyptians to flee their homes. Even more alarming, the war had brought the USA and the USSR closer to their respective allies. In particular, the Soviets had poured weaponry, including sophisticated SAM-3 anti-aircraft missiles, into Egypt. Soviet pilots had even flown Egyptian aircraft over the Canal battle zone.

NASSER AND SADAT

The political geography of the Middle East changed dramatically just after the ending of the War of Attrition when President Nasser died of a heart attack and was replaced by the hitherto unspectacular Anwar Sadat. Egypt's new president was a realist and a pragmatist. His wish was to do whatever was best for Egypt and thus, inevitably, for his reputation. If this meant playing off the USA against the USSR or side-stepping the plight of the Palestinians, so be it. War with Israel, he believed, was a costly and dangerous mistake that could bring the people of Egypt only suffering, economic hardship and political instability. Sadat's primary aims, therefore, were the restoration of his country's economy and a secure peace with Israel.

It did not take Sadat long to realize that his two objectives were closely linked. Slowly unpicking Nasser's state-centred socialism brought little if any quick economic benefit to the mass of the people, and poverty, unemployment and discontent remained rife. Only a cut in military expenditure and a redirection of funds and energies into peaceful productive enterprises could revive Egypt, Sadat determined. And that meant peace. But when he approached Prime Minister Golda Meir and her cabinet with a peace offer based on UN Resolution 242 (peace for land – see pp. 124–5), they flatly turned him down.

The Egyptian premier had to think again. Because of Israel's overwhelming military might and confidence, he realized, it had no need of peace because it had nothing to fear from war. What if that were to change? What if Sadat managed, somehow, to prove the equal of the Israelis in battle? Might that not induce a change of heart in them? Musing along these lines, Sadat began to contemplate a most cunning and desperate plan.

TOWARDS WAR

In the early 1970s, eager for Jewish votes, US President Richard Nixon significantly increased his country's military aid to Israel, including production technology as well as actual arms. In little over one year, the total value of US aid to Israel rose from $93 million to $634 million, of which $545 million was military aid. Simultaneously, National Security Advisor Henry Kissinger reached an agreement with the USSR to maintain the status quo in the Middle East. This infuriated Sadat as it implied Soviet acceptance of Israeli occupation of Arab lands, including the Egyptian Sinai. Sadat responded in July 1972 by expelling thousands of Soviet military advisors. The USA rejoiced, believing it had scored a major diplomatic victory over its communist adversary and had made yet another Middle East war distinctly less likely.

American assumptions were wildly optimistic. Although for a moment taken aback, the Soviets responded to Sadat's snub by making Syria their principal recipient of arms in the region. Syria was now in the hands of its hard-nosed ex-minister of defence, Hafiz Assad, who had engineered his own election as president in 1971. His goal was simple: the expansion of Syrian power and the enhancement of his own glory. The destruction of Israel would suit his needs perfectly. As that was unrealistic, at least in the short term, the recapture of the Golan Heights would do – nothing would boost the prestige of the new and still vulnerable dictator more than a short, sharp victory.

Assad and Sadat began planning in late 1972. The following January, their forces were put under joint overall command. Both wanted a swift triumph, but for different reasons. The former sought prestige, the latter hoped to force Israel to make peace. (Israel rejected an Egyptian peace offer as late as February 1973.) After recent re-arming, the two Arab countries' forces were now significant: Syria had more tanks on the Golan Heights than Israel and Egypt's sophisticated anti-aircraft defences now extended 16 kilometres beyond the Suez Canal. Beneath that protective umbrella, its ground forces would be able to face the Israelis on equal terms. Convinced they could reverse the Arab fortunes of the three previous wars, the two presidents sought only one last piece to make their jigsaw complete: surprise.

The October War

SURPRISE

The Arab attack began on 6 October 1973. They chose their moment well. Many Israelis were at home celebrating the Jewish Yom Kippur (Day of Atonement) festival with their families. Although the intelligence services had reported a build up of forces in Egypt and Syria, the reserves had not been mobilized and the danger of an Arab pre-emptive strike, 1967-style, had been rejected. Golda Meir's government had simply not taken the threat seriously. On the ground, the routine maintenance of some tanks and other vehicles had been let slip. In short, the Israeli war machine, previously the epitome of ruthless efficiency, had grown over-confident and slack.

Thousands of kilometres to the west, Israel's principal succour and support, the USA, was enmeshed in the final stages of the Vietnam conflict, as well as the navel-gazing complexities of Watergate and the tax affairs of Vice-President Spiro T. Agnew. Sadat and Assad could hardly have chosen a more opportune moment to strike.

THREE-PHASE WAR

The brief war (6–24 October) may be outlined in three phases.

Phase one was marked by striking Arab advances on the Golan Heights and across the Suez Canal. Reinforced by Jordanian and Iraqi tanks and token forces from Kuwait and Saudi Arabia, the Syrians drove the Israelis back towards the steep western escarpment of the Heights, destroying many tanks and inflicting heavy casualties. In the south, the Egyptians and their Algerian and Moroccan allies crossed the Suez Canal by blasting through the Bar Lev barrier of sand, steel and concrete with high-pressure hoses and blocking pipes designed to flood the Canal with burning oil. Overhead, Soviet-built SAM-3 missiles kept the soldiers free from attacks by Israeli aircraft.

Insight

In 2010, as Egypt was constructing an iron wall between itself and Gaza, opposition MPs condemned the action as unworthy of the nation that had won honour for breaching such barriers – notably the Bar Lev line along the Suez Canal.

After three days, Israel had lost about 50 planes and around 500 tanks. Defence minister Dayan told his prime minister that he believed they were 'heading for a catastrophe'. The myth of Israeli invincibility had been destroyed and Arab military prestige restored. For the first time, Arab forces had inflicted a major defeat upon the Israelis. His point proved, Sadat would have been happy to end the war there and then. Assad had other ideas – he had not yet managed to recapture all the Golan Heights, the territory seized by Israel when he had been Syria's defence minister.

Phase two saw the Arab offensive grind to a halt. The USA had organized a massive and immediate airlift to Israel of $2.2 billion's worth of military equipment of every kind except nuclear. Nixon, like all US presidents, was determined to enable Israel to survive without having to resort to the ultimate weapon. Re-equipped and now fully mobilized, the IDF was able to stop the Arab advance and plan one of its own. In Sinai, as the front moved beyond the narrow defensive screen offered by the SAM-3s, the Egyptians lost dozens of aircraft to superior Israeli planes.

Phase three was the Israeli offensive. Despite fresh Soviet armaments worth even more than those provided to their enemies, by the second week of the war the Arab armies were being driven back on all fronts. A breakthrough on the Golan Heights was prevented from becoming a drive to Damascus only by heroic Syrian defence. In the south, after a delay while a 400-tonne temporary bridge was laid over the Suez Canal, General Sharon crossed into Africa and encircled the Egyptian Third Army. With the Soviets threatening to send in troops to save the Egyptians and both the superpowers on alert, a ceasefire was finally agreed by all the belligerent states apart from Iraq.

AFTERMATH

Technically speaking, the October War was another Israeli victory: they beat off Arab attacks and advanced beyond the 1967 frontiers at the time of the ceasefire. Their casualties, although high at 2,700 killed, were less than those of the Arabs (8,500 killed). However, from a political point of view it was the Arabs who had come out on top. Sadat – now the 'hero of the crossing' – claimed victory in the first part of the war and said that the subsequent reverse had occurred only because Egypt could not compete with the combined strength of Israel and the USA. The outcome was just what he had wanted: Israel had to take Egypt and its peace proposals seriously.

The war had troubled Israel domestically, too. Its self-confidence had been badly shaken and the traditional ruling Labour elite discredited. Prime Minister Meir resigned in 1974, making way for Yitzhak Rabin. The Israeli economy was in turmoil and more dependent than ever upon US aid. This was partly because its enemies had seriously deployed the 'oil weapon' for the first time. The Organization of Arab Oil-Producing Countries (OAPEC) imposed a boycott of crude oil sales to the USA and the Netherlands, and cut overall production by 25 per cent. World oil prices soared from US$3 to over US$11 a barrel. Israel was hit harder than most by the major world recession instigated by OAPEC's action.

Insight

Some commentators expressed surprise that it had taken so long for the oil-producing nations of the Persian Gulf to realize their potential power. The 'oil weapon' has remained a potent threat in the Arab armoury ever since.

Because the war had yet again threatened to spark a superpower confrontation and because of the recession caused by OAPEC, it was now in almost everyone's interest to get Israel and her Arab neighbours to make peace. The exception, as so often in the past, was the Palestinians. As members of the PLA and smaller bands, they had fought and died beside their fellow Arabs. Yet in the aftermath of the war – including UN Resolution 338, which harked back to Resolution 242, and a peace conference that met in Geneva, Switzerland – the Palestinian issue was very much secondary. Despite all the protests, the cries, the reasoned arguments and the bombings, the Palestinians were being shifted further and further from the centre of the stage.

In depth: West Bank

The term 'West Bank', meaning 5,880 sq km (2,270 sq miles) of rugged land to the west of the River Jordan, was coined by the Jordanians in 1948. It is now in general use, although 'Palestine' and the older 'Judea and Samaria' are also employed. Rising to 1,022 metres (3,353 ft) at Tall Asur on the central mountainous spine and falling to 409 metres (1,341 ft) below sea level at the Dead Sea, this much-coveted territory is hardly the most agreeable place to live. Less than 40 per cent is used for agriculture, its only natural resource; the rest is barren scrub or covered by human dwellings. Water is scarce and getting scarcer; sewage disposal is a serious problem.

By 2009, the West Bank's population was reckoned to include around 2.1 million Palestinians and, if the population of East Jerusalem is included, approaching 370,000 Israelis (CIA Factbook – the figures are estimates only). The holy city of Jerusalem, Israel's capital, is by far the largest city in the region. Technically speaking, only the east of the city lies within the West Bank. The surrounding area teems with places of deep significance to Christianity, Islam and Judaism. Hebron, Bethlehem and Jericho are among the better known.

Before the establishment of Israel, it was generally agreed by all parties, including the Jewish Agency, that the area now called the West Bank should be part of an Arab state. Amid the turmoil of 1948–9 it was seized by Jordan. Israel then overran it in the war of 1967 and administered it as Occupied Territory. Jordan gave up its claim to the West Bank in 1988 and seven years later Israel and the Palestinians agreed a new administration. The West Bank was divided into three sectors. One (the smallest in area) was fully

(Contd)

administered by a Palestinian National Authority; another was wholly Israeli-administered; and the third was under joint administration. Israel kept control of all borders, roads, airspace and, crucially, water. In international law, the West Bank still belongs to no one.

Talks on allowing the West Bank to form the basis of a Palestinian state have been seriously hampered by the growing number of Israeli settlements there, most controversially along the Jordan Valley. In recent years, the region's bleak, camp-like status (some 30 per cent of the Palestinian population are refugees from Israel) has been enhanced by the massive 'security fence' that Israel has constructed along much of the border between itself and the Palestinian-occupied areas.

In depth: Golan Heights

A raised plateau of dark stone and soil, the Golan Heights is bordered by Syria, Lebanon, Israel and Jordan. Rivers mark its limits on three sides, while the indistinct eastern edge merges with the broad Syrian plain. Although only around 520 metres (1,700 ft) above sea level at its highest point, the steep escarpment on the Golan's western side commands spectacular views over northern Israel. The slopes of Mount Hermon, to the north of the Golan, are Israel's only ski resort. The region has many underground springs and receives more annual rainfall than the surrounding areas. The fertile plateau's plentiful water supply and strategic importance have ensured that ownership of the Golan Heights has been the subject of international dispute for many years.

Because of the comparative richness of the soil, until the fighting of the mid-twentieth century the Golan Heights were relatively densely populated. Today the region is home to only about 40,000 people, about half of whom are Druze (see Glossary). Muslims number not more than a couple of thousand.

After some argument, the Golan became part of the French mandate of Syria in 1923. The formation of Israel led to further conflict in the area, especially about water. In the Six-Day War of 1967, Israel captured the Golan after fierce fighting, during which around 100,000 locals fled. They have yet to be allowed to return. Over the following 40 years, some 20,000 Israelis established themselves in new settlements, and the Knesset's Golan Heights Law of 1981 made the region administratively part of Israel.

Ownership of the Golan is not a straightforward Israel–Syria issue. Lebanon also has a claim on a small area in the north known as the Shebaa Farms. Both Israel and Syria say the farms are theirs. Indeed, Syria states unequivocally that it is legally entitled to ownership of the entire Golan Heights and insists that their return is a prerequisite to peace with Israel. The Israelis are extremely wary of handing back all the Golan to a potential enemy because of the way the western escarpment dominates north-east Israel. Israel's critics, on the other hand, say that it hangs on to the Golan less for strategic reasons than for the district's rich soil and plentiful water.

10 THINGS TO REMEMBER

1. *From 1968 onwards, Israelis starting building settlements in the land seized during the 1967 war.*
2. *The PLO, chaired by Arafat from 1969 onwards, acted as an umbrella organization for numerous Palestinian fedayeen groups, including Fatah, the PFLP and the DFLP, which carried out attacks on Israeli targets, including hijacking aircraft and hostage-taking at the Munich Olympics (1972).*
3. *Arafat's PLO sought a secular, multi-racial and democratic Palestine in which Jew and Arab would live side by side.*
4. *In 1970, after a brief but bloody civil war, the PLO was forcibly driven from Jordan to Lebanon where it proceeded to construct a state within a state.*
5. *Between 1968 and 1970, Israel and Egypt fought a low-intensity War of Attrition along the Suez Canal.*
6. *By the early 1970s, when US aid to Israel was increasing dramatically, President Assad of Syria and President Sadat of Egypt planned a swift, surprise attack on Israel to reverse the humiliation of the Six Day War.*
7. *At the start of the October War (1973), the off-guard Israelis suffered heavy losses as Arab forces made significant advances on the Egyptian and Syrian fronts.*
8. *When a ceasefire came into force on 24 October, the IDF was on the offensive once again, driving deep into Egyptian territory in the south and towards Damascus in the north.*
9. *Although technically another Israeli victory, Arab successes at the start of the October War had removed the myth of Israeli invincibility and enabled the two sides to view each other on a more equal footing.*
10. *By supporting the Arab cause with an oil boycott of countries backing Israel, the Organisation of Arab Oil-Producing Countries (OAPEC) threw the world economy into turmoil.*

9

Peace from war 1974 to 1979

In this chapter you will learn about:

- ***the aftermath of the 1973 October War***
- ***the advance of Israel's right wing***
- ***the search for peace, 1976 onwards***
- ***Camp David and its immediate consequences.***

Like the 1967 Arab–Israeli War, the conflict of 1973 made a long-term solution to the Israel–Palestine conflict easier to envisage yet harder to bring about. Optimism stemmed from the fact that because of their first credible military performance the Palestinians' Arab backers now had some political authority. The willingness of the PLO to accept a compromise settlement was also encouraging for the peace process.

At the same time, the mid- and late 1970s saw major developments that made a settlement much harder to achieve: the rise of the uncompromising right in Israel; the isolation of Egypt within the Arab world; open armed confrontation between Israel and the PLO in a war-torn Lebanon; and ominous signs of a further fragmentation within the Arab world with the rise of Islamic fundamentalism.

Possibilities for peace

SHUTTLE DIPLOMACY

Although the post-war Geneva conference fizzled out almost before it had started, it was not in the interests of the major players to let the peace process die. The Nixon administration in the USA, although beset with domestic difficulties that would eventually bring it down (Watergate), was keen to keep Middle East negotiations going. The task fell to ex-academic Henry Kissinger, who was both Assistant to the President for National Security Affairs and, from 1973, Secretary of State.

Kissinger saw the Middle East situation as part of the Cold War. His view was essentially this: with the USA backing Israel, there was a tendency for Israel's enemies also to be hostile towards the USA and therefore obvious targets for Soviet blandishments. Consequently, peace in the Middle East was needed to undermine the power of the USSR. To this end, employing his famous 'shuttle diplomacy' and 'step-by-step' approach, Kissinger flew back and forth between Jerusalem, Cairo and Damascus. The result was two significant agreements known as Sinai I and Sinai II (1974 and 1975). By these agreements' terms the Israeli and Egyptian armies disengaged, a UN force was installed between them, and the IDF withdrew to a significant distance east of the Suez Canal. Both sides also agreed publicly that the conflict between them should henceforth be resolved by peaceful means.

Insight

The new practice of shuttle diplomacy, pioneered by Henry Kissinger, was made possible only by the development of swift, comfortable and reliable air transport. It enabled diplomats to act as go-betweens in circumstances where it was not practicable or realistic to bring the opposing parties together on one site.

Negotiations with Syria were trickier because President Assad, who had ambitions to take over Nasser's mantle as leader of the

Arab world, was loath to be seen to back down. Eventually, a disengagement agreement was reached in May 1974 that separated the two forces on the Golan Heights, imposed UN observers between them, and allowed only limited armaments on either side of a demilitarized buffer zone.

STAGNATION

After Sinai II, the peace movement lost momentum. Kissinger and President Gerald Ford, who had replaced the disgraced Nixon, blamed the new Israeli Prime Minister Rabin for intransigence. In fact, neither the Israelis nor the Egyptians were ready at this stage to commit themselves publicly to one-on-one treaty negotiations. The premiers of both countries feared domestic hostility and Sadat was worried about leaving his Arab partners behind.

Therefore, though impressive, the Kissinger settlements went nowhere near the heart of the Arab–Israeli problem. Israeli–Egyptian relations definitely improved and Egypt was brought closer to the US sphere of influence. Syria, on the other hand, did no more than grudgingly accept reality. In addition, nothing was done for the Palestinians. Indeed, Kissinger told Rabin that the USA would not even talk to the PLO until it accepted UN Security Council Resolution 242.

FEDAYEEN *AND TERRORISTS*

Arafat and the PLO had kept a low profile during the 1973 War. Such relatively quiescent tactics cut no ice with Kissinger, who smartly rebuffed Arafat's tentative approaches for talks. As far as the US secretary of state was concerned, Arafat was a close friend of the Kremlin and many of his fellow Palestinian activists were unashamedly communist. Moreover, Kissinger saw the PLO and all its official and unofficial *fedayeen* offshoots as tarred with the same evil brush of terrorism.

As if to support Kissinger's thesis, in April 1974 a small band of PFLP-General Command *fedayeen* descended on the northern Israeli village of Qiryat Shemona. Here 18 Israelis died, many of them children, before the intruders were themselves shot dead. The next month, 21 Israeli schoolchildren perished when security forces attacked a school in which *fedayeen* of the Democratic Front for the Liberation of Palestine (DFLP) were holding over 100 children hostage. Israel responded with a ferocious strike into southern Lebanon, from where the attacks had come, killing at least 60 civilians.

A major problem for those Palestinians seeking a settlement with Israel was that their movement was so fragmented. The PLO and Fatah offered a degree of leadership, but Arafat lacked that indefinable presidential quality that might have persuaded all parties to coalesce around him. Consequently, he was torn between trying to exert his authority over breakaway groups and giving them coded or half-hearted praise when their actions won the applause of his fellow Palestinians.

We need to remember that deeds dismissed as despicable terrorism in the West were seen by many Palestinians as heroic. *Fedayeen* who died in 'battle' were hailed as martyrs for the Palestinian cause and quickly became the stuff of song, poem and legend. This was not because the Palestinians were particularly insensitive or bloodthirsty. Like the Catholic supporters of the IRA in Northern Ireland, they were desperate people who believed they were being oppressed by a cruel and overbearing tyrant. In such dire circumstances, they declared, any tactic was permissible.

'TWO-STATE SOLUTION'

An Arab summit in Algiers shortly after the end of the 1973 War made a number of secret yet highly significant decisions. Two were especially important. First, the PLO was to be the sole representative of the Palestinian people. Second, for Israel to live at peace with the Arabs it had first to surrender the lands it had conquered in 1967. This was a decidedly more realistic aim than persuading Israel either to return to the UN partition arrangement of 1947 or to accept the PLO idea of a single secular state of Palestine.

These two decisions put the PLO in a very strong position – as long as it was prepared to alter its aim of one Palestine for Jews and Arabs. If it would accept the implied 'two-state solution' – an Israel separate from a Palestine based on the West Bank and Gaza Strip – then it would get the backing of major Arab governments and, very likely, the majority of other world powers too. At a meeting in the summer of 1974, the PLO hinted that it was moving towards the proposed compromise. The new Palestine, it declared, would begin in 'liberated' Palestinian territory. Needless to say, this idea was not accepted by all Palestinians. A number of hardliners, led by George Habash of the PFLP, rejected the compromise. Not long afterwards, this 'Rejectionist Front' left the PLO. Such internal bickering only added to the Palestinians' difficulty of being taken seriously on the international stage.

It should be noted that Arafat, leader of the PLO, continued to tread his equivocal path between aggression and peace-seeking. He would not openly condemn 'terrorist' acts and in public he still promised audiences the eventual 'destruction' of Israel. Such uncompromising rhetoric ensured that in Israel he and his supporters continued to be seen as a murderous threat.

'OLIVE BRANCH AND GUN'

Moderate talk of a two-state solution bore rich fruit in November 1974 when Arafat was invited to speak to the General Assembly of the United Nations. Israel and the USA had resolutely opposed the invitation, which proved to be a major diplomatic rebuff to them both. With a pistol ostentatiously showing, Arafat said he dreamed and hoped that one day there would be a single secular Palestine. However, he also intimated, with talk of peace, that there might be a compromise: 'Today I have come bearing an olive branch and a freedom fighter's gun. Do not let the olive branch fall from my hand.'

It was dramatic stuff and well received around the world. Not long afterwards, the PLO was given 'observer' status at the UN – this was tantamount to official recognition that Palestine was a nation-in-waiting. A year later, the USA finally accepted the inevitable and admitted that the Palestinians were more than just 'refugees' (as they had been described in UN Resolution 242). It happened in a low-key manner when Deputy Assistant Secretary of State Harold H. Saunders declared that in a general Middle East settlement, 'the legitimate interests of the Palestinian Arabs must be taken into account'. It was also suggested that the USA might help the Palestinians if they accepted Resolution 242 and recognized Israel's right to exist.

It was a very small step on a very long journey, but at least it was movement.

Israel turns right

LABOUR'S DIFFICULTIES

The nature of the 1973 October War had been a shock to Israelis. The greatest power in the region had been taken by surprise and brought perilously close to defeat. It had been saved not just by its own steadfastness but also by the USA. For the first time since 1948, Israel's citizens had seen just how vulnerable their little state was.

The war left Israel even more dependent upon the USA for diplomatic and military help, as well as more general aid. The conflict also undermined national confidence. This had two effects. One was a widening of the rift that was already a marked feature of Israeli political life: conservatives and traditionalists moved further to the right, while moderates and those on the left showed a greater willingness to compromise for peace. The second was mounting dissatisfaction with the Labour-based coalition that had been in power ever since the country's formation.

Golda Meir found it difficult to form a government and resigned in the spring of 1974. After a fiercely contested vote, she was replaced as head of Labour by Yitzhak Rabin, the first locally born politician to head the country's government. A native of Jerusalem, he had fought with the Haganah against the Palestinians and, latterly, had served as Israel's ambassador to the USA. Elected to the Knesset only in 1973, his lack of political experience was compounded by an awkward manner.

Things went badly for Rabin and his Labour-led administration. When the troubles in Lebanon finally flared into civil war in 1975, for a while there was a very real fear that Israel's northern neighbour might fall into the hands of the PLO. To prevent this happening, Israel felt obliged to intervene actively in the Lebanese conflagration (see Chapter 10). This put still further strain on an overstretched economy.

Nearer home, the government submitted to constant pressure from extremist Zionists and accepted the first Israeli settlements in the occupied West Bank. Constructed contrary to international law, the new Jewish outposts worried moderates and infuriated the Palestinians. In the longer term, they would make it considerably more difficult for future Israeli administrations to find a compromise peace deal acceptable within Israel and with the PLO. From November 1975 onwards, there was serious protest against the new settlements and against a plan to grant 'civil administration' (limited autonomy) to residents of the Occupied Territories. The latter was interpreted as simply a way of preparing the Palestinians for permanent occupation.

The world's press, once sympathetic towards 'plucky little Israel', was now increasingly likely to label Israel a bully state. This change of mood was reflected in a resolution passed by the General Assembly of the UN in November 1975: 'Zionism is a form of racism and racial discrimination.' Israel's sense of international isolation grew still more painful.

Insight

Normally speaking, resolutions of the General Assembly of the UN – where a simple majority is needed for a measure to pass – carry far less weight than those of the Security Council, where a resolution may be blocked by the veto of a single country.

PALESTINIAN IDENTITY

1976 was even grimmer for the Israeli government than 1975 had been. As the slaughter in Lebanon intensified, so Israel's commitment there grew (see pp. 171–2 and p. 178). In March, the Arabs living within Israel called for protests and a general strike to show disapproval of the government policy of appropriating land in Galilee for Jewish settlers. Six Arabs died when troops fired on a demonstration and the date – 30 March – became 'Land Day', an annual day of Palestinian protest.

From inside Israel, the commemoration of Land Day spread to the Occupied Territories. Here it became part of a swelling sense of Palestinian nationalism and identity. It was fostered by students, especially those of the new Palestine National University at Ramallah, by expanding trade unions and by women's groups. It expressed itself in protests, in art and literature. As we have seen, the *fedayeen* provided an endless stream of folk heroes (see pp. 94–5). Poets, gifted and otherwise, immortalized their legendary qualities and exploits. Songs such as 'Biladi, Biladi!' ('My Country, My Country!'), sung to an Egyptian tune, roused the spirits of a people that for generations had found little to smile about or feel proud of.

The stirring of the national consciousness expressed itself in the Occupied Territories' municipal elections of April 1976. Although Israel had deported many community leaders, the turnout was high and the PLO and nationalist candidates swept the board. Two years later, the new mayors of Nablus, Ramallah and other large towns formed themselves into a National Guidance Committee. Thus slowly, almost imperceptibly at times, the spirit was growing that would eventually burst out into the Intifada (see Chapter 11).

ENTER LIKUD

Harassed from abroad and unsure at home, Rabin's cabinet found little to quicken the pulse. Its one relief came in the summer of 1976, when Israeli commandos made a daring and successful raid on Entebbe airport, Uganda, to rescue 98 Israeli and Jewish passengers who had been on board an Air France plane hijacked by the PFLP. Less than a year later, Rabin resigned over accusations of an illegal overseas bank account. The following month, following a sharp electoral turn-around, the Labour party failed to gain sufficient Knesset seats to set up a new coalition. Consequently, for the first time since its formation, Israel had a right-wing government. This illustrated the division within Israeli society about the very nature of the new country. The rift, profoundly harmful to the peace process, remains to this day.

The right-wing party Likud had been formed four years earlier. At its core were the old Liberal and Herat ('Freedom') Parties, the heirs of Irgun and Lehi, and its principal electoral support came from the growing number of Sephardim who felt shabbily treated by successive Labour administrations. Intellectually and practically, Likud was hard line: Israelis had a religious duty to take back and settle all the lands given to them by God in Old Testament times; He had allowed them to conquer the West Bank ('Judea and Samaria'), Gaza and the Golan Heights – now it was up to them to go and live there; as for the Palestinians, they were not a nation but simply Arabs who had been living in the province of Palestine; if they needed a homeland, then they had one in Jordan; there was nothing to be gained by negotiating with them, especially as they were led by *fedayeen*.

Such views were hardly conducive to the long-term peace of the Middle East. What with the Palestinians' growing nationalism, their sense of outrage at the continued neglect of their plight, the ongoing *fedayeen* campaign, and the bitter fighting in Lebanon, the outlook was decidedly gloomy.

The new prime minister was Menachem Begin, a man against whom Ben-Gurion had warned several years before. Having lost family members in the Holocaust, been detained by the Soviets, fought with the Polish and with Irgun, he was a tough, suspicious, hard-headed individual. He saw anti-Semitism in all opposition to Israel, no matter how reasonable, and he believed that to survive in the sea of enemies that surrounded it, Israel had to stand firm behind an iron wall.

Begin's cabinet contained, somewhat surprisingly, the Labour Foreign Minister Moshe Dayan, Ezer Weizmann in charge of defence and Ariel Sharon as Minister of Agriculture. This last post encompassed settlement – what was coming to be known as 'facts on the ground'. Within 35 years, there were 220,000 Israeli settlers living in 'Judea and Samaria' and Gaza, another 200,000 in and around East Jerusalem and a further 15,000 on the Golan. Eighty per cent of the West Bank's precious water was piped to Israeli settlements or to Israel itself.

The quest for peace

JIMMY CARTER

Before Israel's elections had signalled a move to the right, the USA had moved towards the centre of the political spectrum with the 1976 election of Democratic President Jimmy Carter. Whereas Nixon and Ford had been pragmatists, focusing on the immediate problems of the Cold War, Carter was a 'big picture' man. Deeply religious, scrupulously honest and perhaps at first a little naive, he thought in terms of universal peace and moral justice, especially for the developing world. He was the first US president openly to acknowledge the sufferings of the Palestinians, declaring shortly after taking office that he believed they should have a 'homeland'. Later, when Israeli settlements in the Occupied Territories were declared technically illegal according to international law, the US State Department called on Israel to withdraw from the land it had seized in 1967. The European Community echoed the same request and by the end of 1977 there was talk of restarting the Geneva Peace Conference.

It is now clear – as it was to many at the time – that the chances of getting all the parties involved in the Israel–Palestine problem – not just Israel and the PLO, but Syria, Egypt, Jordan and Lebanon as well as the USA and the USSR – round the same table, let alone talking constructively to each other, was negligible. There was hope, however, if the scale was reduced and the targets simplified.

At the end of the 1973 October War, the Egyptian Chief of Staff had observed to his Israeli deputy counterpart, 'Look… a war between us has ended in equality… From here we can negotiate.' From such sentiments had stemmed Sinai I and II before the process had ground to a halt (see p. 151). Sadat was keen for it to continue. Egypt's economy was suffering badly and in early 1977 there had been food riots in Cairo. As Carter was prepared to offer aid for peace, talks with the USA were clearly to Sadat's advantage. A few hundred kilometres to the north, Prime Minister Begin was having similar thoughts. His prime concern was to secure his southern frontier so that the IDF could concentrate fully on the threat from the PLO in Lebanon. In other words, both Sadat and Begin wanted peace for their own very limited and practical reasons – and the Palestinians did not feature prominently in the thinking of either of them.

DEADLOCK

The autumn of 1977 saw a flurry of diplomatic activity in which Morocco's King Hassan II acted as a sophisticated go-between. Despite his best efforts, though, by November negotiations appeared to be grinding to a halt again. Sadat could not be seen openly to abandon the Palestinians, while Begin could not accept any formula that accommodated them. On 9 November 1977, Sadat broke the impasse in the most dramatic manner possible. Speaking before the Egyptian National Assembly, he declared himself prepared to go 'to the ends of the earth' to find peace, even 'to the Knesset itself'. Astonished, the world awaited Begin's response. He dared not refuse the challenge and the Egyptian president was duly invited to Israel and asked to address the Knesset.

Sadat's speech was broad-ranging, talking of a general peace in the region, self-determination for the Palestinians and a return of the Occupied Territories. Deeply suspicious, Begin replied that certainly there could be talks, but with no pre-conditions. He did not once mention the Palestinians.

Insight

Egypt's antipathy towards extremist militia is understandable given that many of these militia trace their roots back to the Muslim Brotherhood. This Egyptian opposition group, founded in 1928, was the first Islamist organization of the modern age.

As if to emphasize Begin's uncompromising position, not long after Sadat's momentous initiative, new Israeli settlements were authorized in the Occupied Territories and further help was given to Christian militia fighting the PLO in Lebanon. Meanwhile, the Arab world had roundly condemned Sadat for breaking ranks. Israeli–Egyptian talks, begun in Ismailia in December 1977, meandered on into 1978. The atmosphere was not helped by the reuniting of the PFLP and PLO, the assassination of PLO leaders who had talked of reconciliation with Israel, and the murder of a Ramallah politician accused of collaborating with the Israelis.

In March 1978, Fatah *fedayeen* attacked a bus near Haifa in northern Israel. The ensuing slaughter saw 37 Israelis and 6 hijackers killed. Apparently, the aim of the attack had been to demonstrate that, to be meaningful, any talks about peace had to include the PLO. The raid had the opposite effect: the chances of the PLO now being involved in any formal discussions with the Israelis were non-existent. Begin likened Arafat to Adolf Hitler.

Camp David

SHANGRI-LA

Jimmy Carter saved the day. In a move almost as startling as Sadat's invitation to visit Jerusalem, he invited Sadat and Begin to discuss their differences at the presidential country retreat of Camp

David, Maryland. Neither leader dared refuse. Originally named Shangri-La, Camp David was an excellent choice of venue. Its atmosphere was informal, relaxed even; there was sufficient suitable accommodation for each delegation to have its own separate building; above all, it was remote. This had two advantages: there was not a press microphone, TV camera or journalist's notebook for miles, and it was a very difficult place to leave. One could not simply storm out of Camp David because access was by helicopter and there was nowhere in the immediate vicinity to storm to. Begin even described it as an 'elegant jail'. Once Carter had got the two leaders inside the perimeter fence, he was determined not to let them go until they had reached an agreement.

The three heads of state were accompanied by extensive retinues that included, on the American side, Secretary of State Cyrus Vance, National Security Advisor Zbigniew Brzezinski and, towards the end, Vice-President Walter Mondale; the Israeli contingent contained Foreign Minister Moshe Dayan, Defence Minister Ezer Weizmann and Attorney General Aharon Barak; among President Sadat's advisors were the minister Muhammad Ibrahim Kamil and the Senior Presidential Advisor Osama El-Baz.

Consequently, although the Egyptian and Israeli premiers clearly disliked each other, there were enough wise men present for a number of mutual understandings to develop. For 14 days, Carter and his aides shuttled back and forth between the two sides, cajoling, suggesting and even threatening. Eventually agreement was reached and everyone was allowed to go home.

ACCORD

The Camp David Accords, which were formalized in a peace treaty the following March, had essentially two components.

The first was that henceforth Israel and Egypt would be at peace. Egypt received about $1 billion a year from the USA for much of the 1980s and Israel withdrew from the Sinai, dismantling its settlements and bases there. The USA compensated their losses with a $3 billion loan. Relations between Israel and Egypt were restored to normality, with an exchange of ambassadors, air links and so forth.

The second part of the agreement – a 'Framework for Peace in the Middle East' – was a good deal less concrete. Israel accepted the 'legitimate rights' of the Palestinians, whatever that might mean, and agreed to their having 'full autonomy' after a transitional period – another equally vague phrase. Nothing was said about Jerusalem, the right of return for Palestinian refugees or Israeli withdrawal, although Begin had at least recognized that the Palestinians existed. In practical terms, though, he had committed to nothing, and he did nothing. Like Sadat, he had got what he wanted. The IDF now had a free hand to tackle the PLO in the north.

THE AFTERMATH

Begin and Sadat were both awarded Nobel Peace Prizes, although President Carter probably deserved one more than either of them. In 1981, Sadat paid for his with his life when he was assassinated by Muslim fanatics. By this time, Egypt had been ejected from the Arab League and subjected to sanctions from other Arab states. Significantly, Arafat, still keen to get on the right side of the USA, maintained secret links with the Egyptian government.

Begin was criticized by Zionist extremists who called for the agreement with Egypt to be scrapped. They were to some extent mollified when it became clear that Begin planned to do nothing about Palestinian 'autonomy' (which he defined as a purely personal matter) and when Israelis were allowed to make private purchases of land in the West Bank. After Camp David, despite an Israeli High Court ruling that settlements made for political purposes were illegal (1979), the number of Jewish villages in the West Bank doubled and the total number of Israelis living within the Occupied Territories rose five-fold. In protest, Moshe Dayan resigned from the government in 1979 and Ezer Weizmann followed him a year later.

And how were the Palestinians affected? When post-Camp David talks for a wider peace in the Middle East collapsed in 1979, their worst fears were confirmed: in the last instance, their fellow Arabs would always put national and self interest before that of the wider Arab world. Palestinian condemnation of the Camp David Accords was almost universal and there were violent attacks on those who showed any inclination to support them. Yet the Egyptian 'sell-out' brought a wave of Arab sympathy for the Palestinians and Gulf funding for the PLO increased. Furthermore, an Israeli government had at least mentioned Palestinian autonomy. That, at the very least, was a start.

Insight

Israeli sources – hardly likely to underestimate – state that the PLO received 'at least US$100 million a year from the Arab states' after 1973, with the total approaching '$250-300 million a year by the early 1990s'. (www.palestinefacts.org/pf_1991to_now_plo_finances.php)

A start it might have been, but there it would rest for a long time. The Camp David Accords were not the only dramatic change taking place in the region. Civil war still flared in Lebanon, and the PLO and Israelis were both heavily involved. Even more significant, at the beginning of 1979 the Shah of Iran was overthrown and his country became an Islamic republic. The age of militant Islam was dawning, bringing a new spirit of fiery intolerance to the already intractable Israeli–Palestinian confrontation.

In depth: Gush Emunim

Gush Emunim was the most prominent of several extreme Zionist religious groups that led the settlement of lands occupied by Israeli forces during the Six-Day War of 1967. Its work infuriated the Palestinians and made any long-term solution to the problem of the Occupied Territories much harder to achieve.

The fervent Zionist Rabbi Zvi Yehuda Kook (1891–1982) taught that in returning to the land of Israel, given to them by God in Biblical

(Contd)

times, the Jews had hastened the coming of the Messiah (Saviour). The remarkable conquests of 1967, he believed, had instigated the Messianic Age, which would be crowned by the Saviour's arrival. Therefore, it was the duty of all those of Jewish faith to settle (or resettle, as they saw it) the land that God had placed in their hands.

Gush Emunim ('Block of the Faithful', also known as 'Those Who Are Faithful to the Land of Israel') was established to see Rabbi Kook's teaching put into practice. In 1968, led by Rabbi Moshe Levinger, a small band of Gush Emunim fanatics established a presence at Kiyat Arba, just outside Hebron. They were returning, they said, to where Jews had lived before the 1929 massacre. The site comprised no more than temporary shelters until 1971, when more permanent structures were begun on an abandoned army base. By 2005, the population of the settlement and surrounding homesteads was over 9,000.

Even more significant was the offshoot of Gush Emunim that attempted to settle at Elon Moreh, a kilometre or so north of the Palestinian town of Nablus. Israeli troops forced them to leave seven times before Prime Minister Rabin, pressured by Ariel Sharon, relented and let the settlers stay. The permission, temporary at first, soon became permanent. Thereafter, Israeli settlements on the Occupied Territories mushroomed. To his dying day, Rabin bitterly regretted having given way to Gush Emunim, a movement that he believed was a threat to Israel's democracy. Whether it was or not, its band of dedicated followers had altered the course of the country's history and with it the history of the whole region.

In depth: PFLP

Nowadays, the Marxist-Leninist Popular Front for the Liberation of Palestine (PFLP) appears rather old-fashioned, although it retains a surprisingly large following among better-educated Palestinians, especially students. The movement was founded in 1967 by George Habash, a Palestinian Christian whose family the Israelis had forced into exile in 1948. In keeping with its founder's far-left, secularist views, the Front called for Palestinians to join an armed pan-Arab, anti-capitalist movement to crush Israel and all other reactionary and West-favouring regimes in the Middle East. A confusing array of splinter groups, such as the Popular Front for the Liberation of Palestine – General Command (PFLP-GC), the Maoist Democratic Front for the Liberation of Palestine (DFLP) and the Popular Revolutionary Front for the Liberation of Palestine (PRFLP) all broke away from the PFLP during the 1960s and early 1970s.

The Front, which was second in size only to Fatah within the PLO, first came to public attention with its attacks on aircraft and airports. It was bitterly opposed to the Camp David and Oslo Accords but found the rise of Islamist groups, which shared many of its political aims, a difficult challenge to meet. Regarding itself as scientific and modern, the Front held that a return to beliefs and practices of former times would in the long run do nothing to help the cause of Palestinians and the working-class in general. This was an awkward stance because the bulk of the Islamists' support came from the very people – the poor and ill-educated – for whom the Front professed to be fighting.

The PFLP boycotted the 1996 Palestinian elections but backed Marwhan Barghouti in the 2004 vote to replace Arafat. It then contested the 2006 elections to the Palestinian legislature, winning 4.2 per cent of the vote and gaining three seats. Such moderate success may have been due to the way it had resumed its guerrilla campaign with fresh energy at the onset of the Second Intifada, claiming the lives of over 20 Israelis.

10 THINGS TO REMEMBER

1 *Henry Kissinger, key foreign affairs plenipotentiary for US President Richard Nixon, masterminded the first Arab–Israeli long-term peace agreements: Sinai I (1974) and Sinai II (1975).*

2 *While the USA was seeking further peace negotiations, PLO fedayeen kept up the pressure to be included by launching operations such as the murderous attack on the Israeli village of Qirat Shemona (1974).*

3 *By the mid-1970s, influential Arab states had agreed that a 'two state solution' to the Israel–Palestine problem was the only one that stood a chance of success.*

4 *When Yasser Arafat appeared before the United Nations in 1974 saying he bore an olive branch, he won huge international support for the PLO and the cause of the Palestinian people.*

5 *Focusing around events such as the annual Land Day, Palestinian national identity continued to grow throughout the 1970s.*

6 *In 1976, a new right-wing political party, Likud, formed the basis of a government under Prime Minister Menachem Begin.*

7 *For their own very different reasons, by 1977 both Egypt's President Sadat and Israel's Prime Minister Begin both wanted a permanent peace deal. The Palestinians featured very low on their list of priorities.*

8 *President Sadat's visit to Israel (1977), where he spoke of peace before the Knesset (Israeli parliament), was one of the more dramatic developments in the post-war history of the Middle East.*

9 *During a summit at his summer retreat of Camp David, US President Jimmy Carter managed to broker a land-for-peace deal between Israel and Egypt that established normal relations between the two states but which largely skated over the needs of the Palestinians.*

10 *The Arab world outside Egypt condemned the Camp David Accords unreservedly and increased its support for the PLO.*

10

Lebanon 1970 to *c.* 1985

In this chapter you will learn about:

- ***Lebanon, the PLO and civil war***
- ***Israel and the Occupied Territories, 1979–87***
- ***Israel's invasion of Lebanon***
- ***further international attempts to make peace.***

The compromise state

UNEASY STABILITY

The modern state of Lebanon was created by the French after World War I. Forty years later there lived within its boundaries a diverse and potentially explosive collection of peoples and faiths that may be simply categorized as Palestinians, Christians, Druze, Sunnis and Shia. Tragically, by the 1970s, the conditions that enabled the subtle power-sharing constitution to hold the country together were rapidly breaking down.

The Christians, once in a slight majority but now no more than 40 per cent of the population, had always been the wealthiest sector and had traditionally cornered the most influential positions, including the presidency. Among the Christians, the Maronites, numbering perhaps a quarter of all Lebanese, were particularly prominent. As the population grew, the proportion of comparatively poor rural Muslims also increased. Beirut, the capital, had expanded to the point where almost one half of all Lebanese lived within or close to its perimeters. It had also grown into a divided and increasingly wary city in which the different ethnic and religious communities inhabited distinct and discrete quarters.

Lebanon's refusal to join with the other Arab nations in their wars with Israel in 1967 and 1973 angered many Lebanese Muslims. There was also the problem of Palestinian refugees. Since 1948, around 270,000 of them had found shelter in Lebanon, some doing well (Lebanon's largest construction company was Palestinian-owned) but the vast majority remaining poor and landless. Like the majority of Lebanon's Muslims, the Palestinians felt their interests were ignored by the ruling class.

ENTER THE PLO

Into this dangerous mix came the PLO. Driven from Jordan at the end of 1970, it arrived in Lebanon with its weapons, its separate organization and, above all, with its independent, aggressive attitude. Many Lebanese, especially the Christians and the more intellectual, better-educated Palestinians, regarded the intruders as little more than bandits who levied taxes, set up road blocks and generally behaved as if they owned the place. The PLO was tainted by corruption, too, and it was rumoured that some of its bureaucrats earned a private income by selling arms to Lebanese Christians. To add to the frustration of the PLO's opponents, Palestinian cross-border sallies against Israel drew disproportionately violent and destructive reprisals.

That, however, is only part of the story. To many of the refugees the PLO was, almost literally, a godsend. It had money and confidence, commodities a generation of camp-dwellers singularly lacked. The Palestine National Fund, mostly Gulf money, which the PLO had at its disposal, reached about US$233 million a year by the late 1980s. Long before that, its members had infiltrated themselves into all aspects of camp life, making and mending roads, providing electricity, running schools, clinics, hospitals and even their own revolutionary courts. Equally significantly, they fostered a sense of Palestinian nationalism, flying the Palestinian flag at every available opportunity, teaching nationalist songs, publishing nationalist stories and poetry. The young, especially, were fostered for the cause: for the boys there was the *Ashbal* (Lion Cub) movement, for the girls the *Zahrat* (Flowers) movement.

Much of the PLO's work was crude, ignorant and bullying. There was corruption and internecine squabbling, which on occasion became violent. Yet overall the effect was to build up a sense of steely purpose and hope among a downtrodden people. Small wonder Menachem Begin had signed the Camp David Accords in the belief that they would free him to turn north and tackle the PLO's state within a state.

CIVIL WAR

One more piece of the Lebanese collage remains to be explained: the paramilitary Phalange. This was a right-wing, Christian, military-political organization whose 10,000-strong militia was as ruthless as it was well-armed. With a neo-fascist motto that proclaimed 'God, the Fatherland, and the Family', they believed themselves to be descended from the ancient Phoenicians, not the Arabs; they rejected Pan-Arabism and hated the PLO.

In 1975, Lebanon slid into civil war: the fishermen of Sidon went on strike; clashes with the authorities turned violent; a prominent Muslim was assassinated; shots were fired in a church; the Phalange ambushed a busload of PFLP supporters... and by May the country was tearing itself apart. Central government collapsed and local warbands imposed what order they could. Arms, ranging from sophisticated rocket launchers to simple rifles and grenades, flooded into the country, particularly from Syria, Iraq and Israel. Planeloads of Lebanese fled the mayhem, destruction and slaughter. Of those who could not get away, some 70,000 lost their lives. Most were innocent civilians.

Lebanon's neighbours and others, all with their separate agendas, inevitably kept a close eye on the situation. Initially, Syria helped the PLO against the Christian militias, who were backed by Israel. However, when by mid-1976 it looked as if the Christians might be wholly defeated and Lebanon might fall into the hands of the PLO and its Muslim allies, the Syrians made common cause with the Israelis to prevent this happening. President Assad had long regarded Lebanon with covetous eyes and had no wish to see his prosperous neighbour become a left-wing Palestinian stronghold. Therefore, in the most Machiavellian of moves, a secret deal was brokered by the USA in which Syrian forces entered Lebanon, ostensibly as peacekeepers but really to fight alongside the Christian Tiger and Phalange militias. That summer, the Palestinian losses were horrific.

Insight

Lebanon and Syria were originally part of 'Levant', a single League of Nations mandate put under French control. The division of Levant into two states in 1920 is still regarded by many Lebanese and Syrians as a high-handed imperialist gesture that ought to be reversed.

IMPASSE

A ceasefire agreed in October 1976 reduced the violence but did not stop it. Broadly speaking, the Syrians remained in control of the east and north of the country – the Christian bases were north of Beirut – while the PLO had strengthened its positions in the south. Despite the warfare, Arafat was trying to present the PLO as a reasonable organization willing to come to terms with Israel. This may have been true, but there were many under the PLO umbrella (the 'Rejectionists') to whom accord with the enemy was impossible, and from 1977 Israel had a prime minister who considered accord with the PLO unthinkable. The old cliché was painfully relevant: Arafat was between a rock and a hard place.

The autumn of 1977 saw a number of bloody incidents on the Israel–Lebanon border. On one occasion the IDF advanced towards the Litani River, only to be recalled when an irate President Carter learned that the Israelis were deploying US equipment provided for strictly defensive purposes. The following March, the IDF again drove into what it called 'Fatahland', this time reaching the Litani. Perhaps 1,000 Palestinians and Lebanese were killed, including 75 when an air strike hit a mosque. A ceasefire was quickly called, accepted by Fatah and policed by the UN. The Rejectionists turned it down and attacked the UN peacekeepers. In the far south, Israel established a 'good fence' policy, providing Lebanese Christians just across the border with aid of every kind, including weaponry, in return for help against the PLO. This led to the formation of the Christian, Israeli-backed South Lebanese Army (SLA).

That, more or less, was where things stood as Begin signed his Accords with President Sadat. Likud and its right-wing backers in the Knesset wanted the PLO eliminated and a pro-Israeli Christian government firmly established in Beirut – at almost any cost. Moderate-minded Israelis were worried at their country's new aggressive posture and the more active of them had joined a growing Peace Now movement. Arafat, boosted by understanding noises coming out of the Carter White House, seemed genuinely keen to find a peaceful solution to his people's difficulties. He was increasingly isolated from the sentiments of the people of the Occupied Territories, however, where Palestinian nationalism was becoming more anti-Israeli (see Chapter 11); he was also unable to control or convert the more hard-line Palestinian factions, who were pledged to settle for nothing less than the destruction of Israel. In the short term, it seemed, diplomatic solutions were out of the question. It was down to sheer brute force.

Israel, Likud and the Occupied Territories

DIVIDED ISRAEL

This book is essentially the story of two competing nationalisms, two peoples contesting ownership of the same piece of land. During the 1920s and 1930s, it was hoped the two could live together in the same state. When that was seen to be clearly impossible, partition was suggested. This was rejected by those who owned the great bulk of the land, the Palestinians. In the fighting that followed over the next 25 years, the Palestinians lost control over all their land and found themselves either in exile or under foreign domination. They had never been a self-governing nation and now, in the 1980s, they were a scattered and divided people.

This is roughly how the Jews had been before 1948. Since then, although bound together by a distinctive religion, a common language and an ancient heritage, they had found nation-building a difficult process. Israel in the mid-1980s was a mini-United Nations: under 20 per cent of the population were Israeli-born; slightly more were of Asian (largely Russian) or African origin, and just under 40 per cent came from Europe or the USA. Each sector brought with it distinctive customs and attitudes.

Broadly speaking, Sephardim Israelis (see Glossary) were conservative, less well educated and inclined to be less tolerant than their Ashkenazim counterparts. Many had come from cultures where life for Jews had been hard – and cheap. They had had to fight to survive. When aligned with the religious zealots who came to Israel from all parts of the globe determined to fulfil what they believed were holy Biblical prophesies and commands, they created a powerful and illiberal bloc that democratic politicians ignored to their cost. Under its influence, Israel followed aggressive policies that the state's founding fathers would never have considered. Much of the remaining international sympathy for Israel drained away, and across the country the deep and grievous socio-political divide widened.

> ***Any plan that includes handing over parts of the western Land of Israel to foreign rule ... undermines our right to the land... and ultimately jeopardizes the existence of the state of Israel.***

This is an extract from the manifesto of the Herut party, 1988. It amalgamated with Likud in the same year.

LIKUD RETURNS

The elections of the summer of 1981 gave Likud one more Knesset seat than Labour and enabled Begin to remain as prime minister. The opposition had been hampered by squabbling between its two senior men, Yitzhak Rabin and Shimon Peres, and by votes going to Peace Now. In contrast, at the last minute Begin had used a daring display of military machismo to pick up the votes of wavering right-wingers who disapproved of the Camp David Accords: three weeks before the elections, Israeli bombers had penetrated Iraqi air space and destroyed a reactor said to be capable of producing nuclear warheads.

Secure in the cabinet, Prime Minister Begin, Foreign Minister Shamir and Defence Minister Sharon were free to pursue their policies of confrontation and containment of the Palestinians. The emotional and economic strain these put on Israel was enormous. Over 600 soldiers were killed, international opprobrium soared, and the economy came close to collapse as unemployment rose and inflation topped a staggering 400 per cent per annum. The strain on Begin was great too, and, depressed by the death of his wife, he broke. After resigning in August 1983, he had some sort of collapse and disappeared from public life.

Shamir took over as prime minister in October and invited Labour to join a government of national unity to sort out the mess. Unpopular economic austerity measures were one reason why Likud won fewer seats than Labour at the 1984 elections. More significant in terms of the way Israeli society was now divided, Shamir lost votes to the crypto-fascist ultranationalists. Nevertheless, Labour did not have enough support to form a cabinet of its own and so a unique power-sharing device was organized. A unity government would be headed by Labour's Peres for two years, then Shamir would take over for the next two years. Rabin was Minister of Defence under both. The new administration took the necessary steps to restore the economy but did nothing to placate the rising sense of furious frustration in the Occupied Territories.

SETTLEMENT

Before 1981, the man with the most influence in the Occupied Territories was Agriculture Minister Ariel Sharon. His policy was simple: settle the West Bank and Gaza with Israelis, making the future establishment of a purely Palestinian state there impossible; clamp down on Palestinian nationalism; and, where practicable, encourage Palestinians to emigrate to other parts of the Arab world. Though pleasing to Israel's hard-right, such as the influential National Religious Party, in the long run these tough measures proved painfully counter-productive.

The 'creeping annexation' of Gaza and 'Judea and Samaria' was speeded up by the giving of financial incentives, such as cheap mortgages, to those willing to go and live there. Sharon's policy took over eight per cent of Israel's budget. Its consequences were dramatic: the proportion of the West Bank under direct Israeli control, either through ownership or by military order, rose from about one-third in 1983 to almost nine-tenths by 1988.

Settlements on open hilltops were less controversial than those in or very close to large Palestinian conurbations, such as Hebron, the 'City of the Patriarchs' holy to Jews, Muslims and Christians. For instance, a decision to restore the centre of old Hebron in 1983 and to maintain an Israeli presence there was highly contentious. Even more so was the Basic Law (equivalent to a constitutional amendment) of July 1980 that annexed all Jerusalem to the State of Israel, although maintaining open access to believers of all faiths. The extension of Israeli law to the Golan region the following year provoked a furious reaction from the local Druze. Their strikes and other protests drew fierce repression.

'IRON FIST'

To counter the influence of the PLO and rising Palestinian nationalism, in 1978 the Israeli government appointed a secular governor of the West Bank and sought to establish pro-Israeli

'Village Leagues'. The experiment was a complete failure and was abandoned in 1981. Instead, the occupiers came to rely on a repressive policy known as the 'iron fist'. From a purely practical point of view, the policy made sense: if the Israelis let Palestinian nationalism grow unchecked, they would quickly find the Occupied Territories slipping from their grasp. However, they soon discovered that harshness only increased the sentiments they were trying to crush.

'Iron fist' measures included cancelling municipal elections in the West Bank, banning all contact with the PLO, censorship, curfews, the use of live ammunition when quelling riots, bulldozing or blowing up the houses of those taking part in or suspected of taking part in anti-Israeli activities, and banning display of the Palestinian flag. In 1982, the National Guidance Committee of elected mayors was outlawed and several mayors sacked and replaced by appointed Israeli officials. The clamp-down became even tighter in the mid-1980s, with detention of suspects without trial and deliberate breaking of the bones of those detained.

When two Palestinian *fedayeen* were taken alive after a failed hijack in 1984, it was announced shortly afterwards that they had died of their gunshot injuries. Because many had testified to the men being uninjured at the time of their capture, suspicions were raised. A committee of investigation found that members of Shin Bet, the Israeli internal security agency, had killed the prisoners while they were held in custody. Ten years later, it was revealed that their skulls had been crushed between massive stones, apparently a common Shin Bet practice.

In contrast to the heavy-handed treatment of the Palestinians, Israeli military and legal officials tended to treat lightly settlers who perpetrated violence. Even so, in 1984 they did foil an attempt by the Jewish 'Terror Against Terror' group to blow up Jerusalem's Al-Aqsa mosque. Less impressive was the way Israeli troops stood by when, in 1980, militant Islamists burned down the Gaza offices of those associated with the secular Fatah.

At this point, it should be emphasized that in no way did Israel have a monopoly on violence or cruelty. Indeed, it may be argued that in striking indiscriminately at civilian Israelis – women and children as well as men – the *fedayeen* were the more reprehensible. Moreover, they were accountable to no one. Israel was at least a democracy where the rule of law was supposed to run. But it was a democracy permanently at war, and in those circumstances normal decent and humane standards are invariably lowered. We may also add in defence of Israel that, however unpleasant its policies and tactics, outside the Occupied Territories the freedom of the press was not curtailed and the people were allowed to protest at what their government was doing. And many surely did, loud and long.

Israel remained a free enough society for army reserve officers to make a public protest in 1982 against what they were being asked to do in the West Bank. Acting with 'violence and brutality' against crying women and stone-throwing children, they complained, 'we are losing our humanity'. One cannot imagine such public statements being allowed in any other Middle Eastern state at the time, let alone in an area controlled by the PLO. On 2 March 1986, the PFLP assassinated the Israeli-appointed but PLO-approved mayor of Nablus, Zafir al-Masri. What was his crime? He built links between West Bank leaders and Jordan with a view to a possible confederation of the two. Certainly, the Palestinians had no more reason to be proud of their behaviour than had the Israelis.

Invasion of Lebanon

CEASEFIRE AND BREACH

When Ariel Sharon was installed as Israeli Defence Minister in mid-1981, Prime Minister Begin had a man after his own heart in the key position for a final push against the PLO. Despite Arafat having said privately that he would recognize Israel in return for Israel recognizing a Palestine in the West Bank, Begin was convinced that the PLO was a 'terrorist organization' dedicated to the 'destruction of the Jewish state'. To a Jew of his generation, with such people there could be no compromise.

Israel had been active in Lebanon before Sharon took over. In April 1981, Israeli jets supporting the Christian militia shot down two Syrian helicopters. In July, following attacks with Soviet-made Katyusha rockets into Galilee, the IDF bombarded Southern Lebanon and launched an air attack that obliterated the PLO headquarters in Beirut. The USA then brokered a ceasefire, which Arafat was intent on keeping. Eager for a peace deal, he was desperate to prove himself a man of his word. It was later revealed that the PLO and the USA were actually holding secret peace talks at the time. For the moment, therefore, Begin and Sharon were stymied.

The Israeli cabinet was buoyed by the recent election of Ronald Reagan. The Republican president had already expressed a strong dislike of all things left of centre, including the PLO, and of any organization that smacked of terrorism, which also included the PLO. Moreover, his unsophisticated secretary of state, Alexander Haig, regarded Israel as a 'strategic asset' in the USA's Cold War. Begin was sure that, in public at least, his actions would be supported by the White House.

Nevertheless, although all the world knew Israel was bursting to send its troops into Lebanon, a viable pretext for invasion was still required. Despite provocation, it took a while. In October 1981, a car bomb wrecked a PLO base in Beirut. The following spring, Israel twice attacked PLO strongholds in Lebanon and at one stage shot down two Syrian MIGs. But still the PLO abided by the ceasefire. Eventually, Begin and Sharon got what they needed from an ex-Fatah fighter by the name of Abu Nidal. Rejected by mainstream Palestinians, this near-psychopathic killer was pursuing his own trail of murder and on 21 April he shot the Israeli ambassador in London. The man survived. To Begin and Sharon this was irrelevant, however, as was the fact that Abu Nidal had been thrown out of the PLO for attempting to assassinate Arafat himself. Declaring 'they're all PLO', Begin ordered the IDF into Lebanon.

PEACE FOR GALILEE

Announcing that they were advancing 40 kilometres into Lebanon to make the 63 settlements in northern Israel safe from PLO attacks, Israel launched Operation Peace for Galilee with overwhelming force: 80,000 troops, 1,240 tanks, 1,520 armoured personnel carriers and hundreds of artillery pieces. Reaching the 40 kilometre mark in a matter of hours, Sharon commanded the IDF to press on. By 13 June, they had surrounded Beirut. Most of the PLO and thousands of civilians were trapped inside the city. On the road, the Syrians had been pushed back to the east and the PLO crushed.

Before it happened, the invasion idea had general approval within Israel. Now it had clearly gone further than many expected, support began to waver. Abroad, condemnation of blatant aggression against a sovereign state was almost universal. The major exception was the USA. While saying that the Israeli action was 'deplorable' and banning the shipment to Israel of certain exotically cruel weapons such as cluster bombs, President Reagan vetoed the Security Council resolution excoriating his ally's behaviour. And it was US funds that permitted Begin and Sharon to continue their $1 million-a-day campaign.

Beirut and to a lesser extent Tyre and Sidon were besieged, bombed and shelled for two months. To add to the misery, water and electricity supplies were cut. Lebanon's capital, once the proud 'Paris of the Middle East', was reduced to a scarred and stinking ghost town of rubble, pock-marked concrete and dark, sinister voids. Around 33,000 died, mostly civilians, and at least 100,000 were made homeless. As the conflict was conducted before the world's TV cameras, Israel's international reputation reached its nadir.

MISSION FAILURE

The added tragedy of operation 'Peace for Galilee' was that it failed. First, the Lebanese Christian leader, Bashir Jemayel, refused to play the part the Israelis had assigned to him. He would not send his men into Beirut to drive out the remains of the PLO.

Neither, later, would he make peace when Begin wanted him to. Sharon's dream of a compliant puppet state on Israel's northern border remained unfulfilled.

Nor was the PLO destroyed. In mid-August, to prevent what he termed another Holocaust, President Reagan finally called the Israelis off. After one last day of horrendous bombardment, Sharon silenced his guns and the PLO warriors, who had fought with remarkable courage and bravery, were allowed to leave by sea. Taking their small arms with them, most made their way to Tripoli, where Arafat established a new headquarters. By destroying the PLO, Sharon had hoped to cut Palestinian nationalism off at the root. Instead, the PLO had survived and Palestinian nationalism, boosted by 1,000 new martyrs and stories of legendary heroism, was stronger than ever.

MASSACRE

Lebanon's tale of horror was far from over. Before the arrival of an international peace-keeping force of largely American, French and Italian troops, the Israelis made themselves masters of much of the south and west of the country by occupying Beirut. The previous day, Bashir Jemayel, now president elect of Lebanon, had been killed by a bomb that blew up his party headquarters. The Syrians were implicated, and the outraged Phalange thirsted for revenge.

In West Beirut, four kilometres north of the airport, lay the two large Palestinian refugee camps of Sabra and Shatila. They were filled not only with their normal incumbents but with Muslim refugees – including Palestinians – who had fled there during the recent fighting. Among them were some PLO and other *fedayeen*. The day after the Israelis took charge of the area, heavily armed Christian militia entered the camps to weed out the guerrillas. They did so with Israeli consent and approval. At night fall, the Israelis even lit the scene to assist their allies.

As soon became obvious from the pandemonium within the camps, the militia had not gone in simply to hunt down a few paramilitaries but to indulge in wholesale slaughter, rape, mutilation and other ghastly crimes. Men, women and children all suffered. No one knows how many died. The Lebanese Army said the figure was 474, including 16 children, 14 women and 21 Iranians. The IDF's figure was 700–800 dead. Other sources, talking of mass graves, said the number was between 1,800 and 3,000.

Whatever the true figure, the slaughter was an inexcusable and horrific crime. It provoked massive protest rallies in Israel and universal worldwide condemnation. Bowing to public pressure, Begin's government announced a full-scale enquiry. The Kahan Commission found that although Sharon and the IDF could not be held directly responsible for the Sabra–Shatila massacre, the Israeli forces could have done more to prevent it. Sharon stepped down as Minister of Defence (1983) but remained within the cabinet.

Insight

Israel's Kahan Commission reported in 1983 that Ariel Sharon had been responsible for the massacres in the Sabra and Shatila camps. He was not dismissed, however, nor did he resign. In fact, 18 years later he became his country's prime minister.

THE SLAUGHTER GOES ON

Following the Sabra and Shatila massacres, Israel negotiated an armistice with President Amin Gemayel, brother of the assassinated Bashir. It lasted, on and off, for about a year and involved the IDF falling back to a line south of Beirut. Eventually, in the spring of 1985, Israel's unity government, headed by Prime Minister Peres, ordered the IDF back towards the frontier with Israel. Its last elements finally pulled out of southern Lebanon in 2000.

In the meantime, the tit-for-tat fighting with various types of *fedayeen* continued. In 1983, open warfare broke out between Fatah groups hostile to and supporting Yasser Arafat. At the end of the year, a bomb destroyed the Israeli headquarters in Tyre, killing 60. Shortly afterwards, six civilians were killed by a PLO bomb on a bus in Jerusalem and, two months later, Katyusha rockets were again falling on Galilee. 1985 saw Israeli–CIA attacks on a new, Iranian-backed force in the region, Hezbollah (see pp. 185–6). There was also more Fatah in-fighting, an Israeli air force attack on the PLO headquarters in Tunis (from which Arafat amazingly emerged unscathed), and a *fedayeen* hijacking of the cruise liner Achille Lauro in which a disabled Jewish-American passenger was killed. At the end of the year, Abu Nidal grabbed the headlines again by bombing Rome and Vienna airports, killing 20 and wounding over 100.

Lebanon's complex and ever-shifting civil war dragged on to the end of the decade, concluding only when the Syrian Army was in a position to impose a ceasefire. This was something the international peacekeepers had singularly failed to do. By the spring of 1983, Americans, Italians and French were being picked off by another, Syrian-based *fedayeen* group, Islamic Jihad (see p. 230). When one of its suicide bombers drove a truck laden with explosives into the American Embassy in Beirut and blew away the central section of the building, human remains were found floating in the Mediterranean. The attack prompted the USA into an ineffective offensive against the Evil Empire of the red flag and its sympathizers. Nothing symbolized the operation's inappropriately heavy-handed impotence more than the *USS New Jersey* lobbing 40-centimetre (16-inch) shells inland in the general direction of Druze positions. Stung into even more determined resistance, in October 1983, suicide bombers slew over 300 American and French peacekeepers in their bases. Within a year, the international forces had gone home.

Searching for peace

THE BITTER FRUITS OF WAR

Intended to end the Israel–Palestine problem, Israel's intervention in the long-drawn-out Lebanese civil war had only made things worse. As we have seen, one effect of the October 1973 War had been to strengthen Israel's political right (see p. 154). This gave political power and influence to hard-line religious Zionists who had little time for compromise. The Lebanese escapade had now brought hard-line fanatical Muslims into the equation on the Palestinian side. The emergence of Hezbollah ('the Party of God'), for instance, appeared to stem directly from the IDF's attacks on Shia communities that had hitherto been neutral. Backed by the theocratic regime in Iran, such zealots barely understood the meaning of compromise.

By the mid-1980s, therefore, it was even more difficult for moderates on both sides – and there were times now when even Arafat was starting to look like a moderate – to find a deal acceptable to all their constituents. This became abundantly clear when a whole series of proposed compromise deals proved stillborn or died in their infancy.

PEACE TALKS

Early in 1981, the Soviet leader Leonid Brezhnev put forward a Middle East peace plan based upon Resolution 242. He hoped to re-fashion his country's image in the Middle East and take back the diplomatic initiative from the USA now that the memories of Camp David were fading and the Americans had been humiliated by the Iranian Revolution. The Soviet plan proved barren. The USA's secret talks with the PLO ended the following year with no agreement. Before that, Crown Prince Fahad of Saudi Arabia had thrown his hat (or rather *gutra*) into the ring by offering an eight-point peace plan of his own. It was rejected by Israel and later, under pressure from Syria and others, by Arafat. Eventually, even Syria came up with a peace-for-land deal. The chances of Begin accepting anything put forward by Assad without US backing were non-existent.

In September 1982, just after the PLO had been forced from Lebanon, President Reagan came up with a new and quite feasible peace proposal. It featured three ideas. First, the Palestinians should have their own self-governing entity, based on the West Bank and Gaza but linked to Jordan. Second, Israel should freeze settlement-building in the Occupied Territories. Third, the future of Jerusalem should be left for negotiations at a later date. For the first time the Americans were formally including the Palestinians in their plans and Arafat gave the proposal a cautious welcome. The Israeli Labour party liked it, too, but not Likud. Begin's immediate response was to approve still more West Bank settlements. Although accepting a settlement freeze would have deprived him of the support of the far right, his reaction was singularly provocative.

Five days after the launching of the Reagan Plan, the Arab Summit meeting in Fez came up with yet another set of proposals. Some believe that if the Americans had leaned a little harder on Israel at this stage, the combined Reagan and Fez initiatives might have got somewhere. Sadly, though, it did not happen. Talks, open and secret, continued over the next two years. Arafat was keen to compromise. The negotiations were serious enough for Abu Nidal to assassinate an important figure in the PLO team and for the PFLP and several similar splinter groups to form a 'Democratic Alliance' against what was happening. This split the Palestinian leadership three ways, between Arafat's compromise-seeking Fatah, the new anti-negotiation left-wing Alliance, and the religious hardliners who were equally unwilling to talk to Israel.

The closest the negotiators came to agreement was in 1985, when Arafat and King Hussein produced an Aman Accord for a confederacy between Jordan and the Occupied Territories. Although not acceptable to the PFLP and its associates, Prime Minister Peres of Israel at first reacted to the proposal with a degree of flexibility. The optimism was short-lived. Arafat would not accept Resolution 242, as it did not mention Palestinian self-determination, and Peres agreed to the bombing of the Tunis headquarters of the PLO in retaliation for the murder of three Israelis in Cyprus. This 'Israeli state terrorism', as the PLO put it, badly soured relations once again. Finally, an agreement between Peres and King Hussein, made in October 1986, drowned in a sea of acrimony when it was revealed to Yitzhak Shamir, who had just replaced Peres as prime minister under the terms of their 1984 post-election pact.

If all this seems complicated, tortuous to the point of irritation and ultimately deeply frustrating, it was. Particularly to the pawns in the middle of it all, those whom all the fighting and talking were about: the ordinary Palestinian men, women and children of the West Bank and Gaza Strip. In the end, tired of being ignored, fought over and bullied, they decided to take matters into their own hands. The result was one of the most extraordinary demonstrations of people power since World War II – the Intifada.

In depth: Hezbollah

Hezbollah – the 'Party of God' – emerged in 1982 out of a group of around 2,000 Iranian revolutionary guards sent to Lebanon to fight the Israelis. A band of leading Shia clerics acted as midwives for the birth. The movement's original aim was to help drive the invader from Lebanon. After that, it grew into a huge military, religious, socio-economic and political force within that country. It won 14 seats in the Lebanese Parliament in 2005 and was rewarded with two ministerial portfolios.

Within Israel and in the West, Hezbollah was known as a terrorist organization dedicated to carrying Iran's Islamist revolution across the face of the globe by whatever means it deemed necessary. This included the use of extreme violence in the form of guerrilla warfare and suicide bombings. Hezbollah operated primarily in Lebanon with support from Syria and Iran. Western security services also believed it had managed to establish cells in Europe and the Americas. Among its notable operations were the spate of kidnappings of Westerners in Lebanon in the 1980s, the truck bombing of a US marine barracks in Beirut in 1983, attacks on Israeli-Jewish targets in Argentina in 1992 and 1994, and the capture of two Israeli soldiers in the summer of 2006, which led to the Israeli bombardment and invasion of Lebanon.

(Contd)

By the 1990s, Hezbollah, which had a political as well as a military wing, was a potent force in Lebanese politics. Its support was strongest among exiled Palestinians and native Lebanese from the impoverished Shia community. Adherents were attracted by the group's programme of social welfare, providing help with schools, houses, mosques, medical centres and other such facilities. There was evidence that those not wedded to Hezbollah's extreme religious views were prepared to pay lip service to them (wearing 'seemly' dress, for instance) in order to receive assistance. Hezbollah showed itself capable of acting independently of Tehran and Damascus. Indeed, its relationship with the secular Syrian regime was complex, revealing a degree of pragmatism among its leaders that hinted at the possibility of a compromise peace with Israel one day.

In depth: the Herut and Likud parties

Founded by Menachem Begin in 1948, Herut or 'Freedom' was one of Israel's earliest right-wing parties. Its roots lay in the Irgun paramilitary group that had fought the British before Israel's independence, and all its life Herut maintained an uncompromising attitude towards anyone or anything that might imperil the State of Israel. Its right-wing mix of nationalism, Zionism and racism so worried some prominent American Jews that in 1948 they openly condemned the party as neo-fascist.

Throughout Labour's long dominance of Israeli politics, Herut controlled between 10 and 20 Knesset seats and hounded successive governments with assiduity. For example, it helped bring down the ruling coalitions in 1954 and 1961. Herut's support came mainly from Sephardim and blue-collar workers resentful at the perceived dominance of a wealthy, liberal-minded Ashkenazi elite. In the 1970s, Herut merged with other right-wing parties to form first the Likud coalition, then a distinctive Likud Party.

Likud ('Consolidation'), led by Begin, formed Israel's first right-wing government in 1977. Not until 1988, however, was it formally instituted as a single political party. Its policies were anti-socialist and, in matters of security, largely against any compromise with the Palestinians. Three of its four leaders – Menachem Begin (1973–82), Yitzhak Shamir (1983–92) and Ariel Sharon (1999–2005) – were robust military men who had seen action at first hand. Together with Benjamin Netanyahu (leader 1993–9 and 2005 onwards), they openly opposed the establishment of a Palestinian state and were highly reluctant to surrender any of the Golan Heights, Gaza Strip or West Bank.

Yet it was Likud's Menachem Begin who signed the Camp David Accords with Egypt and Yitzhak Shamir who agreed to meet with the Palestinians (but not the PLO) at the 1991 Madrid Conference. Moreover, Sharon's controversial acceptance in 2004 of unilateral Israeli withdrawal from some of the Occupied Territories (the Disengagement Plan) sent shivers of horror through Likud ranks. The party was thrown into further disarray when Sharon left to form Kadima at the end of 2005.

The 2006 Knesset elections gave Likud only 12 seats, its lowest ever total. At the time, some said this was the end of Likud and of a major right-wing power bloc in Israeli politics. They were proved wrong when, having done well in the 2009 elections, Likud leader Benjamin Netanyahu became prime minister at the head of a right-centre coalition administration.

10 THINGS TO REMEMBER

1 *Already an unstable state, Lebanon was thrown into turmoil by the arrival there of the PLO in 1970.*

2 *Lebanon endured a long, brutal and debilitating civil war between 1975 and 1990.*

3 *By 1977, Israel was making retaliatory strikes against Palestinian insurgents in southern Lebanon.*

4 *Israel became a more divided society as Sephardim immigration increased the power of the political right.*

5 *In 1980–1, the government of Prime Minister Begin endorsed legislation that annexed all Jerusalem to the State of Israel and extended Israeli law to the Golan region. East Jerusalem and the Golan had both been acquired by force of arms.*

6 *Israel's 'iron fist' policy, introduced in the early 1980s, involved clamping down on all manifestations of Palestinian nationalism and retaliating to* fedayeen *activity with disproportionate force.*

7 *Intending to wipe out the PLO, which it condemned as a 'terrorist' organization, in 1982 the IDF launched a massive invasion of Lebanon.*

8 *After being besieged in Beirut amid terrible slaughter and destruction, in August 1982 Arafat and the PLO were permitted to flee into exile in remote Tunis.*

9 *Shortly afterwards, the Israelis were blamed for standing by as Christian extremists carried out terrible massacres in the Sabra and Shatila refugee camps outside Beirut.*

10 *The slaughter in Lebanon inspired several new attempts to broker an Israeli–Palestinian peace deal. All failed.*

11

Intifada early 1980s to 1993

In this chapter you will learn about:

- ***the causes of the Palestinian uprising ('Intifada')***
- ***the nature of the First Intifada and its effects***
- ***the impact of the end of the Cold War and the First Gulf War, 1991***
- ***the Madrid peace process, 1991–3.***

The forgotten people

DEPRESSION

By the end of 1967, the original Arab population of Britain's Palestinian mandate had been divided four ways. During the years between 1967 and 1986, there were some changes in the size of these groupings. Slightly over 150,000 remained in Israel, some eventually accepting Israeli citizenship, others remaining what the government had enigmatically called 'present absentees'. By the end of the century, the total Palestinian community within Israel had risen to about 1 million. A larger number of Palestinians, fed by emigration of around 20,000 a year from the Occupied Territories during the 1970s, lived in neighbouring states. The remainder were divided between the Occupied Territories: the tiny Gaza Strip and the larger West Bank. In 1986, the former contained around half a million native Gazans and a slightly smaller number of refugees, half of whom still lived in camps. Of the West Bank's 372,000 remaining refugees, some 100,000 were still camp-dwellers. Since about 1980, the mood within the Occupied Territories had become one of mounting despair.

As we have seen on several occasions, for all their fine talk about solidarity, neighbouring Arab states appeared to be unwilling to exert themselves to help the Palestinians. Nothing had epitomized this apparent betrayal more than Egypt's separate peace with Israel and its vague, swiftly evaporating talk of sorting out the problem of Palestine. The Palestinian leadership, the PLO, had been driven first from Jordan, then from Lebanon and was now in remote, impecunious and largely impotent exile in Tunisia. The Palestinians of the Occupied Territories felt trapped in a political cul-de-sac.

The economic situation had deteriorated, too. After the oil-price boom of the 1970s, remittances sent home by Palestinians working abroad had fallen. Unemployment rose four-fold between 1980 and 1985, fed by Jordan's economic problems and the growing tide of Soviet immigrants (not all of whom were Jews) looking for work in Israel. Some sources say that the unemployment rate in the Gaza Strip reached 50 per cent. Rising poverty brought with it the usual portmanteau of difficulties: crime, depression, drugs, deteriorating health and so forth.

CHANGING ATTITUDES

At the same time, Israel's attitude towards the Occupied Territories had shifted, mirroring changes within Israel itself. The State of Israel had been founded on European secular, liberal principles dating back at least to the eighteenth-century Enlightenment. Although at times these had been seriously compromised, they remained more or less intact. By the 1980s, however, they were coming under pressure from a massive influx of Sephardim and Soviet Jews largely alien to the essentially open-minded ideas of Western Europe. One consequence was the Likud-led coalition, a more religious, intolerant and hard-hearted administration than most of its predecessors. This reflected a broader change in attitude towards Palestinians in general: racism was on the rise.

Insight

For several years, despised Sephardim were sprayed with disinfectant when they arrived in Israel. By 2010 20 per cent of marriages are mixed Ashkenazi–Sephardi.

New Jewish settlements in 'Judea and Samaria' proliferated and the settlement population trebled between 1982 and 1986, by which time half the land within the West Bank was under direct Israeli control. Some settlements were provocatively close to established areas of Palestinian habitation. New Israeli roads, regularly patrolled by the army, cut off Palestinian areas from each other. The aim, sometimes known as the 'Drobles Plan', seemed to be to squeeze the Palestinian settlements, like toothpaste in a tube, until those who lived there either became totally submissive or emigrated in despair. To make matters worse, Israel was still taking more than three-quarters of the West Bank's water for its own use. In fact, the area provided Israel with over 30 per cent of all its water. This was reason enough to explain its extreme reluctance to lose control there.

TAKING NO MORE

In the 1980s, as we have seen (pp. 175–6), Israel had begun its 'iron fist' policy towards the Palestinians within the Occupied Territories. The foremost exponent of the approach was a Labour politician, Yitzhak Rabin, Defence Minister within the unity administration. His approach was to substitute the stick for the carrot whenever feasible.

Israel proper remained a state in which the rule of law was paramount, but the Occupied Territories, under military command, did not come under the same jurisdiction. On occasion the judiciary seemed to turn a blind eye, or at least to act with unwarranted lenience when confronted with unacceptable behaviour. Deportations (illegal according to the terms of the Geneva Convention), press censorship, demolition of their homes, closure of facilities like schools and colleges, curfews, road blocks, searches, petty cruelties and humiliations – all these and more became part of everyday life for many Palestinians.

In the end, unloved, ignored and downtrodden, the Palestinians of the Occupied Territories spontaneously decided they would take no more. Spectacularly taking matters into their own hands, they rose up against their perceived persecutors. There had always been acts of violence against the forces of occupation, averaging 350 recorded incidents a year between 1968 and 1976. This had risen to 700 a year over the next seven years, then to around 3,000 a year in the early 1980s. These figures were nothing compared with what happened next. In the first six months of 1987, the IDF reported no less than 42,355 cases of active hostility towards it. The rebellion had begun.

Intifada

RUMOUR AND RIOT

On 6 December 1987, an Israeli trader was stabbed to death in a Gaza market. This was not unusual. However, the next day an Israeli tank transporter collided with two vans carrying Palestinian workers back to their homes in Gaza's Jabaliya refugee camp. Four workers were killed, seven seriously injured. Rumour – always wickedly at work in such situations – said that the collision had not been an accident but was a planned revenge for the stabbing. Riots broke out at the funerals held that evening and an Israeli guard post was stoned. Tensions rose sharply.

Three days later, another resident of the Jabaliya camp died – shot dead by Israeli soldiers chasing stone-throwing youths. Hundreds of Palestinians took to the streets in protest. The security forces were reinforced. There was more stone-throwing, more firing. The conflagration soon spread to the West Bank and within two weeks the situation had flared out of Israel's control. The Palestinians called their extraordinary uprising – similar in some ways to what was to happen in parts of Eastern Europe two years later – the *Intifada* or 'Shaking Off'.

Insight

The word 'intifada', deriving from the verb *nafada* 'to shake', can be used as a verb or noun. Meaning while the verb means 'to shake', as so often in Arabic, the noun's connotations are broader and more poetic. One meaning is 'an awakening' in the sense that sleep has been shaken off. Hence its use for the rebellion that sought to shake off the heavy hand of the Israelis.

STICKS AND STONES

The Intifada was a widespread, long-drawn-out campaign of civil disobedience and constant harassment of the occupying forces. It lasted until around 1992, by which time its nature had changed. At first spontaneous and leaderless, it soon came under the loose direction of the United National Leadership of the Uprising (UNLU). Comprising second-rank, local officials of existing groups such as Fatah, it put forward a 14-point plan for Palestinian self-determination. Its principal instrument was the clandestinely printed letter carrying instructions, suggestions and exhortations. Letter 40, for example, urged Palestinians to kill an Israeli soldier or settler for every Palestinian slain in the Intifada. The Israeli media, of course, described such action as 'terrorism', while Palestinians claimed simply to be responding to Israel's 'terrorist' act of stealing their country.

When the PLO leadership in Tunis realized that the uprising was more than just another bout of rioting, it became more closely involved. Iraq and Iran provided funds totalling an estimated US$40 million, while Baghdad Radio gave the movement a source of information and propaganda beyond Israeli control. Most significantly, within a year, a new-style, Islamist leadership had emerged in the form of Hamas and Islamic Jihad. Over time the nature of the Intifada changed, too. The heavy economic and personal toll of gestures such as strikes, boycotting Israeli goods and refusal to work in Israel were self-defeating. Greater emphasis was placed on acts of aggressive defiance such as knifings, arson and kidnap.

The icon of the uprising was the stone-throwing youth or child. Often adorned with the distinctive kafiya head-dress and frequently egged on by their elders, the young emerged in their thousands to taunt the occupying forces with sharp words and stones. Stone-throwing was a traditional Islamic practice to ward off evil spirits. One of the remarkable features of the Palestinian experience after 1967 had been the emergence of a 'literature of resistance'. A key image in much of this work was the martyred stone-throwing child.

The children of the Intifada were a desperate generation that had grown up amid violence and cruelty. Lacking any concept of a better future on earth, they were fearless. Fleet of foot and knowing the terrain far better than their enemy, they made an impossible target. When the panicking Israeli conscripts employed excessive force – live ammunition was increasingly used against stone-throwers – they appeared before the world's media as child murderers. The only Israeli alternative was to hand back the streets, alleyways and markets to the Palestinian mob – an admission of failure. Practically, the Intifada gave the Israelis an insoluble problem: unless they resorted to genocide on a Holocaust scale, there was no way 3.5 million of them could hold down 1.5 million Palestinians determined to resist. For the first time, Israel was in a battle it could not win.

BULLETS AND BROKEN BONES

Shamir's government responded to the Intifada in the usual no-nonsense manner. Reservists were called up and the security presence within the Occupied Territories increased significantly. Schools, colleges and other places where crowds might gather were closed down. The uprooting of 120,000 precious fruit trees deprived many Palestinians in rural communities of their living. The bulldozing of their houses left them homeless. All forms of media were heavily censored. Ringleaders were identified, rounded up and detained without trial. Crowds were broken up with tear gas, rubber bullets and, sometimes, live ammunition. Deportation was also used, although it flouted international law. Suspected bases of the insurgency's leadership were bulldozed or blown up, even when they were private houses inhabited by women and children. Upon Rabin's instruction, the limbs and fingers of stone-throwers were deliberately broken to prevent them from continuing their assaults.

The Israelis were not above employing their own form of 'state terrorism' in the battle, too. Although there is no definitive proof of Israeli participation, it is widely agreed that Abu Jihad, the PLO mastermind organizing the Intifada, was taken out in Tunis by Mossad-led commandos. The operation, launched in April 1988, was supervised by Ehud Barak, a future prime minister of Israel. The piercing of Abu Jihad's body with 150 bullets before the terrified gaze of his wife and child ensured that the act was widely condemned, even in the USA, and provided the Palestinians with yet another martyr.

The Intifada accounted for 396 Palestinian deaths in the first year and over 1,200 by 1992. It is essential to bear in mind that only slightly over half of these were at the hands of the Israelis. Intra-Palestinian bloodletting was also escalating alarmingly. The most serious single Israeli-on-Palestinian incident was the shooting dead of 21 Palestinian protestors and the wounding of 150 others when an Israeli extremist group calling itself the Temple Mount Faithful tried to lay the foundation stone of a new Jewish temple on Temple Mount (1990). Yet again the world condemned what it saw as Israeli over-reaction. As well as the shootings, some 40,000 Palestinians were detained during the first two years of the insurrection. Thereafter, they were joined by tens of thousands of others.

ISRAELI DISLOCATION

The Intifada hit Israelis and Palestinians alike. In the long run, it was probably the latter who came off worst. Nevertheless, Israel's international reputation struck an all-time low. At the end of 1987, even the USA was not prepared to veto a Security Council resolution condemning Israeli violence against protesters. The economy was badly dented, too. Security costs soared. The call-up,

Palestinian boycotts and frequent border closures deprived Israeli businesses of labour. The country's total national wealth fell by an estimated 1.4 per cent. As a consequence, the opinion of a significant number of Israelis about the Occupied Territories began to change. Originally seen as essential to the country's security, they were now more likely to be regarded as a liability, actually weakening the country and its economy.

Equally serious was the divisive effect of the Intifada on Israeli society, which, as we have seen, was already riven by a painful left–right schism (see for example p. 173). Those of a liberal persuasion, including President Herzog (re-elected in 1988), believed that the measures taken to control the Occupied Territories were undermining the country's democracy and its key virtue of tolerance. Others went further, saying that Israel's tactics were horribly reminiscent of those employed by the Nazis. Several Israeli groups were formed – such as Hotline – with the specific intention of assisting distressed Palestinians. The Israeli right, on the other hand, horrified by Palestinian killings and lawlessness, urged still sterner measures to restore law and order and protect the burgeoning Jewish settlements in 'Judea and Samaria'.

The two contradictory currents were reflected at election time. The 1988 vote gave Likud 40 Knesset seats and Labour 39. By allying with a number of small, right-wing religious parties, Shamir was able to install another unity government. This time, however, the premiership was not for rotation. The election also saw a rise in the number of seats for religious parties, and the emergence of Shas, a party of Orthodox Sephardim. Predominantly Arab parties won six seats, and after the election a Labour Knesset member, Abdel Wahab Darawashe, left Labour to form the Arab Democratic Party. This was the Knesset's first purely Arab party. Another post-election development was the creation of Meretz, a coalition of left-leaning peace parties.

The stresses of the Intifada and US pressure for peace talks gradually pulled the unity government apart. Shamir lost a vote of confidence in 1990 but, after much political wrangling, managed to remain in power at the head of a Likud-led right-wing government. This survived until 1992, when Labour, led by 'iron fisted' Yitzhak Rabin, won 44 Knesset seats. Joining with Meretz and the Arab Democratic Party, a new administration was formed intent on hammering out some form of peace deal with the Palestinians.

PALESTINIAN PROBLEMS

If Israel was shaken up by the Intifada, the Palestinians were even more so. Its internal effects were essentially four-fold:

- *As we have already seen, individuals and families suffered serious physical and emotional hardship (pp. 194–5).*
- *The economies of the Occupied Territories were shattered and Palestinian wealth dropped sharply. The GNP of the Gaza Strip and the West Bank fell an estimated 30 per cent in three years. Retailers' turnover fell by 80 per cent. There was an increase in economic self-reliance, the West Bank producing four-fifths of its dairy needs, for instance, but this was scant compensation. Ominous for the future was the closure of many schools and colleges for weeks on end, thereby depriving the next generation of key skills and training.*
- *The sudden violent upsurge of desperate feeling within the Occupied Territories drew the world's attention to these 'forgotten people' and forced the PLO to reconsider its position on a number of issues in order to retain the support of fellow Palestinians. Most importantly, it had to listen to the message coming from Gaza and the West Bank: the people had had enough of suffering. The PLO's refusal to recognize Israel was all very well as a political gesture but in practical terms it made no sense at all. Palestinians worked in Israel, traded with Israel and in many cases had relatives living in Israel, some as Israeli citizens. Like it or not, the Jewish state was a very real fact of their lives. The armed struggle had failed. From such thinking came a major strand of what came to be known as the 'peace process'.*

  In June 1988, the PLO representative at the Arab summit in Algiers demanded a two-state solution to the Israeli–Palestinian problem. That was the closest it had yet come to recognizing Israel. A few weeks later, King Hussein renounced all claim to lands beyond the River Jordan, allowing the PLO to say it was formally taking control of the West Bank and Gaza. The most significant move came on 15 November, at a meeting of the Palestine National Council. Here, speaking to an astounded world, Arafat announced that henceforth Palestine was an independent state with East Jerusalem as its capital. Much more dramatic was the ex-fedayeen's renunciation of all forms of terror, his acceptance of UN Security Council Resolution 242 as the basis for talks, and the recognition of Israel within the pre-1967 borders. Before long, 100 states had formally accepted Palestine as an independent country. After all those dark years, the first rays of peace were finally peeping over the horizon.

- ▶ *The Intifada proved fertile ground for Islamists. Their rapid advance, advocating principles very different from those of the essentially secular PLO, meant that Arafat's change of heart may have come too late for an all-embracing peace.*

To understand the significance of what was going on, we need to stand back and take in the broader context.

During the second half of the twentieth century, militant Islam emerged as a radical alternative to both communism and liberal capitalism. Its appeal was particularly strong in those cultures whose social customs, academic norms and entrepreneurial achievement seemed at odds with the world of the late twentieth century, engendering a feeling of unease, even inferiority. Unable to compete with the modern, rational world on its own terms – unlike many Asian cultures – whole segments of the Middle East turned to the past for solace and meaning.

The first important manifestation of the new movement (or, rather, the revival of a very old one) was the Iranian Revolution of 1979. Next came the emergence of Hezbollah in Lebanon (see pp. 185–6). Palestine's turn came with the appearance of the Hamas Islamic Brotherhood in 1988. The more militant Islamic Jihad emerged slightly later. By the time Arafat was making his dramatic gestures, these contrary but equally revolutionary forces had reached the Occupied Territories and were taking root within Palestinian society. The Islamists challenged the PLO at every point. They rejected its secular stance, its left-leaning politics, its nationalism, its local corruption, the self-seeking of some of its leaders, and its Western views on matters such as female emancipation.

As an alternative to the PLO mind-set, the Islamists offered the idea that Palestine was part of a larger Islamic Trust (*waqf*) that would be held by the faithful until the Day of Judgement. To this end, nation-states, especially infidel ones like Israel, had to be cleared away. On this sacred duty there could be no compromise. Although many Palestinians, especially women, whose lives it threatened to ruin, remained sceptical or even hostile to the Islamists' religious teaching, the new movement rapidly gained support. Its strengths were grass-roots knowledge, energy, less corruption (initially, at least) and laudable programmes of practical assistance funded by Iranian money. It opposed strikes as a weapon against Israel, for example, because they hit the strikers harder than those they targeted.

Fighting between the Islamists and the PLO had already broken out in Lebanon and it was not long before it spread to Palestine. As each side sought to dominate the other in the battle for hearts and minds, killings, maimings and blackmailings rose. The Israelis, who first saw the Islamists as a useful ally against the PLO, soon realized the danger they posed. After the first Hamas *fedayeen*-style action in April 1989, the kidnapping and killing of two Israeli soldiers, membership of Hamas was outlawed and 300 of its activists arrested. Their number included Sheikh Yassin, one of the movement's founders.

Cold war and hot war

END OF THE COLD WAR

The emergence of militant Islam was not the only change sweeping the globe during the last quarter of the twentieth century.

Even more significant, in the short term at least, was the collapse of Soviet communism and the end of the Cold War. This had a massive impact on the Arab–Israeli confrontation. Previously, with the USA standing unflinchingly behind Israel, the Palestinians and many Arab states had turned to the Soviet Union for arms and aid. The PLO had been formed as a left-wing organization – Arafat had been a guest of Moscow – and the whole panoply of offshoot *fedayeen* groups were similarly socialist-orientated.

All this now changed. Socialism and talk of revolution and the people's armed struggle was replaced by praise for market forces, liberal democracy and diversity. There was now only one superpower, too. For a short time, until the Islamists became a global nuisance, US presidents no longer felt obliged to support Israel as an unshakeable ally in a world threatened by communism. They could now lean on Israeli administrations as never before, threatening a variety of economic sanctions safe in the knowledge that there was no one else the Israelis could turn to. The result was the 'peace dividend' that emerged in the late 1980s.

THE FIRST GULF WAR

By 1990, attempts to cajole the Shamir government and the PLO into finding at least some common ground between them had ended in deadlock. This was broken, somewhat surprisingly, by the Iraqi dictator Saddam Hussein.

For a series of reasons, none of which make sound political or military sense to the outsider, in the summer of 1990 Hussein sent his well-trained and well-organized army into Kuwait. Within hours he was master of the small but oil-rich sheikhdom. When this blatant aggression was condemned by just about every country in the world, including the wealthy oil-producing Arab states, he offered to pull out if Syria left Lebanon and Israel returned to its pre-1967 borders. This unsubtle attempt to link his conquest to others' was a failure, and a mighty coalition began assembling under the auspices of the UN to drive him out.

All this while, the PLO, the PFLP and the Palestinian people in general had remained steadfastly behind the Iraqi president. In a way this was wholly understandable and even laudable: Hussein was one of the few world leaders who had openly declared his support for the Palestinian cause – and backed up his words with arms and money. In practical terms, however, support for Iraq was an act of political suicide. Not only was Hussein reviled almost universally, but his cause was hopeless.

The US-led coalition attacked in January 1991 and within days the Iraqis had been driven from Kuwait and were in headlong retreat towards Baghdad. Desperate to destroy his enemy's solidarity, Hussein bombarded Israeli cities with Scud missiles. What he wanted, of course, was for Israel to retaliate, thereby presenting the coalition Arabs with the unenviable choice of siding with Israel against an Arab state or changing sides and joining him against the traditional enemy. As it was, although 4,000 Israeli flats were destroyed (but only one person killed), the Shamir government resisted the calls of warmongers like Ariel Sharon to retaliate. Israel's planes remained on their runways and its tanks behind its borders. Hussein's gambit failed.

Iraq was crushed and Arafat and the PLO, having made considerable headway over the previous few years, were utterly discredited. The PLO was financially bankrupt, too. Arafat's decision to back Hussein was probably the worst he had ever made. By the summer of 1991, impecunious and impotent, he had no option but to swallow his pride and return to the negotiating table.

The peace process

ARAFAT'S INITIATIVE

Back in November 1988, Arafat had won international acclaim for declaring Palestine an independent state, denouncing terrorism outside Israel and calling for peace talks based on Security Council

Resolution 242 (see p. 124). Even so, the climb-down had cut no ice with the USA and Israel, both of whom still insisted that the PLO was a terrorist organization and therefore not one with which talks could be held.

In December, Arafat made the USA–Israeli position even more awkward. Speaking before the UN, temporarily transferred to Geneva as the USA would not allow him into New York, he spoke of the 'State of Israel', called for a comprehensive Middle East peace conference, openly accepted Resolutions 242 and 338, and again condemned terror. At a news conference held afterwards, replying to questioners who asked how far he was prepared to go to meet US demands, he made his famous reply, 'Enough! Do you want me to do a striptease?'

Shortly afterwards, Arafat did clarify his position a little by declaring the original PLO charter, calling for the destruction of Israel, null and void. By now the UN General Assembly had accepted Palestine's declaration of independence. Within weeks, finally convinced of Arafat's good intentions, the USA began indirect, preliminary talks with representatives of the PLO. After decades of impasse, this was indeed a momentous move.

Prime Minister Shamir, on the other hand, still would not budge. Then Labour's hard-handed Defence Minister Yitzhak Rabin, realizing perhaps that settling the Intifada required something other than just brute force, suggested that they might at least try talking to some Palestinians. Shamir played for time. He talked vaguely of granting Palestinian 'autonomy' – but only after the Intifada had been called off – and ruled out the possibility of direct negotiations with the PLO. Meanwhile he pressed ahead with yet more settlements in the Occupied Territories. As immigration from the former USSR was now approaching an average of 100,000 a year, he argued, new living space was essential. Privately he believed 'facts on the ground' would eventually make return of the conquered land impossible (see Figure 11.1.)

In the autumn, US Secretary of State James Baker came up with various peace plans. Shamir stalled then rejected them in March 1990.

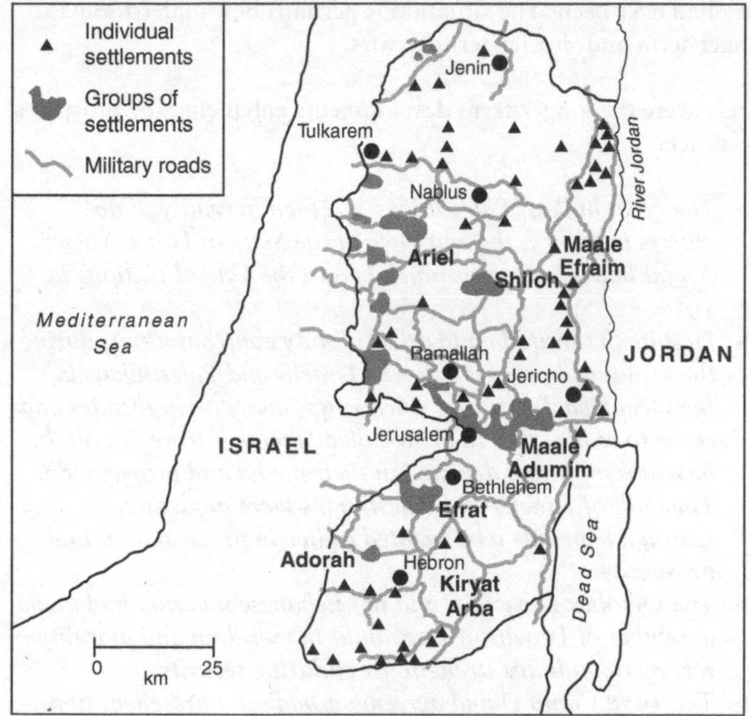

Figure 11.1 Facts on the ground – The extent of Israeli settlements in the West Bank.

In the ensuing chaos, all talk of resolving the half-century dispute came close to collapse. First, a deranged Israeli reservist deliberately shot dead seven Palestinian workers. Ten days later, Israeli security forces killed an entire Palestine Liberation Front (PLF) *fedayeen* group attempting an attack on Tel Aviv. Two weeks after that, James Baker stormed out of talks with the Israelis, infuriated by their lack of flexibility. When the PLO failed to condemn the failed *fedayeen* assault, Baker broke off talks with them too. Middle East peace-making had never been easy.

A CHANGING WORLD

Nevertheless, despite immediate problems, by the end of the First Gulf War (spring 1991) the broader circumstances for a peace deal between the Israelis and Palestinians were more favourable than they had ever been. The situation is perhaps best understood as longer-term and shorter-term factors.

These were the longer-term developments enhancing the prospects for peace:

- *The great bulk of Palestinians accepted in reality, if not always in theory, the existence of the State of Israel. Yasser Arafat had admitted as much before the United Nations in 1988.*
- *Despite the Intifada and other bloody confrontations, during the prolonged contact between Israelis and Palestinians in the Occupied Territories since 1967, many on both sides had come to realize that their so-called 'enemies' were not all the heartless monsters depicted in their media and propaganda. The bulk of Israelis and Palestinians were moderate, reasonable people who wanted to live in peace and mutual prosperity.*
- *The October 1973 War and the Lebanese invasion had made a number of Israelis unsure about the wisdom and morality of relying on military strength for enduring security.*
- *The 1978 Camp David agreement had set a precedent of a land-for-peace compromise deal.*
- *The collapse of Pan-Arabism had lowered the external threat to Israel and increased the Palestinians' drive to initiate a settlement for themselves.*
- *After exile from Lebanon, from where the last vestiges of PLO forces were finally driven in May 1991, the PLO was a homeless and impoverished organization urgently seeking to return to the centre stage.*

The shorter-term factors hastening the peace talks were as follows:

- *The disintegration of the USSR and the end of the Cold War had two effects. First, it deprived militant Palestinians of Soviet backing. Second, it enabled the USA to put pressure on Israel because it was no longer a key Cold War ally.*

- *In the emerging global economy, Israel had to find a new economic role and economic stability. Globalization was not compatible with its previous aid-dependent existence.*
- *The sudden appearance of local leadership at the beginning of the Intifada had threatened the PLO's position at the head of the Palestinian movement. It now needed to rediscover its links with the people it claimed to serve in order to fulfil their wishes.*
- *As far as the White House was concerned, the Gulf War had shown Israel in a new light. For the first time, especially when Sharon was calling for retaliation against Iraq's missiles, Israel had been a dangerous liability. Consequently, for the next few years, US administrations felt an urgent need to pressure Israel into accepting peace terms.*
- *At the same time, the Gulf War had gone some way to reversing the way the Israelis and Palestinians were viewed globally. By siding with Hussein – the man the world loved to hate – Arafat had undone much of the good of his previous peace initiatives. The image of Israel, on the other hand, had lost some of its militaristic tarnish: by not attacking Iraq, for the first time it had shown that it could be a nation of peace.*
- *Finally, there was the emergence of fundamental, radical Islam as a powerful new force in Iran, then in Lebanon and then in Palestine. Slowly, Israel and the USA were starting to realize that their real enemy was no longer Arafat, with his outdated, Soviet-style socialism, but determined Islamists who rejected many of the principles and values of the democratic-capitalist, post-Cold-War world. Against such a fundamental new threat, the West called on all who prized its values to unite.*

MADRID

After the liberation of Kuwait, US President George Bush Sr proposed a combined US–Russian peace conference, or series of conferences, to tackle the entire range of Middle East issues. Secretary of State James Baker drew up a nine-point plan embracing Syria and Jordan as well as Israel and the Palestinians.

It was based on the idea of bilateral (two-sided rather than multi-sided) talks between Israel and the various Arab teams, interim agreements and eventual final, permanent settlements.

Initially the Palestinians were offered 'less than a state' but 'more than autonomy' but without the PLO being directly involved in the negotiations. Arafat refused to participate on these terms, but was forced to back-track on account of the weakness of his position. The PLO eventually attended the opening conference as part of the Jordanian delegation, although a number of leading PLO figures resigned rather than accept this perceived humiliation. The compromise was too much for Shamir, who for a while also refused to take part. He eventually gave way when the USA threatened to withhold loan guarantees to Israel worth $10 billion.

Insight

The linking of Palestinian representatives to the Jordanian delegation at Madrid was more than just an acceptable way of getting them to the conference table. For years a number of prominent Israelis had argued that the best solution for Palestinian Arabs was to become part of a Kingdom of Jordan that might include parts of the West Bank.

On 30 October 1991, the conference opened in Madrid before a worldwide live TV audience of many millions. After Presidents Bush and Gorbachev had made their opening addresses, each participating nation was given 45 minutes to set out its position. Following these acerbic and often inflexible pronouncements, the conference ground to a halt in a series of procedural wranglings. Shamir had actually gone home after barely 24 hours in the Spanish capital. In the hope of finding a way forward, the bilateral talks reopened in Washington in December.

BACKGROUND OF VIOLENCE

The talks dragged on throughout 1992 but progress was painfully slow. A major handicap was what was going on elsewhere: time and again events on the ground, often violent, poisoned the atmosphere between the negotiating parties, making it impossible for even a semblance of cordiality to develop.

In February 1992, for example, an Israeli helicopter gunship killed the Hezbollah leader in Lebanon, Sheikh Abbas Mussawi, together with his wife and five-year-old son. In October, a large bloc of non-PLO Palestinian groups that included both the secular and Islamist wings of the movement (the 'Damascus 10'), united under the banner of the National Democratic and Islamic Front to oppose the peace process. November saw several shootings of Palestinian stone-throwers and others. A month later, when Hamas kidnapped an Israeli soldier, Israel deported 415 suspected Hamas militants to southern Lebanon, which refused to accept them. This provoked an Arab walk out from the talks then taking place in Washington.

The situation was no better in 1993. *Fedayeen* slew 13 Israelis early in the new year, causing Prime Minister Rabin to seal off the West Bank. Bending to international pressure, he then said he would allow back 100 of the previous year's deportees. They refused to return without their colleagues. Eventually, they all returned. Ominously, April saw the first Hamas suicide bomb attack, killing one Israeli, while July witnessed heavy fighting between the IDF and Hezbollah in southern Lebanon. Against such a backdrop, talk of peace often sounded decidedly hollow.

IRRECONCILABLE DIFFERENCES

In early 1992, the Palestinian delegates at the Washington talks had suggested the formation of a Palestinian Interim Self-Government Authority (the future Palestinian National Authority or PNA) of 180 elected officials to guide Palestinian territory towards full independence. The Israelis had not welcomed the proposal but the USA thought it had some mileage. An Israeli counter-proposal, considerably watering-down Palestinian autonomy, was immediately rejected by the Palestinians.

At this point, a fortuitous accident gave Arafat's position among Palestinians a considerable boost. His plane crashed in the Tunisian desert and for some hours he and all on board were missing, believed dead. Obituaries were written. When he reappeared, as if miraculously rising from the dead, in the eyes of many his immortality was confirmed.

The formation in Israel of a Rabin-led Labour administration at the end of July gave the peace talks a new impetus. Rabin's foreign minister, Shimon Peres, was a known 'dove'. Agreement was further helped when Democrat Bill Clinton assumed the US presidency at the beginning of 1993. Rabin froze new settlement in the Occupied Territories and accepted Palestinians at the talks, as long as they were not PLO or PLA. Interestingly, prominent among the Palestinian delegation was Faisal al-Husseini, from the same family as the noted Palestinian leader of a previous age (pp. 50–1). At the start of 1993, the Knesset repealed the law that had made all contact with the PLO illegal.

For all these favourable signs, the formal talks remained shrouded in mistrust and progress was dreadfully slow. The PLO knew that Rabin put Israel's security before peace and even as he negotiated he was instigating a massive new road-building programme across the West Bank, for military purposes. Settlements planned before the freeze were going ahead, too. On the other hand, the Israeli premier knew that the PLO would probably return to violence if things did not turn out as it wished. Moreover, its members were under growing pressure from the Islamists to be seen as true warriors in the Palestinian–Islamic cause. Even at this stage, accord with the PLO would not automatically mean peace for Israel.

In depth: Hamas

Hamas was created in 1987, early in the First Intifada, as a Palestinian offshoot of the Sunni Muslim Brotherhood. Rumours abound about its early years, for there is evidence that it received funding from Israeli secret services hoping to set up a Palestinian movement to counter-balance the influence of the PLO and portray the uprising as an Islamist-led movement. If this was indeed Israel's policy, then it backfired disastrously. Hamas expanded steadily, boosted by fresh funding from Iran and private sources around the Middle East, and waged a devastating Jihad against Israel. By 2006, it had been democratically elected to govern the PNA.

Employing tactics similar to those of Hezbollah in Lebanon, Hamas gained the support of Palestinians – mainly from Gaza – by using around 90 per cent of its multi-million dollar annual budget to fund social services. These ranged from immediate relief for the impoverished to longer-term programmes such as provision of mosques, schools, orphanages and even sports' leagues. Before its electoral triumph in 2006, Hamas was acting as virtually the surrogate government within Gaza.

Inevitably, Hamas' advance brought it into conflict with the PLO and Fatah. The two sides were opposed on a number of theoretical grounds, most obviously the position of Islam within Palestinian politics. On a more practical level, the rivalry was a power struggle for the hearts, minds and votes of the Palestinians in the Occupied Territories. The rivalry came to a head in 2007 when Hamas forcibly seized control of Gaza, giving a geographical dimension to the debilitating Palestinian divide.

In Israel and the West, Hamas was seen as an Islamist organization dedicated to the destruction of the Jewish state and the humbling of its allies, especially the USA. The Hamas covenant, drawn up in 1988, had renounced all compromise in its holy mission. That said, the leadership had accepted ceasefires and in 2007 was prepared to share power with non-Hamas politicians so that the PNA's foreign aid could be restored. Moreover, it also suggested it might accept some form of peace with Israel if it accepted the 2002 Saudi proposals.

Hamas began with guerrilla-style warfare against Israel. From 1993 it added suicide bombings to its armoury, sometimes employing women and children on these gruesome missions, while it was responsible for hundreds of cross-border rocket attacks from Gaza. Over the years, Hamas killed dozens of Israelis, civilians as well as military, and in return saw several of its leaders assassinated.

In depth: Yitzhak Rabin (1922–95)

Yitzhak Rabin is remembered as a man of both peace and war, the complex, sometimes tortured, Israeli minister who ordered his soldiers to break the bones of Palestinians and then, a few years later, signed Israel's first peace deal with them. His character, difficulties and career epitomized the bitter tragedy of the Israeli–Palestinian confrontation.

Born in Jerusalem to parents of Russian stock, Rabin was raised in Tel Aviv and ended his formal education at the age of 18. The next year he joined the Haganah, the first step in a long and distinguished military career. He fought in the 1948–9 war and later expressed reservations about the policy of ethnic cleansing of Arab areas in which he had participated. Staying in the IDF after the war, he rose to become its Chief of Staff in 1964. He is reported to have had some sort of breakdown during the extremely stressful build-up to the 1967 Six-Day War, but he quickly recovered and was bathed in glory after remarkable success in a conflict he may not actually have wanted.

Rabin served as Israeli Ambassador to the USA from 1968 to 1973, before being elected to the Knesset as a member of the Labour Alignment. Within a year, he had become party leader and then prime minister. His first premiership, which featured growing accord with Egypt, ended in disillusionment and scandal and was followed by the country's first Likud-based administration.

On returning to office in 1984, Rabin found himself minister of defence in the unity governments of Shamir and Peres. He supervised the drawback in southern Lebanon and then the fierce Israeli reaction to the First Intifada (1987).

His policies were described as those of the 'iron fist', earning him a reputation as an implacable enemy of the Palestinians. Beneath the surface, though, he was beginning to accept the need for compromise – but strictly on Israel's terms. The opportunity arose when he became prime minister for a second time in 1992.

Rabin's dramatic premiership saw the acceptance by the PLO of Israel's existence and its renunciation of violence, the establishment of the PLA, and a formal treaty between Israel and Jordan. If Rabin's peace deal with the Palestinians appears to outsiders a bit one-sided, it did not look so to many Israelis. The radical nature of the Oslo Accords, for which Rabin was awarded the Nobel Peace Prize, was confirmed when a Jewish Orthodox extremist assassinated his prime minister for betraying what he saw as the Jewish people's sacred trust.

10 THINGS TO REMEMBER

1. *By 1986, half the land in the West Bank was under direct Israeli control.*
2. *Palestinian attacks against Israelis rose from around 350 incidents a year in the early 1970s to nearer 3,000 a year by the early 1980s.*
3. *Between December 1987 and 1992, the Palestinians of the West Bank and Gaza rose in protracted rebellion, the First Intifada, against the occupiers. The violence cost over 1,000 lives, mostly Palestinian.*
4. *During the Intifada, militant Islamism in the shape of Hamas and Islamic Jihad first became a major influence among Palestinians.*
5. *The Intifada damaged Israel's economy and sharply divided opinion over the tactics used to counteract it.*
6. *In 1978, Arafat renounced violence, accepted UN Security Council Resolution 242 and declared Palestine to be an independent state based on the West Bank and Gaza.*
7. *Arafat made the mistake of backing Iraq during the First Gulf War (1990–1); the reputation of Israel, on the other hand, improved considerably when it refused to retaliate against Iraqi scud missile attacks.*
8. *Labour Prime Minister Yitzhak Rabin came to power in 1992 intent on striking a peace deal with the Palestinians.*
9. *Taking advantage of the 'peace dividend' that followed the ending of the Cold War and the collapse of the Soviet Union, a massive USA-initiated peace conference opened in Madrid in October 1991.*
10. *As the peace talks dragged on with little sign of real progress, tit-for-tat violence flared again between Palestinian* fedayeen *and Israeli security forces.*

12

Oslo and after 1993 to 1998

In this chapter you will learn about:
- ***the signing of the Oslo Peace Accords, 1993***
- ***attempts to implement the Oslo agreements***
- ***mounting violence and the slowing of the peace process.***

The 1990s were a desperately tragic decade for Israel–Palestine relations. They began with such high hopes: the two sides talking to each other for the first time and actually reaching agreement on some issues. These included very limited but nevertheless genuine Palestinian autonomy, and the promise of further steps towards permanent agreement and peace. Yet by 2000, the bright optimism had all but melted away, destroyed by the fiery hatred of the rival hardliners, leaving the chances of a permanent and total settlement as remote as ever.

Oslo

SECRET MEETINGS

By the summer of 1993, the series of formal Middle East peace talks, begun in Madrid and continued in Washington, seemed to be going nowhere. Israelis and Palestinians were sharply divided between those prepared to compromise for peace and those to whom rational agreement was an anathema. There was bitter fighting in southern Lebanon, Israeli settlements were still being built in the Occupied Territories, and Hamas had begun its campaign of suicide attacks. Beneath the surface, however, new life was stirring.

As the opening remarks of the Madrid Conference had showed, public negotiators always had more than one eye on their broader constituency. Israeli spokespeople had to demonstrate that they were not giving way to 'terrorism', while their Arab counterparts needed to remain true to the mantra of Palestine for the Palestinians. In other words, public talks were as much about rhetoric as compromise. As the Camp David talks that produced peace between Egypt and Israel had shown, true progress was generally possible only beyond the reach of the cameras and microphones of the media.

In late January 1993, a group of like-minded Palestinians and Israelis had met in Sarpsborg, Norway. For the first time, leading figures from both communities actually sat and talked peace together. Assisted by tactful and light-handed Norwegian mediation and without the full knowledge of the USA, a PLO delegation that included the prominent pragmatist Mahmoud Abbas (Abu Mazen) and an Israeli delegation featuring the respected academic Yair Hirschfeld began by exploring the topics on which they could find common ground. Both realized that at this stage, for instance, there was little point in talking about the future status of Jerusalem (see Figure 12.1) or Israeli settlements in the West Bank. On the other hand, an end to violence was a common desire. Gaza was another topic on which progress might be made. Given that most Israelis had little desire to retain the overpopulated strip and the Palestinians did not want them there, a solution was at least within the bounds of possibility.

Insight

The breakthrough Sarpsborg talks have been described by Professor Hilde Henriksen Waage of Oslo University as a 'shining moment' in Norway's history. It is a considerable surprise, therefore, to find that the entire records of the process by which two implacable enemies learned to talk together has disappeared from the archives.

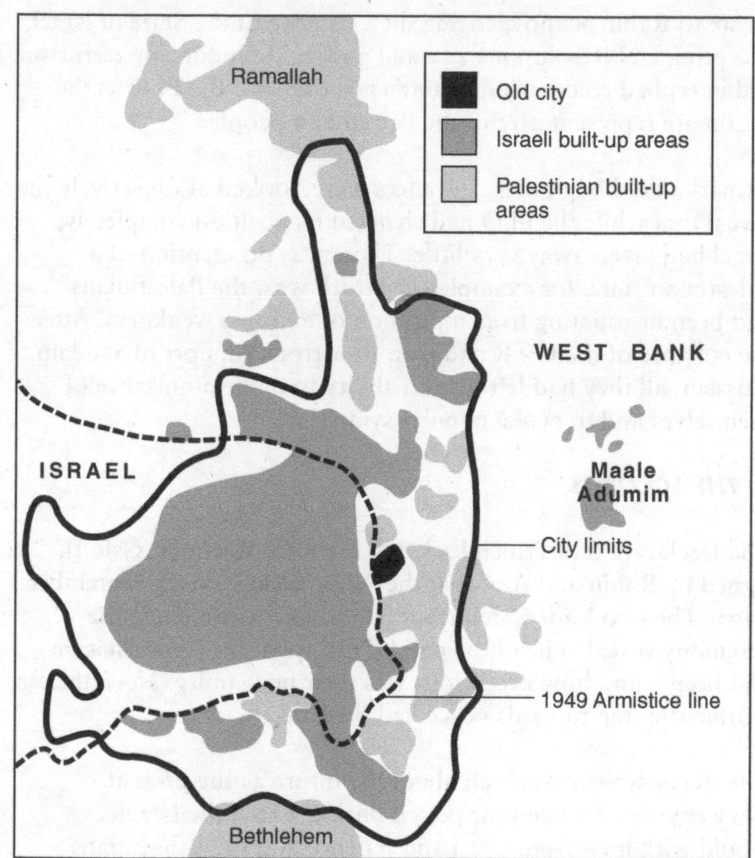

Figure 12.1 Jerusalem, 2006.

This step-by-step approach produced a series of principles that was revealed to a startled world on 20 August 1993. By now the major players, including Arafat, Rabin and the new US president, Bill Clinton, were on board. Moderates everywhere welcomed the extraordinary news. The reaction of hardliners was equally predictable. The Israeli far right denounced those who had talked with 'terrorists'; Islamist extremists, members of the old-style far left and radical representatives of the Palestinian diaspora condemned negotiation with 'infidels' and 'imperialists'. Nevertheless, events moved fast. In early September, Arafat wrote to Rabin acknowledging the existence of the State of Israel, accepting UN Resolutions 242 and 338, and renouncing terrorism. Rabin replied recognizing Arafat's position and the PLO as the legitimate representative of the Palestinian people.

Remarkable though these advances were, looked at objectively they reveal that while the PLO had changed its position completely, Israel had given away very little. There was no mention of a Palestinian state, for example. The truth was, the Palestinians had been negotiating from a position of extreme weakness. After the collapse of the USSR and their disastrous support of Saddam Hussein, all they had left was an ability to make a nuisance of themselves and to evoke popular sympathy.

THE ACCORDS

The Declaration of Principles led to the Oslo Accords (Oslo I), signed by Rabin and Arafat at the White House on 13 September 1993. The two leaders' reluctant handshake to conclude the ceremony revealed just how painful the apparent reconciliation had been – and how precarious was their new amity. Nevertheless, a dramatic step towards peace had been taken.

The Accords were as much about the future as the present. They envisaged a five-year period during which the Israelis would withdraw from Gaza and Jericho, and the Palestinians would establish an elected Palestinian National Authority (PNA) to manage internal affairs, including policing, tax and health, in the areas they controlled. The agreement foresaw the Israelis gradually pulling out of further areas in the West Bank and handing them over to the PNA. Negotiations between the two sides would continue with the aim of concluding a permanent and comprehensive settlement within five years. Meanwhile, a liaison committee would help resolve practical disputes between the two sides. The Knesset ratified the Accords on 23 September and the PLO Executive Committee (minus several high-profile opponents of the deal) did the same by one vote on 11 October 1993.

The success or otherwise of the rapprochement would depend on what happened next. Even so, its critics were many, particularly in the Palestinian camp. A step-by-step approach was all very well, they pointed out, but so far the steps had been mostly side-steps. Their objections were powerful: there was no programme for the formation of a Palestinian state; Israel still controlled all security and external affairs in the Occupied Territories, where its authority had now been legitimized; the Palestinians were to be held responsible for all acts of violence against Israel while violence towards Palestinians by Israeli settlers or security forces was deemed merely retaliatory; a long list of practical issues had been left open: the distribution of water, frontiers, the right of Palestinian refugees to return to Israel, and Israeli settlements on occupied land were among the most prominent. Small wonder that, referring to the treaty imposed on Germany after World War I, a number of Palestinian opponents of the Oslo Accords referred to them as 'Palestine's Versailles'. Israel had not only won its wars with the Palestinians; it now seemed to have won the peace, too.

Accord and discord

IMPLEMENTING OSLO

Whatever its critics said, the great majority of Palestinians and Israelis welcomed the Oslo agreement and sincerely hoped that it would herald a new era of peaceful co-existence between the two peoples. Therefore, despite huge opposition, violent and otherwise, the peace-making progress went forward. In April 1994, Israeli and Palestinian negotiators reached a deal on economic relations between the two peoples. A month later, some Oslo principles were turned into a concrete agreement for the IDF to pull out of Gaza and Jericho and be replaced by Palestinian forces.

Israel released 5,000 prisoners and detainees and cancelled a number of military orders used to govern the West Bank. Arafat, who was only too aware that Palestinian extremists were now labelling him a traitor, made his reluctance to sign the agreement patently obvious. At this stage, though, he had no choice. He was wedded to the peace process: if it collapsed, so would his credibility. All the same, he still sought to keep a foot in both camps, speaking of the Palestinian Jihad shortly after signing. In the end this sort of double-dealing led both Israelis and the USA to lose all faith in him (see pp. 246–8).

For the time being, however, Arafat was a hero. In July 1994, when after a Tunisian exile of many years he returned to Gaza, ecstatic crowds greeted him as the long-lost saviour. Further agreements followed in that year: the Israelis gradually handed over to the Palestinians local responsibility for education, health, tax, tourism and social welfare. Matters such as commerce, industry, agriculture, local government, post and insurance followed the following year. The process culminated in an agreement known as Oslo II, signed in September 1995.

OSLO II

The new deal, the product of months of painstaking negotiation, divided the West Bank into three zones. Zone A, comprising some seven per cent of the region's territory but containing the refugee camps and seven large cities in which the bulk of the Palestinian population lived, was to come under the direct control of the PNA. A small Jewish community remained within the largely Palestinian city of Hebron and the many thousands of Palestinian citizens of Jerusalem were still under Israeli governance. Israel and the PNA were to share responsibility for Zone B (about 23 per cent of the region), while Israel would retain its total control over Zone C (the remaining 70 per cent of the region) until final status talks had been concluded. Within Zone C came Jewish settlements and the militarily sensitive Jordan Valley.

As in Oslo I, Oslo II left aside the thorny questions of refugees, Jerusalem, water, and the settlements. Prisoners were released and optimistic noises made on both sides. In reality, though, all that had been done was implement some of the ideas of 1993 – and they had by no means pleased everyone. Prime Minister Rabin was openly called a 'traitor' and 'murderer'; furious extremists attacked his car and at a protest meeting paraded a coffin with his name painted on the side. It was ominous indeed. On 4 October 1995 Yitzhak Rabin, winner of the Nobel Peace Prize, was shot dead by a Jewish extremist. A crowd estimated at 300,000 attended his funeral.

Shimon Peres, always less hawkish than his dead colleague, took over as prime minister. As agreed, the IDF withdrew from the Palestinian towns of Nablus, Bethlehem and Ramallah, and from Taba on the border with Egypt. An international force moved into Hebron to ensure the maintenance of peace between the two communities. Meanwhile, an 88-seat Palestinian Legislative Council was elected. The turnout was high and all but ten seats went to Fatah. Yasser Arafat realized one of his lifetime ambitions when he was elected president of the PNA with 88 per cent of the vote.

Insight

The PNA lost the confidence of its people almost from the moment it was established. 1996 opinion polls in the Occupied Territories showed that while 63.7 per cent opposed the continuation of *fedayeen* attacks on Israel, 52.7 per cent believed the PNA was corrupt and over 56 per cent believed that a personal connection was the only way to get a PNA job.

NETANYAHU

By now the peace process was rapidly running out of steam. The prospects of reaching the much vaunted 'final status' agreement within the specified five-year period grew more remote by the day. Within Israel, the ceaseless waves of Islamist violence (see pp. 221–2) had turned people against the Oslo process. What was the point in talking to the PLO, they argued, if it couldn't control its own people? Gangs of youths roamed the streets of Israeli towns, condemning peace as weakness. Some rabbis even declared that a vote for right-wing Likud would ensure a blessing. As never before, Israel was bitterly, irreconcilably divided.

The elections of May 1996 were held on a new basis: one vote for a party and another for the post of prime minister. Likud's Benjamin Netanyahu narrowly defeated Shimon Peres in the latter, while Labour won slightly more Knesset seats than Likud. However, the backing of religious and other right-wing parties (including a new Russian immigrant party) enabled Netanyahu to form a coalition. Having opposed Oslo from the outset, the new prime minister was not going to make any compromises to carry the peace process forward.

THE PLO AND HAMAS

The peace process had divided Palestinians as sharply as it had Israelis. There were other difficulties, too. A Palestinian National Authority might have been created on paper but institution-building is a long and difficult process. Too few Palestinians, from Yasser Arafat downwards, had the necessary experience to construct a stable and reliable bureaucracy for the new administration. Although foreign aid poured into Palestinian coffers, gross maladministration resulted in frequent chaos and massive corruption. When in 1996 the head of the Independent Commission on Citizens' Rights in Palestine publicly criticized elements of the PNA for being crooked and repressive, he was unlawfully arrested.

The formation of a Palestinian Police Authority offers a good example of the sort of thing the commissioner was complaining about. It was initially envisaged that around 9,000 police would be required to look after the areas under PNA control. As suitable men had to be found relatively quickly and Arafat had large numbers of Fatah *fedayeen* who needed rewarding for their loyalty, the obvious solution was to turn ex-freedom fighters into salaried police. However, not only did they bring their *fedayeen* attitudes with them, soon dividing into semi-autonomous bands that interpreted the law as they saw fit, but their numbers swelled alarmingly to over 45,000. This made PNA territory one of the most heavily policed regions in the world.

In effect, the PNA police force and PNA militia became a sort of private security force for Arafat. Before long the inevitable happened. From early 1994, under pressure to be seen upholding his pledge to prevent attacks on Israel, Arafat ordered the periodic rounding up of Hamas militants. This heightened tension between Fatah and Hamas. At the end of the year, the issue suddenly escalated when PNA police shot and killed over a dozen fellow Palestinians outside a Gaza mosque. Another 200 were wounded. Shortly afterwards, up to 20,000 Gazans attended a mass Hamas rally. Tragically, instead of uniting the Palestinians, the peace process was fragmenting them, making further progress all the harder. As we shall see, the situation got so bad that by the mid-2000s the Fatah–Hamas rivalry periodically flared into full-scale combat and separate administrations were created in Gaza and the West Bank.

THE SUICIDE CAMPAIGN

While the peace process was still slowly and hesitantly developing, various groups were doing their best to make it fail. On the Arab side, this included the Lebanon-based, Iran-backed Hezbollah. Israel responded to Hezbollah provocation with its traditional no-nonsense harshness. Rabin's self-professed policy was to pursue peace as if there were no *fedayeen* campaign and pursue the *fedayeen* as if there were no peace process.

1994 saw a number of tit-for-tat attacks and raids in Lebanon and northern Israel. Then, when Hezbollah launched 28 Soviet-designed Katyusha rockets into northern Israel in the spring of 1996, Rabin decided it was time for another major Israeli reprisal. Operation Grapes of Wrath involved a naval blockade of the Lebanese coast as well as heavy air strikes. Beirut and 147 other towns and villages were hit, almost half a million Lebanese fled their homes and around 200 lost their lives alongside several Hezbollah fighters. A UN-monitored ceasefire was eventually put in place. Katyushas may have stopped raining on Israel for a short while, but as events were to show, in the long run the assault had done nothing to further either peace or Israeli security.

Hamas and Islamic Jihad suicide attacks killed far more Israelis than did the occasional Hezbollah rocket. Within a year of Oslo I, they had become a regular occurrence. In 1994, bus bombs slew 15 in April, and 22 in October. The next month a suicide cyclist killed three IDF troops at a checkpoint. Earlier in the year, an IDF attempt to rescue a soldier kidnapped by Hamas had left five dead. The next year saw bombs on buses, in a snack bar and in other public places. As the death toll mounted, so did Israeli public disillusionment with the peace process, precisely as the Islamists intended. The violence reached a new peak in early 1996, when 58 deaths in attacks on four separate venues paved the way for Netanyahu's election victory.

It might be helpful at this point to remind Western readers just how Islamist leaders managed to find so many young Muslims prepared to sacrifice themselves in such a grisly manner. The reason was as simple as it was abhorrent. Certain Islamic mullahs had declared the struggle with Israel to be a Holy War. Although suicide under normal circumstances was a sin, in such a cause it became the opposite: those who died while fighting the enemy had all their sins immediately forgiven and were guaranteed a direct path to heavenly life. To the idealistic young of a religious disposition, the teaching had a certain appeal.

Insight

Popular media in the West, eager to belittle the motives of suicide bombers, have readily accepted recruiting mullahs' sexist assurances that the Islamic heaven (the assured destination of martyrs) is peopled by 70 alluring 'virgins'. Such dubious blandishments are based on poor scholarship and even poorer translation. (See Ibn Warraq in the *Guardian*, 12 January 2002.)

ISRAEL: PEACE AND PROVOCATION

Accord with the PLO brought Israel benefits in several quarters. Diplomatically the pariah state came in from the cold, receiving recognition in states like Morocco and Tunisia that had hitherto sided unequivocally with the Palestinians. The Arab boycott of Israel was lifted, too, freeing major international companies to trade there. Israel also struck a valuable commercial and military deal with Turkey, and signed a long-desired peace with Jordan. Israeli–Jordanian talks had begun even before the ink was dry on the Oslo Accords. A common agenda was agreed in September 1993, an economic agreement the following January, and a full-scale peace treaty that ended 46 years of war was signed in October 1994.

Compared with the sacrifices made by the PLO, the Israeli government gave little away. It made a few gestures, such as outlawing one or two fanatically extreme Jewish religious groups and not pressing ahead with fresh settlement plans. But, as noted, there was no freeze on existing settlement plans – near Bethlehem, for example – and this fed Palestinian resentment.

Palestinian disillusionment was all too understandable. Instead of finding themselves with something approaching a state of their own as a result of the Oslo process, they were now living in ever more fragmented communities, separated by heavily patrolled Israeli roads and a constantly growing number of Israeli settlements. Some commentators compared what was happening to the policy of South Africa's apartheid governments: setting up 'Bantustans' or areas of native settlement. This concept has been labelled 'structural violence'.

Occasional acts of aggression by Israeli settlers against their Palestinian neighbours persisted. Far more terrifying was the slaughter carried out by Baruch Goldstein, a fanatical immigrant doctor from New York. Wearing an IDF uniform, he entered Hebron's Ibrahimi Mosque at dawn prayers on 25 February 1994.

The building held the tombs of Abraham and Jacob, prompting Goldstein to convince himself that it should be cleared of all Muslims. Firing an automatic rifle, he slaughtered 21 worshippers and injured a further 300 before being overpowered and killed by the incandescent mob. Some of those present claimed that Israeli guards positioned nearby deliberately chose not to hear what was happening. The massacre came close to ending the peace process there and then.

As before, the Israelis rounded up suspects en masse after *fedayeen* attacks: 370, for instance, after the suicide assaults of February–March 1996. In total, between 1967 and 2007, the Israelis imprisoned over half a million Palestinians. Nor did the peace process stop the Israelis continuing with what the Palestinians designated 'state terrorism' – singling out key leaders of opposition groups for assassination by bomb, gun or even poison. The head of Islamic Jihad was killed by a car bomb in November 1994. More noteworthy was the assassination – probably by Israeli agents, although this has not been proved – of Yihyeh Ayash. Known as the 'Engineer', Ayash was believed to have been responsible, in one way or another, for at least 60 Israeli deaths. Not surprisingly, his removal did not lead to a reduction in attacks in Israel. Quite the opposite, in fact: the pantheon of Palestinian 'martyrs' was thereby furnished with yet another figure to inspire would-be terrorists/freedom fighters.

Netanyahu, Arafat and Clinton

THE OPPORTUNITY PASSES

By May 1996, the date of Netanyahu's election, the high hopes of the early 1990s were fading fast. For a few years following the collapse of the Soviet Union, there had been a genuine sense of global optimism in international affairs. The USA, the sole remaining superpower, had been free to concentrate its massive resources and political clout on solving world problems rather than focusing on the sterile struggle of the Cold War. As far as the Middle East was concerned, now that Israel was no longer required as an ally in the fight against communism, the USA had been able to bring greater pressure on it to reach an accord with the Palestinians. Without Soviet backing, the PLO and its supporters had been similarly susceptible to US arm-twisting. Yet even as the Accords were being hammered out, a new power was once again reshaping the face of international affairs.

In 1978, militant Islam had expressed its dislike of the West when a group of fervent Iranians took hostage the entire staff of the US embassy in Tehran. Islamist hostility towards the USA grew and, by the 1990s, Muslim extremists were striking at American as well as Israeli targets. In their eyes a democratic, capitalist, pro-Israeli, pro-female-equality and essentially Christian America was the principal enemy of a worldwide fundamentalist Islamic revival. 1993 saw the first attack on the World Trade Center, New York. Then came assaults on US facilities in Saudi Arabia and two US embassies in Africa. In 2000, a US warship was bombed in Aden harbour. By now the CIA and other Western intelligence services were collecting an ever-growing volume of evidence relating to the extreme danger posed by fanatical Muslims.

As Israel's principal enemies – Hamas, Hezbollah and Islamic Jihad – were linked to this Islamist movement, the USA reverted to its previous position of seeing Israel as a key ally in a global struggle. This made it more difficult for American administrations to pressure Israel into coming to terms with the Palestinians. As ever, it was the bulk of ordinary Palestinians – in the Occupied Territories, in foreign refugee camps and even within Israel – who suffered most.

'PEACE WITH SECURITY'

Benjamin Netanyahu was the first, and to date, the only Israeli prime minister born since the founding of the State of Israel. His background was atypical for an Israeli political leader, too. He lived, studied and worked in the USA for many years before deciding to serve his country as a diplomat and then as a politician.

His successful US-style premiership campaign had shocked many Israelis unused to such a very personal, media-savvy approach. Nonetheless, it had proved effective and he had come to power promising to 'make a safe peace'.

Peace and security were, of course, what all Israelis wanted. Ultimately the former was required in order to guarantee the latter. Netanyahu's problem was that instinctively he wanted things the other way round, putting security before peace. Moreover, his Likud-based coalition's reliance upon the support of Ultra-Orthodox Jewish parties gave him little option but to strike a hard line. In the end, he was able to provide neither peace nor security and fell from power after only three years.

Across the divide, Yasser Arafat similarly felt himself pulled in two directions. On the one hand, there was the painfully slow peace process that he had helped set up and which still offered the prospect of a fully independent Palestinian state one day; on the other hand were the increasingly influential Islamist groups, hostile to a submissive compromise with Israel and determined to continue their armed struggle for a fully integrated, independent Palestine. By the end of the millennium, Arafat was clearly worried that Hamas, in particular, was undermining his PLO–Fatah organization, thereby weakening his control over the Palestinian movement. Ever the wily master of pragmatic scheming, it has been suggested on quite strong evidence that the Palestinian president reacted by secretly backing the Islamists in the hope of forcing Israel to make concessions. Evidence has been uncovered showing that he was even more duplicitous, allowing *fedayeen* under his direct or indirect command to conduct Hamas-style raids to show that the Islamists were not alone in their militant hostility towards Israel.

ANTI-OSLO

Netanyahu had never approved of the Oslo process and his premiership was dotted with incidents that served to stoke up Israeli–Palestinian ill-feeling. Security was toughened, with the

Israeli borders being closed to Palestinian workers on several occasions. Suspects were rounded up, homes searched and buildings flattened. In September 1996, the prime minister personally authorized the opening of a 2,000-year-old tunnel that passed near the Al-Aqsa Mosque. Muslims were incensed at what they believed was a threat to the foundations of the mosque and a stone-throwing mob assembled near the archaeological site. Israeli and Palestinian police arrived. Shots were fired, and by the time order had been restored, 75 people lay dead. As was invariably the case in such situations, most of those killed were Palestinians.

Meanwhile, the Netanyahu coalition had further inflamed Palestinian feelings – and made a full peace deal even less likely – by lifting the freeze on Israeli settlements within the Occupied Territories. Jewish encroachment was particularly unwelcome around East Jerusalem and on land confiscated from Arabs. The Oslo Accords had specifically forbidden all such development. Other incidents played their part in souring relations. Certain court decisions did not help, for example, as when soft sentences were passed on Israelis found guilty of harming Palestinians. Other provocative acts were more violent. In 1997, an Israeli gunman opened fire on Palestinian shoppers in a Hebron market. Later in the year, Mossad – Israel's secret service organization – bungled an assassination attempt on a Hamas leader sheltering in Jordan. King Hussein made return of the Israeli agents he had captured conditional on the release of the Hamas leader Sheikh Ahmad Yassin. The Sheikh promptly went on a tour of Arab capitals to raise funds for Hamas.

The following year, another Hamas leader was less fortunate when he was shot and then blown up in the Palestinian-controlled town of Ramallah. Palestinians blamed Israeli agents for the assassination; Israelis said it had been carried out by Fatah. Two weeks earlier, there had been serious rioting in Hebron after the IDF shot dead three Palestinians at a checkpoint.

Despite Netanyahu's security clamp-down, Palestinian attacks on Israel were maintained. The targets were invariably intended to provoke maximum outrage: a restaurant in Tel Aviv, a market, a shopping centre. Such acts fostered a fresh approach to the security situation as a growing number of Israelis began taking seriously the idea of 'separation': permanently dividing themselves from the Palestinians by the erection of impenetrable walls and fences. Nonetheless, Israelis were not the only targets. In 1997, Palestinian estate agents were killed for selling land to Jewish settlers.

THE CLINTON INITIATIVE

For all the problems on the ground in Israel, the Occupied Territories and in the areas controlled by the Palestinian Authority, President Clinton was still pressing resolutely ahead with the peace process. Although they had to keep a wary eye on their constituencies, neither Netanyahu nor Arafat wanted to see the process collapse completely. The Israeli premier was only too aware of the economic dislocation that prolonged violence inevitably brought, while his Palestinian counterpart knew that a failure of the peace talks would be hailed as a victory for the Islamists.

Insight

Like nearly all his predecessors, President Clinton found he could achieve far more in foreign affairs, where he had a relatively free hand, than in domestic matters, where the president's authority was severely restricted by the US constitution and the workings of the country's checks-and-balances political system.

Arafat's reputation among his own people was suffering, too. The frequent closure of crossing points into Israel hit Palestinian workers particularly hard. Increasingly disillusioned and desperate, they did not take kindly to the findings of a report, published in 1997, that declared two-thirds of the PNA budget to have been misspent or mismanaged. The Palestinian National Assembly voted almost unanimously for all PNA personnel to be replaced.

Less than a year after coming to office, under massive US pressure, Netanyahu withdrew the IDF from Hebron. This completed the handover of territory to the PNA envisaged in the Oslo Agreements' first phase. The Israeli premier then made it clear that this was about as far as he was prepared to go. He made a number of provocative statements about Israel remaining permanently in the West Bank and about power being the only guarantee of security. Arafat responded by releasing Hamas suspects and by rejecting further co-operation on security matters.

In the fall of 1998, President Clinton broke the deadlock by holding a Camp-David-style summit at Wye Plantation, Maryland. Jordan's King Hussein, in the USA for cancer treatment, was on hand to lend such assistance as he could. After long hours of talks, Arafat and Netanyahu eventually agreed to take up the peace process where it had broken off. The Wye River Memorandum, signed later in Washington, spoke of prisoner release, co-operation on security, safe passage between Gaza and the West Bank, and the PLO cutting back on anti-Israeli rhetoric. More significantly, Israel agreed to hand over to the PNA a further 13 per cent of West Bank Zones B and C in return for greater US involvement in Israel's security.

Moderates on all sides welcomed the Wye River undertaking as another important step towards a lasting settlement. The Palestinian National Assembly and the Knesset both accepted it and attempts were made to start implementing some of its terms. Inevitably, though, there was fierce opposition. Islamists and the anti-Oslo 'Damascus 10' (see pp. 207–8) condemned it outright, pointing out that there was still no mention of a Palestinian state. Ultra-orthodox Jews fulminated against handing over still more of their sacred homeland to Muslims. To mollify his supporters, Netanyahu began to renege on parts of the deal by imposing fresh conditions for Israeli withdrawal. Beset by allegations of corruption and stories about his private life, he lost a vote of confidence in the Knesset and his ill-fated administration fell.

In depth: Islamic Jihad

Islamic Jihad, also known as PIJ, had its origins among enthusiastic Palestinian students studying in Egypt. Although they were Sunni, the young men were inspired by the revolutionary activities of the Shia who had overthrown the Shah of Iran in 1978.

The movement took a while to crystallize and organize itself, not claiming its first Israeli victim until 1987. PIJ followers said their campaign was a Holy War (*Jihad*) against all Western and pro-Western regimes, especially Israel. Negotiation it eschewed as useless – the only way to triumph was through an armed struggle, if necessary sacrificing oneself in the holy cause. Consequently, Islamic Jihad would have nothing to do with the Oslo Accords or other peace movements, meaning its relations with Yasser Arafat's Fatah and the PLO were always strained. On the other hand, as their aims and tactics have converged, so relations between Islamic Jihad and Hamas gradually became more cordial.

Islamic Jihad carried out a number of attacks during the First and Second Intifadas, some of them truly ghastly. It was responsible for suicide nail bombs, for example, and for stoning to death young Israeli settlers it had captured. Inevitably its leadership became a primary target for the Israeli security services who, in 1995, are believed to have had a hand in the shooting dead of the PIJ's commander in Malta. His Gazan replacement, the Western-educated academic Ramadan Abdullah Sallah, rapidly rose to the top of the Israeli and US most-wanted-terrorists lists and was said to have taken refuge wisely in Syria.

In depth: Ariel Sharon (1928–)

Few Israelis provoked stronger feelings than Ariel Sharon. A huge man of huge drive, he was loved and hated in almost equal measure during a long and highly controversial career as soldier and politician, warrior and peace-seeker.

Born in the Palestinian mandate to parents originally from Russia, Sharon joined the Haganah and fought with distinction during Israel's War of Independence. After serving as an intelligence officer and trying to catch up on his education, he returned to the army to lead the new anti-terrorist Unit 101. In this post he began to build a reputation as a fearless, utterly ruthless defender of Israeli interests, even at the cost of the lives of Palestinian civilians.

Sharon served in the 1956 Suez campaign and finished his university education before commanding a powerful armoured division with flair in 1967. He briefly entered politics, then rejoined the IDF for the 1973 October War in which his unorthodox leadership earned him both high praise and strong criticism. Back in politics, he served as a right-wing member of the Knesset and helped form Likud. For almost all his time in government, in several offices, he used a variety of tactics to increase the number of Israeli settlements within the Occupied Territories, especially the West Bank. A number of settlers came to see him almost as their patron.

Appointed minister of defence in 1981, Sharon was architect of the following year's invasion of Lebanon that led to the defeat and expulsion from that country of the PLO. He was also widely seen as responsible for the massacres within the Sabra and Shatila refugee camps, although the actual killing was done by Christian militia. As a result, he was deprived of his post but remained in the government as minister without portfolio.

In the years that followed, Sharon became a more and more divisive figure. Rumours spread of personal corruption; he opposed Oslo yet participated in the Wye River talks; he put enormous energy into housing Israel's recent immigrants yet gave them sub-standard caravans. In 2000, his tactless behaviour almost single-handedly started the Second Intifada. He remained resolute through all difficulties, however, and his aura of unflinching strength won him the prime ministerial election in 2001.

Sharon saved his greatest and most enigmatic of surprises to the end. At first he toed the traditional Likud hard line in the face of

(Contd)

fedayeen attacks. Then, in late 2003, he announced a unilateral Disengagement Plan. This involved pulling out of Gaza and small areas of the West Bank and relying on the security barrier to defend the homeland. The Knesset backed him and after Israeli settlers had left their Gaza settlements – sometimes only when forced to do so – the Strip was handed back to the Palestinians. Next, seeking support for further unilateral withdrawal from the West Bank, Sharon announced the setting up of a new political party, Kadima ('Forward'). This advance was his last, for he suffered a massive stroke that plunged him into a coma from which there was no hope of recovery.

10 THINGS TO REMEMBER

1 *Secret and informal talks held in Sarpsborg, Norway, early in 1993 made more serious progress towards a framework for peace than all previous peace conferences of a more formal nature.*

2 *The ground-breaking Oslo Accords of September 1993 established an elected National Authority to run internal Palestinian affairs in the West Bank and Gaza.*

3 *Oslo was a starting point: key issues such as water distribution, frontiers and the right to return were left for future negotiation.*

4 *Oslo II (September 1995) divided the West Bank into three zones: one entirely Palestinian administered (7 per cent), one entirely Israeli administered (70 per cent) and one under joint administration (23 per cent).*

5 *On 4 October 1995, Prime Minister Yitzhak Rabin, key architect of the Oslo peace agreements, was assassinated by a Zionist extremist.*

6 *The first half of 1996 saw Arafat elected as President of the PNA and the Likud prime minister Benjamin Netanyahu form a right-wing coalition government in Israel.*

7 *By the mid-1990s, the Islamist group Hezbollah, acting out of Lebanon, had joined with Hamas and other* fedayeen *in terrorising Israel with rocket attacks and suicide bombings.*

8 *As ever, Israel responded to attacks with disproportionate violence. Palestinian towns were re-occupied, thousands arrested and* fedayeen *leaders assassinated.*

9 *Netanyahu, who had never publicly approved of the Oslo Accords, broke them by permitting further settlements to be built in the Occupied Territories. By the end of 1997, hope of further peace deals had almost completely evaporated.*

10 *Approaching the end of his presidency, in 1998 Bill Clinton tried to breathe new life into the peace process by brokering the Wye River Memorandum. It was immediately rejected by extremists on both sides.*

13

Terror 1999 to 2004

In this chapter you will learn about:

- ***attempts at a negotiated settlement, 1999–2001***
- ***the outbreak of the Second Intifada***
- ***9/11, the 'war on terror' and the proposed Roadmap to peace***
- ***the close of the Arafat era.***

To solve the unsolvable

This chapter covers the years between the collapse of Benjamin Netanyahu's first term as prime minister in May 1999 and the death of the Palestinian leader Yasser Arafat in November 2004. In a story already vividly marked with bitter and bloody turbulence, the period witnessed a plethora of incidents of murder and mayhem. Tragically, there was no inevitability about what happened. As the second millennium was drawing to a close, in fact, two – possibly even three – highly influential middle-aged men were trying hard to go down in history as those who succeeded in solving the unsolvable. US President Bill Clinton, Israeli Prime Minister Ehud Barak and Palestinian President Yasser Arafat, all hard-headed realists, wished to be remembered as peacemakers.

BARAK'S INITIATIVES

Ehud Barak, the most decorated soldier in his country's history and now leader of its Labour party, was the second Israeli prime minister to be elected under the presidential-style system first used in 1996. Its advantage was that it produced a leader who could boast reasonably widespread popular support. The disadvantage was that an incoming prime minister, whatever his national backing, could not automatically command a Knesset majority. This fact had led to the collapse of Netanyahu's frail coalition, and now it left his replacement with the guaranteed support of only the 26 seats of his One Israel three-part coalition of Labour, Gesher (a short-lived Likud break-away) and Meimad (an equally short-lived left-wing Zionist group). Prime Minister Barak, already handicapped by his own inexperience as a politician, had to depend on a coalition cobbled together with six other parties.

But the man credited with masterminding the Entebbe airport raid (see pp. 156–7) and several other such daring operations was nothing if not confident. He had campaigned on a pledge to end his people's 100-year conflict with the Palestinians, and a guarantee to withdraw the IDF from Southern Lebanon within a year. He may well have believed he could achieve it. President Clinton, sullied by scandal, was similarly eager to make 1999, the final year of his presidency, something of an *annus mirabilis*. Yasser Arafat, too, needed a masterstroke to counter the growing swell of religious and moral outrage at the corruption within the Palestinian National Authority that he headed.

Insight

A number of liberal-minded Israeli commentators, such as the Tel Aviv University professor Tanya Reinhart (author of *The Road Map to Nowhere*, 2006), have bemoaned what they see as the unhealthy influence of the military within the Israeli political system.

Barak pressed ahead on three fronts. November 1999 saw Israeli–Palestinian negotiations, brokered by the USA to further the Wye River Accord (pp. 228–9), in which the parties discussed what form a final peace settlement might take. In January 2000, formal peace talks, again brokered by the USA, were reopened with Syria. Meanwhile, Barak tried to put military pressure on the Lebanese government to take firmer control over Hezbollah in preparation for an Israeli withdrawal from the south of the country. But the Lebanese could do nothing without Syrian backing and when Israeli failings led to the collapse of negotiations with Syria's President Hafez Assad in March, Barak was left with an awkward choice. He could either renege on his promise to leave Lebanon or do so with his northern frontier yet unsecured. He chose the latter and the Arab world, led by Hezbollah, proclaimed a great victory. President Assad died a fortnight later. The succession of his rather less forceful son Bashir Assad did not augur well for improved relations in that direction.

What particularly pleased the Iranian-backed Shia of Hezbollah was that although the IDF and its ally the South Lebanese Army had gone, the border question was not quite settled. Still in dispute was an area of 22 square km at the northern end of the Israeli-occupied Golan Heights known as the Shebaa Farms. Marked as Syrian on UN maps, it was claimed by Lebanon. Thus Hezbollah had an excuse to maintain its armed wing, whose express purpose was to drive Israeli forces from all Lebanese territory. The UN troops posted along the frontier were unable to prevent periodic Hezbollah rocket fire into northern Israel, but not until 2006 did the frontier once again hit the world's headlines.

CAMP DAVID II

Meanwhile, progress on the Palestinian front had been grinding to a halt. Barak's Foreign Minister, David Levy (ex-Likud), had held fairly fruitless discussions with the PLO plenipotentiary Mahmoud Abbas about what a 'final status' agreement between Israel and the Palestinians might look like. Arafat's position had been weakened, too, when in November 1999 a group of 20 of his leading opponents produced a petition entitled 'The Homeland Calls Us', which apparently had thousands of Palestinian signatures. It damned in no uncertain terms the Oslo Accords, the PLO chairman and all compromise with Israel. In an attempt to demonstrate to the USA and Israel that he was still in charge of the situation, Arafat ordered the arrest of eight of the signatories from the petition. It was not a convincing gesture. Nor were even moderate Palestinians impressed by Barak's failure to do anything about the relentless expansion of Israeli settlements in the West Bank.

Nevertheless, President Clinton was desperate for a breakthrough, for the place in history he craved as one of the great peace-making statesmen of modern times. Surprising though it may seem, he came closer to achieving this than many thought possible.

To break the deadlock, in July 2000 Clinton tried a Carter-style summit amid the pines and golf buggies of the luxurious but remote Camp David (see pp. 160–2). Barak and Arafat were there, complete with their teams of advisors. The Palestinian leader was unhappy from the start, feeling that he had been 'summoned' to appear rather than attending of his own free will. His mood was not helped by Barak, apparently still in military commander mode, issuing orders that he expected to be obeyed instantly.

Arafat's problem was that, unlike Sadat in 1978, he had to negotiate from a position of almost total weakness. Egypt's president had been able to remind the Israelis of Arab victories at the start of the October War, implying that without a lasting peace Israel might suffer similar reversals in the future. Arafat held no such stick. Even the threat posed by Palestinian militants had now partly passed out of his control with the growth of Hamas and other Islamist groups. He could reject what was put forward, but he was in no position to suggest viable alternatives. In the end, all he could do was pick up the hand the USA and Israel dealt him or leave the game altogether. He eventually opted for the latter.

Insight

Satisfactory conflict resolution is rarely possible unless each side respects, even fears the other. Ongoing *fedayeen* violence may be interpreted as attempting to make Israelis accept that life would be a great deal more enjoyable if the question of Palestine were resolved.

The Israelis were prepared to concede more than at any time previously. Their offer included returning Gaza and most of the West Bank to the Palestinians, and the establishment of a safe and permanent link between the two. Furthermore, part of Jerusalem would be handed back to form a Palestinian capital. Clinton knew this was as good as he could expect. To get the Palestinians to accept the offer he tried every trick he knew, flattering, hectoring and even shouting at Arafat. But all to no avail. The PNA president, only too aware of the Islamists waiting to denounce him, could not accept a proposal that amounted to a climb-down. There was no right of return for Palestinians exiled from their native land and the West Bank deal was dismissed as establishing 'Bantustan' Palestine. How could the USA call the Israeli suggestion 'generous', asked Arafat, when it proposed returning only some of the land originally stolen from Palestinians?

In the end, the talks broke up without a deal, although both sides agreed to carry on talking. Back home, Arafat was greeted as a hero – the man with the guts to stand up to the Americans and the Israelis. Abroad, USA and Israeli spin doctors portrayed him as the man who had rejected peace.

THE END OF NEGOTIATION

Following an emergency summit in October at the Egyptian Red Sea resort of Sharm El Sheikh, in December Clinton made one last effort. There is some disagreement over the 'Bridging Proposals' that he put forward during his final few weeks in office, although it is generally agreed that they went further than the Camp David offer. Dennis Ross, the chief US negotiator, said afterwards that the USA suggested all of Gaza and 97 per cent of the West Bank be handed over to Palestinian rule. The Palestinian negotiators said no such proposal was made and the new offer still left considerable areas of the West Bank in Israeli hands. Whatever the USA suggested – and both sides agree that the package included no guaranteed 'right of return' – neither side was able to endorse it unequivocally.

In late January 2001, European and Egyptian mediators presided over last ditch talks held at Taba, a small Egyptian town at the northern tip of the Gulf of Aqaba. Apparently the two sides came closer than ever, although they still could not agree a final two-state map or how the right to return might be handled. While there was a basis here for further discussion at a later date, that date was receding fast. Clinton had gone and Barak was facing re-election. Worse still, Palestinian frustration had again exploded into Intifada.

Sharon and the Second Intifada

THE AL-AQSA UPRISING

At this point, we need to try to imagine what the previous five years had been like for the Palestinians of the Occupied Territories. Hopes had been so high in the middle of the decade. Arafat, the near mythical leader, had returned from exile amid hysterical rejoicing. The IDF was going to withdraw, there would be elections, the Palestinians would govern themselves, there would be peace, foreign aid would pour in to stimulate the economy, and before long all Palestinians would enjoy a decent standard of living... And now, at the turn of the millennium, what had happened to all these golden dreams?

As so often, Palestinian dreams had been cruelly dashed. Most still lived in overcrowded cities or in enclaves, surrounded by Israel patrols and divided by heavily guarded Israeli highways; the Authority they had elected had been shown to be impossibly corrupt; internal divisions, particularly between secularists and Islamists, were growing and becoming more serious almost by the day; their desperate attacks, condemned as terrorism, produced fierce, old-style Israeli harassment, detention and targeted killings; Israeli courts seemed to turn a blind, or at least a very myopic eye on settlers who preyed on Palestinians; living standards were as low as ever, especially when the closure of border crossings deprived Palestinians of work in Israel. Surely, they asked, all the pain and suffering of the Intifada had not been for this?

In such an explosive atmosphere, a visit by an Israeli politician to the compound surrounding the Al-Aqsa mosque in Jerusalem was sure to cause controversy. When that politician was the right-wing leader of the opposition and he arrived in the company of a massive bodyguard of armed police, the situation was bound to be even more tense. And when the unwanted visitor was no less a person than Ariel Sharon, the veteran of countless bloody anti-*fedayeen* operations, the destroyer of the PLO in Lebanon and supposed mastermind behind the Sabra and Shatila massacres (see pp. 180–1), Palestinian reaction may easily be imagined. Anyway, there were those among the more extreme Islamists who were waiting for just such an opportunity.

Sharon's visit took place on Thursday, 28 September 2000. Rumours of sacrilege and other misdemeanours were soon flying, fanned by inflammatory words from the mosques the following day. Stones were thrown at the Israeli police, who responded with tear gas, rubber bullets and finally with live ammunition. The rioting spread, and within a week 50 Palestinians had been killed.

So began the Second or Al-Aqsa Intifada. By the end of the year, the death toll stood at 315 Palestinians and 37 Israelis. The Palestinian dead included 66 children. The killing of one boy, 12-year-old Mohammed al-Durrah, as he cowered beside his father amid a hail of bullets, was captured live by a French TV camera crew. The image sped around the world, fuelling the Intifada and raising a massive groundswell of anti-Israeli feeling.

Insight

As with the Americans in Vietnam, the Israelis have often found themselves losers in the media wars. Images and reports are more likely to catch the eye of news desk editors if they offer an easily-grasped story of Goliath bullying a defenceless David.

The Israeli authorities were as unprepared for the second Intifada as they had been for the first. Its ferocity shocked them. It was on a different scale, too. Stones and insults had been replaced by bullets, bombs and suicide attacks. Disparate radical groups like the PFLP, Hamas, and Islamic Jihad competed with Arafat's own terrorist-style unofficial militia, Fatah Tanzim (organized in 1995 to prevent the Islamists from undermining his authority) to inflict the deepest wounds.

Months of shootings, bombings and lynchings left Barak's much-vaunted peace policy in tatters and he lost the support of both left and right in the Knesset. Even the Arab members refused to back him. His resignation, but not the fall of his government, led to the third and final use of the prime-ministerial election process. In February 2001, the 72-year-old Ariel Sharon of Likud overwhelmingly defeated Barak, taking 62.4 per cent of the vote on a broad platform of 'security and true peace' (all things to all people). As his party still commanded only 21 Knesset seats, he was obliged to form a new coalition administration of 'National Unity'.

Peace on our terms

UNILATERAL DISENGAGEMENT

The Sharon government included Labour members like the prime minister's old rival Shimon Peres, who became foreign minister. Compromise on the domestic front, however, did not mean compromise elsewhere and as the Second Intifada continued, the year slid into a grisly mire of tit-for-tat killings.

Where, then, was Sharon's 'true peace'? Although the man who had established his reputation as a doughty fighter for Israel and an implacable enemy of Palestinian independence was now well into his eighth decade, he had lost none of his bite. All the same, as the body-count mounted, his mind inevitably turned to his legacy: how fitting it would be for the man who had done so much to bring Israel victory on the battlefield also to bring his people lasting security.

The way to achieve this, Sharon decided, was not through peace conferences. That had been tried too often and always found wanting. Besides, who was there to negotiate with? Over the past 50 years the Palestinians had been so pummelled and pounded, crushed, harassed, divided and fragmented that it was no longer possible to find a voice that spoke for all of them. Arafat tried desperately to be that voice, which is why he made so many contradictory statements: for example, whereas only a few months before he had been calling warmly for peace, he was now offering the Intifada his wholehearted support. Confusing, maybe, but he was simply expressing different aspects of the Palestinian spectrum.

Sharon's response was to work for peace on his own terms – 'unilateral disengagement'. This meant, first, using all possible means to undermine Arafat and the Palestinian National Authority, for which he had nothing but scorn, so that it could be replaced by a more amenable and moderate alternative; and second, 'decapitating' militant opposition groups by taking out their leadership by armed strike if the PNA would not or could not do the job for him. A third strand to the policy, initially endorsed only warily, was protecting Israel's frontiers with insurmountable physical barriers. In the short term, though, the Intifada battle raged on.

INTIFADA

The suicide attacks were too many to be listed individually. In June 2001, the deaths of 20 Israeli teenagers outside Tel Aviv's Dolphinarium Discotheque caught the world's headlines, as did a similar attack on a Jerusalem pizzeria two months later which left 15 dead. In December, the slaughter reached a ghastly crescendo with 26 Israelis dying in a series of co-ordinated attacks in

Jerusalem and ten deaths when a bus carrying Orthodox settlers was attacked. Before that, Israel had seen its first Israeli–Arab suicide bomber and the killing of a government minister. During this period the attacks were nearly all the work of Islamists, mainly Hamas, although another group supposedly linked to Fatah, the Al-Aqsa Martyrs Brigades, had recently been formed. Its unofficial task was, apparently, to prove to the average Palestinian that Arafat's supporters could be as aggressive towards the Israelis as the Islamists. There was also internecine violence within the Palestinian ranks. To the outside world, this was explained as the PNA exercising its authority over dissident terrorist groups. In reality, it was Arafat striving to maintain his power base.

The Sharon government responded to the attacks as all Israeli administrations had done, with deliberately disproportionate force. Palestinian leaders were targeted for assassination. The more notable victims were Massud Ayyad, a key figure in Arafat's bodyguard and a supposed member of Hezbollah, the Hamas leader in Nablus, the Secretary General of the PFLP, and the Fatah leader in Bethlehem. When internment and other measures failed to curb the daily attacks, more heavy-handed tactics were used. Helicopter gunships were brought in and in May F16 jets attacked targets in the West Bank. Later, heavy armour was employed and areas recently handed over to the PNA were re-occupied. Such ferocious tactics brought short-term lulls in the fighting, but ultimately only added to the number of martyrs and increased Palestinian determination to maintain the Intifada. It was a truly terrible situation.

9/11

The US administration of President George W. Bush (2001–9), Bill Clinton's Republican replacement, was deeply concerned by the shocking scenes from Israel and Palestine that flashed almost daily across US TV screens. In October 2000, former Senator George Mitchell had been dispatched to the region and asked to produce a report on the causes of the Intifada. He duly did so in April 2001, making sensible recommendations that were ignored by all sides. Sharon, Arafat and the Americans all called for ceasefires – and occasionally the firing actually stopped for a day or so. At one stage, Peres and Arafat met to discuss peace and President Bush attempted to mollify the Palestinians by saying that he could envisage a Palestinian state one day. Then some incident would spark off the violence again and each side would blame the other for the fresh flare-up.

It was against this background that news came through of Al Qaeda's September 11 attacks on New York and Washington (2001). Throughout much of the Middle East the reaction was one of shock and horror, just as it was elsewhere in the world. Yasser Arafat and Ariel Sharon condemned the outrages without reservation. Hamas, on the other hand, refused to comment on a non-Palestinian event. This hardly endeared it to the American people. Some Muslim extremists went so far as to endorse the attacks while others claimed the whole thing had been a put-up job, a massive Jewish conspiracy to get the USA to declare war on all Arabs. Quite a few Palestinian hearts had a sneaking admiration at the way so tiny a band had done such enormous damage to so powerful an enemy. They viewed their struggle against Israel in precisely the same David vs. Goliath terms. On the other side of the fence, there were Israelis who felt almost grateful to Al Qaeda for demonstrating to Americans the kind of threat Israelis had lived under for years. The 9/11 attacks, they hoped, would bring the USA and Israel closer still.

In the end, the Al Qaeda attacks had a double effect on the Israel–Palestine situation. In the short term they did indeed bring the USA and Israel closer together, allies against Islamist extremism. In his 2002 State of the Union Address, for instance, US president George W. Bush included Iran and Iraq – two of Israel's foremost opponents – in a supposed 'Axis of Evil'. Over the longer term, though, the USA came to realize that the Israel–Palestine conflict lay at the very heart of much of the misunderstanding and conflict that dogged the West and the wider Middle East. Solve the Israel–Palestine problem, lance that boil, and the sickness that pervaded the rest of the body might clear up.

Arafat sidelined

THE KILLING GOES ON

The prospects for peace were even gloomier at the end of 2002 than they had been at the beginning. The Intifada, punctuated by ineffective ceasefire announcements, continued to reap its grisly harvest: by the end of July it had claimed the lives of almost 1,800 Palestinians and around 800 Israelis. The ratio of Israeli to Palestinian deaths was much higher than in previous violent episodes, reflecting almost daily attacks in the early part of the year. Notable Palestinian outrages were the slaughter of Israelis at a Bar Mitzvah ceremony in January, the murder by a Hamas suicide bomber of 30 elderly Jews enjoying a seaside Passover feast in March, and Islamic Jihad's killing of 12 settlers in Kiryat Arba in November.

Israeli attacks were no less vengeful. The leader of the Al-Aqsa Martyrs Brigades, which at the time were on ceasefire, was assassinated in January 2002, and in July a Hamas leader, Salah Shahada, was blown to pieces by a huge bomb. The explosion also killed 14 others, nine of whom were children. On a far larger scale were two massive counter-Intifada actions, Operation Defensive Wall launched in the spring and Operation Determined Path in the summer. Both involved entering Palestinian areas in the West Bank with massive force, smashing homes, making hundreds of arrests, imposing curfews, shooting suspicious characters on sight and countless other forms of harsh repression. Talk of a massacre of civilians in Jenin was later disproved, although the IDF did kill dozens of militants when it entered the town.

Two incidents in particular captured the attention of the world's media. One was the siege of wanted *fedayeen* inside Bethlehem's Church of the Nativity. The other was the total destruction – apart from a single office in which Arafat was virtually held prisoner – of the PNA president's compound in Ramallah (April 2002). Later, Israeli forces also risked widening the conflict by attacking positions inside Syria (October 2003), claiming that guerrillas were training there for operations against Israel.

It is not easy for outsiders to understand the actions of either side. As the experiences of World War II and Vietnam had shown, civilian casualties served only to increase a determination to resist, not weaken it. Sharon's 'decapitation' policy might have brought some short-term relief, but Palestinians, like the mythical Hydra, were quite capable of producing new heads to replace those they had lost. For their part, the guerrillas knew that military victory was impossible. All their desperate actions might do was to strengthen the Palestinian position in any future negotiations.

Meanwhile, the inhabitants of the Occupied Territories were suffering terrible hardship – unemployment had risen to 50 per cent of the workforce and the region's GNP had more than halved since 1999. But they could not, as some Israelis wished, react by simply packing their bags en masse and going to live elsewhere. Above all, there wasn't anywhere else.

'COMPROMISED BY TERROR'

Amid all this mayhem, Arafat's reputation had been taking a battering in the international arena from which it never really recovered. The tarnishing began in May 2001, when the IDF captured an arms shipment worth an estimated US$10 million on board the *Santorini*. It was supposedly purchased by the PFLP, and PNA officials were lined up to bring it ashore. This was not good news for Arafat, who steadfastly denied any links between the PNA, which he chaired, and armed action.

Far more incriminating was the seizure in January 2002 of a fresh boatload of rockets, mortars, missiles, rifles, mines, ammunition and explosives aboard the Tonga-registered freighter *Karine A*. According to Lloyds Registry, the vessel was owned by the PNA. The crew, too, were allegedly PNA employees and the vessel's cargo was destined, via a sophisticated concealment device, for Al-Aqsa Martyrs Brigades (believed to have links with the PNA leadership). The Israelis immediately announced that they had concrete evidence that Arafat was doing precisely what he had vehemently denied doing: backing *fedayeen* attacks on Israel. So much for Arafat's much vaunted renunciation of terror, snorted Sharon.

In defence of the president of the PNA, two points are worth making. Firstly, the final destination of the captured weapons could never be guaranteed – of Iranian origin, they might have been destined for Hezbollah in Lebanon or even 'planted' by the Israelis themselves; secondly, the PNA president was not the first politician to be economical with the truth. Since his primary duty was to hold together the Palestinian movement, it would have been political suicide to ignore the growing popularity within his constituency of the 'martyrs' and their tactics.

Insight

Institutional corruption was a major reason why the PNA lost favour among so many Palestinians. A Palestinian parliamentary committee, for instance, discovered that part of Israel's detested 'security barrier' was built using cement provided by the Palestinian Al-Quds company, the family business of sometime PNA Prime Minister Ahmed Qurei!

If the arms seizure was bad for Arafat, the contents of documents confiscated by the Israelis when they overran his compound were worse. Again, we cannot be certain that they were not forgeries or 'plants', although they were sufficiently realistic to convince US officials as well as Israeli. Letters, receipts, accounts and a host of other papers appeared to show not only that Arafat's regime was notoriously corrupt, even by local standards, but that he had directly funded *fedayeen* with money for weapons and bomb-belts. Henceforward, Sharon declared Arafat to be 'irrelevant' to the peace process. President Bush, too, refused to have anything further to do with him, urging the Palestinians to find a new leader 'not compromised by terror'.

THE SECURITY FENCE

Despite gaining some Arab sympathy at the way the Israelis were treating him, Arafat was struggling to hold together any sort of effective policy. Sharon's 'security and true peace' initiative was making slightly more progress. The PNA leadership was increasingly marginalized and, following brutal assassinations and incursions into Palestinian territory, by the spring of 2002 a second string of the unilateral disengagement strategy policy was emerging. This was the 'security wall' to physically separate Israel from the West Bank.

A barrier already existed around Gaza and had proved most effective at reducing armed incursion. A similar barrier around the West Bank, demanded by the popular 'Fence For Life' pressure group established after the 2001 disco bombing, was an altogether different question. It had to be much longer for a start. Although for most of its length it would not be an actual wall but more a Western Front-style barrier of barbed wire, it would send out a dispiritingly negative image. In the popular imagination, walls were associated with repression, with apartheid, with prison and above all with the hated communist regime of East Germany. Moreover, was a 'security fence' (as the Israeli government liked to call it) actually legal? The International Court of Justice eventually ruled (July 2004) that it was not and demanded that it be pulled down. The Sharon government, which had started the barrier's construction in June 2002, ignored the decision but did adjust the wall's path to meet the stipulations of its own Supreme Court.

The route was already a *cause célèbre*. The obvious path was along that of the Green Line dividing Israel from Jordan at the time of the 1949 ceasefire. For obvious reasons, Sharon wished it to encompass as many Israeli settlements as possible, even where these had been built on Palestinian land occupied in the 1967 war. Thus places like East Jerusalem, Ariel, Oranit, and Maale Adumim were to find themselves on the Israeli side of the fence while some Palestinian towns like Marda (accessed only through a lockable gate!) were virtually surrounded by it. Disagreement over the barrier was one of many issues that divided Sharon's Unity government and led to its eventual disintegration at the end of 2002.

THE SAUDI PLAN

Meanwhile, anxious politicians outside Israel and the Palestinian Territories were seeking ways of resolving the debilitating and highly destabilizing conflict. In February 2002, Crown Prince Abdullah of Saudi Arabia – a state painfully caught up in the spate of Islamist terror that was now unsettling large swathes of the globe – proposed that in return for withdrawing to its pre-1967 frontiers, Israel might receive full and friendly recognition from the Arab world and beyond. The idea was warmly welcomed and received official endorsement from the next month's Arab summit.

Sharon rejected the Saudi proposal out of hand but, for the time being, the Bush administration kept its opinion to itself. Eventually it incorporated the Saudi initiative into an idea of its own, the 'Roadmap to Peace'. Essentially, this was not very different from the earlier step-by-step approach. The main difference was that the final goal – a two-state solution – was fixed, as were three precise points along the route towards that goal. The Roadmap was not published until the following year, when an alternative to Arafat had been found within the PNA. The Roadmap was now fully backed by powerful 'Quartet' of powers: the USA, the EU, Russia and the UN. Here, perhaps, was a faint glimmer of hope in an otherwise depressingly dark picture.

The Roadmap

AQABA

After Labour left his government in November 2002, Sharon defeated Netanyahu for the leadership of Likud and called for early elections to resolve the impasse. The election of January the following year returned 40 Likud members to the Knesset and Sharon for another term in the prime ministerial office. His conservative coalition included the far-right National Unity Party.

Heading the Roadmap's quartet of sponsors, the Bush administration insisted that there was no point in holding talks to end the bloodshed unless the Palestinians put forward a spokesperson whom all parties could trust. That was not Yasser Arafat. What the USA and Israel were angling for was the appointment of a Palestinian prime minister, a position which, legally speaking, Arafat should have filled years earlier. He continued to dig his heels in, claiming that outsiders were interfering in Palestine's internal affairs. The charade continued until March 2003, when the pragmatic Mahmoud Abbas (aka Abu Mazen, an old colleague of Arafat's and a long-standing PLO member) was finally chosen as Palestinian prime minister. He duly formed a cabinet.

The following month, shortly after the USA had spearheaded a coalition of countries invading Iraq, the Quartet presented a concrete version of its Roadmap. For talks to begin, its first phase called for the Palestinians to end all violence, confiscate illegally held weapons, and as far as possible return Palestinian social and political life to normal channels. Other Arab states were to stop supporting 'terrorist' groups such as Hamas. Israel was to freeze settlement building and withdraw from those built since September 2000. Two further phases of the plan talked of a conference to establish a sovereign and truly democratic Palestinian state, and yet more talks to tackle unresolved issues like the status of Jerusalem and the right of return for Palestinian refugees. With no mechanism for objective verification and only vague statements about key issues, the chances of the more extreme Palestinian groups accepting such terms were slight.

That is precisely how it turned out. In June 2003, Sharon and Abbas met at a USA-brokered summit in Aqaba – the Quartet was already looking decidedly lop sided – and shook hands under the beaming gaze of George W. Bush. Sharon agreed that he would accept a sovereign Palestine, and Abbas called for the Intifada to be halted. Both men agreed to the outline principles of the Roadmap.

Days later the sweet words disappeared in several puffs of acrid smoke as Islamist and Fatah *fedayeen* slew Israeli soldiers and a failed assassination attempt was made on the Hamas leader Ahmed Rantissi. More suicide attacks and targeted assassinations followed, heralding a return to the murderous atmosphere of tit-for-tat slaughter that had been a feature of the years before the Aqaba summit. In September, as Arafat blocked his attempts to clamp down on the *fedayeen*, Abbas resigned and was replaced by the PLO's financial guru, Ahmed Queia (aka Abu Ala).

DISENGAGEMENT

With Abbas sidelined, Sharon reckoned all immediate hope of compromise with the Palestinians was gone. The time had come, therefore, to implement the next and most controversial phase of his unilateral disengagement strategy. The idea, borrowed from the Labour party, was for Israel to withdraw from Gaza and parts of the West Bank, and get on with its own life as best it could behind impenetrable barriers. To international astonishment and the bemused fury of many of his Likud supporters, in November 2003 Sharon announced that he had decided to adopt such a policy: Israeli unilateral disengagement, starting in Gaza, would begin in six months' time. It was hardly an all-embracing peace plan, but it did at least show that even one of Israel's most fervent patriots had begun to accept that it might not be wise to try to hold on to all the 1967 conquests for ever.

On the other side of the expanding security fence, prime minister Ahmed Queia was enjoying his job as little as Abbas had done. Specifically, he was finding it as difficult as his predecessor to get Arafat to relinquish personal control over the PNA security forces. He even submitted his resignation, like Abbas, only for the PNA chairman to reject the submission by allegedly scribbling a large X across the letter. By July 2004, with Fatah factions in Gaza engaged in open conflict, Arafat needed all the support he could get. Seriously ill, his grip on events was loosening fast.

Israeli security forces remained in the West Bank, exacerbating the day-to-day difficulties of ordinary Palestinians. Sporadic suicide attacks continued, as did the occasional rocket attacks on Israel from Gaza and Lebanon. The IDF carried on responding with disproportionate force. Two targeted killings in particular roused Palestinian ire. In March 2004, helicopter gunships killed Sheikh Yassin, Hamas' founder and spiritual leader. On hearing that the wheelchair-bound paraplegic had been hit as he was leaving a Gaza mosque, a Hamas spokesperson declared that Sharon had 'opened the Gates of Hell'. Many who lived in the region had their doubts: those particular portals, they believed, had been swung back long ago. A month later, Israeli assassins took out Abdulaziz al-Rantissi, the head of Hamas in Gaza. That left only one of the original founders of Hamas still alive.

Despite unilateral disengagement winning the approval of President Bush in April, the following month Likud rejected the plan and left Sharon at the head of a minority government. The confusion extended to the Palestinians, too. There were those who saw Sharon's announcement as a welcome concession and a reason to resume settlement talks; others regarded it as proof that the bombing campaign was producing results and, consequently, a justification for continuing it. These different opinions exacerbated Palestinian inter-communal violence, especially in Gaza, between different factions of Fatah and between Islamists and others. At the same time, the firing of numerous home-made Qassam rockets into Israel provoked several massive and bloody Israeli incursions into the territory it was planning to leave.

EXIT ARAFAT

The final months of the year were dominated by the death of Yasser Arafat. Virtually imprisoned by the Israelis within his Ramallah compound for the better part of two-and-a-half years, his health had gradually declined. Finally, his French wife insisted he be flown to Paris for treatment for a mysterious blood disorder. There, on 11 November, he died of multiple organ failure following a massive stroke. For security reasons, the funeral was held in Cairo. Heads of state from all over the world attended, although an official Israeli representative was notably absent. To this day, many Palestinians maintain that their leader had been poisoned.

Arafat's body was flown back to Ramallah for burial, Sharon having vetoed internment within Jerusalem's Al-Aqsa mosque. The decision probably saved a great deal of bloodshed, for the funeral was hijacked by a gun-firing mob. The hysterical screaming, shouting and wailing of the mourners temporarily obscured the dislike that many Palestinians had developed for their president during his final years, allowing the old warrior to be buried as he had lived, in passionate disorder.

Almost everything written about Arafat after his death contained a degree of truth. He was unmistakeably charismatic, remarkably brave, inspiring, devoted and determined. Furthermore, he was a good, probably great guerrilla leader, a powerful orator with a strong sense of humour, and he understood his people and their cause better than anyone. Yet he was neither a diplomat nor an administrator. Rather, he was disorganized, autocratic, corrupt, tactless, unsophisticated and cursed with a furious temper. He did more than anyone to create the modern Palestinian nation and force the world to recognize it. Yet in the end it was his failings as a president that did as much as anything to prevent his people from securing their own homeland.

In depth: the Al-Aqsa Martyrs Brigades

As their name suggests, the Al-Aqsa Martyrs Brigades emerged shortly after the beginning of the Second, or Al-Aqsa, Intifada. Their provenance is somewhat obscure. The Israelis and Americans explain the Brigades' formation as an attempt by President Yasser Arafat to stop the Islamists' monopolizing violent anti-Israeli activity. Yet he had officially renounced violence and his own organization, Fatah, was supposed to adhere to this policy.

Although there is evidence showing PNA funds finding their way into the Brigades' pockets, Arafat denied all links between the two organizations. At one stage, Fatah Prime Minister Ahmed Queia openly contradicted this by admitting that the Brigades were Fatah's armed wing. However, such remarks may have been made for political purposes and offer only circumstantial evidence. In 2002, the Israelis arrested the Brigades' Chief Executive, Marwhan Barghouti, and sentenced him to life imprisonment for multiple murders. Although Barghouti was also a Fatah member, this did not necessarily mean the two organizations worked together. Similar implications, but no proof, may be drawn from the fact that after Arafat's death the Brigades announced a change of name to the 'Brigades of Shahad Yasser Arafat'.

The Brigades were not a specifically Islamist group, but regarded Islam as a useful tool in the war with Israel. Their suicide attacks, therefore, were not religiously motivated. This secular attitude did not rule out joint operations with Muslim extremists such as Hamas and even, on occasion, Hezbollah. When President Mahmoud Ahmadinejad of Iran reportedly said he wished Israel to be 'wiped off the map' in a Holy War, the Brigades supported his Islamist outburst. Moreover, in 2006, bandits claiming to be Brigade members attacked the Gaza offices of the EU and demanded apologies from Denmark and Norway for the publication of cartoons mocking the Prophet Mohammed.

The Brigades, which also built up a feared section of female recruits, were accused of, or claim responsibility for, numerous *fedayeen* activities against both Israelis and Palestinian opponents. These reached a peak in 2004 (36 attacks) but declined markedly thereafter. The group expressed fury at the way it was portrayed in the film *Brüno*, when Sacha Baron Cohen interviewed Ayman Abu Aita, a supposed Brigades' leader.

In depth: Mahmoud Abbas (aka Abu Mazen, 1935–)

Along with many other leaders of the Palestinian movement, Mahmoud Abbas came from a family that the Israelis had forced into exile in 1948. The legacy of bitterness thus created turned the young Abbas into an angry militant. Age and experience quickly mellowed him, and by the twenty-first century he was regarded in Israel and the West as the acceptable face of the Palestinian leadership.

Born in the British mandate of Palestine, Abbas spent his formative years in Syria before completing his education in Egypt and Moscow. He then worked in the Gulf and became heavily involved in Palestinian politics, joining Fatah and rising to become a key member of the PLO under Yasser Arafat. By now a pragmatic academic, he appeared always willing to try a negotiated rather than a military settlement of the Israeli–Palestinian conflict and he maintained links with left-wing Israelis during the darkest years of impasse.

Abbas kept himself in the background, perhaps deliberately, yet played an important role in the Oslo peace process and in mending fences between the PLO and the Arab states that had joined the anti-Iraqi coalition in 1990–1. He finally emerged from the shadows in 2003, when the aging and discredited President Arafat gave him the post of Palestinian prime minister. The appointment was a disaster, as Abbas found himself in almost continual conflict with Arafat on one side and the militant Islamists of Hamas and Islamic Jihad on the other. He quickly resigned his post.

Abbas' second chance came in January 2005 when, following Arafat's death, he was elected president of the PNA. He ran up against the Islamists again when he tried to set up further peace negotiations with Israel. His presidency ran into yet more difficulties when Hamas won a majority of seats in the Palestinian Assembly in January 2006, open fighting escalated between his PNA security forces and militant extremists, and Israel launched all-out attacks on Hezbollah in Lebanon and on Gaza. By late 2009, Abbas was ruling by presidential decree, although his writ ran in parts of the West Bank only. Having failed in nearly all his objectives, he declared several times that his presidency would end with the 2010 Palestinian elections.

10 THINGS TO REMEMBER

1 *Military man turned politician, Ehud Barak became prime minister of Israel in 1999, promising a swift peace deal.*

2 *In the second half of 2001, US President Bill Clinton came close to brokering a deal between Israel and the Palestinians.*

3 *Palestinian discontent flared into the Second Intifada, which was soon dominated by militant fedayeen groups.*

4 *Lasting from 2000 to at least the end of 2004, the Second Intifada was marked by bombings, rocket attacks and gunfire, which drew persistent and deliberately disproportionate Israeli reprisals.*

5 *Prime Minister Ariel Sharon, the darling of the Israeli right, replaced the hope of peace by negotiation with a policy of unilateral disengagement.*

6 *The 9/11 attacks on New York and the USA's subsequent 'Axis of Evil' declaration re-focused the world's attention on the Israel–Palestine impasse.*

7 *As the Palestinian movement fragmented and disillusionment with the Palestinian National Authority grew, Yasser Arafat's reputation and power declined.*

8 *Israel began construction of a highly controversial (and probably illegal) 'security fence' between its own people and the Palestinians of the West Bank.*

9 *A Quartet of powers – the USA, the EU, Russia and the UN – put together a new step-by-step plan, known as the Roadmap, for solving the Israeli–Palestinian problem.*

10 *Yasser Arafat, the dominant figure in Palestinian politics for over 40 years, died in November 2004.*

14

Fresh hopes, old problems 2005 to 2010

In this chapter you will learn about:

- ***the air of optimism that followed Arafat's death***
- ***the plunge into bloodshed and despair, 2006–7***
- ***Palestinian divisions and the Annapolis talks***
- ***where the Israel–Palestine impasse stood at the beginning of 2010.***

After Arafat

As the Arab world mourned the death of one of its most charismatic leaders, in the USA, among the more liberal sectors of Israeli society, and perhaps even among moderate Palestinians, the mood was less distraught. With the intransigent and supposedly unreliable Arafat out of the way, they hoped that wise international mediation would enable Palestinians and Israelis finally to work out some form of settlement to their long-running disputes.

It was not to be. In fact, contrary to expectation, the passing of Arafat introduced an even more bitter and complex dimension to the Israel–Palestine problem. For all his faults, the Chairman of the Palestinian Authority had been a figure of international renown who provided a focus for his people's cause. Palestinian fragmentation had begun long before his demise, but once he was gone the last semblance of unity quickly dissolved. Within a year, would-be peacemakers found themselves trying to bring together not two irreconcilable parties but three. The search for peace was now immensely more difficult.

SHARM EL SHEIKH

After a period in which Mahmoud Abbas and Prime Minister Ahmed Qurei shared Arafat's powers between them, in early January 2006 Abbas was elected President of the Palestinian National Authority with 61 per cent of the votes cast. Given the militants' boycott of the election and the difficulties created by Israeli occupation, the respectable 60 per cent turn out gave the new president a healthy mandate to pursue such policies as he thought fit. Meanwhile, on the other side of the security fence, Sharon was remodelling his administration by forming a National Unity Government that included representatives of Likud, Labour and the left-wing Zionist party Meimad.

Insight

Critics of President Mahmoud Abbas say that he lacks the charisma and steely personality necessary to hold his people together and lead them towards nationhood.

Heartened by Abbas' efforts to discourage Palestinian violence towards Israel, in February the Israeli Prime Minister travelled to the Egyptian resort of Sharm El Sheikh to meet with the new Palestinian leader, President Mubarak of Egypt and Jordan's King Abdullah II. The aim of the conference was officially to end the Second Intifada and to get Israeli–Palestinian negotiations back on the track laid out in the Roadmap (see pp. 250–2).

The first important talks of the post-Arafat era were encouragingly cordial. The Intifada was declared over, ceasefires and prisoner exchanges announced, and Israel said it would leave the Palestinian towns it had re-occupied. Islamic Jihad was quick to puncture the bonhomie with a suicide bombing in Tel Aviv, causing Sharon to postpone the promised withdrawals. Nevertheless, as the attack had been condemned by Abbas, both the Knesset and the Israeli cabinet formally endorsed Sharon's disengagement strategy of quitting all 21 Israeli settlements in Gaza together with four in the West Bank.

Picking up on the new mood, militant Palestinian groups meeting in Cairo agreed a *tahediyeh* (a 'slowing down', commonly interpreted as a ceasefire), resulting in a suspension of violent attacks on Israel for a while. Israel responded by pulling out of Jericho. Optimism remained high as the Palestinian President flew to Washington for a significant meeting with President Bush, at which he received a promise of $50 million in aid for the Palestinians if the lull in violence became permanent.

The next step was a meeting between Abbas, Sharon and US Secretary of State Condoleezza Rice. High though hopes were, it came to nothing. Sharon, increasingly under attack from his own right wing, was worried by falling popularity, and Abbas felt threatened by the growing popularity of the uncompromising Hamas and its militant supporters. Under such conditions, despite Rice's best blandishments, neither side was secure enough to yield anything significant. Like so many others, the summit produced little but platitudes.

OUT OF GAZA

The *tahediyeh* collapsed within a few weeks of the summit's closure when five Israelis fell victim to an Islamic Jihad suicide bomber. Thereafter, things swiftly unravelled. The Israelis resumed the targeted killing of *fedayeen* leaders and reoccupied Palestinian areas, like Tulkam on the West Bank. Hamas launched massive rocket attacks on Israeli towns from across the Gaza border. Still more worryingly, over the summer and into the autumn of 2005 the Fatah–Hamas rivalry began to break into open, armed conflict.

Nothing daunted, Sharon retained the support of the IDF and so was able to press on with the Gaza withdrawal. There was inevitable Israeli opposition, some of it violent, but in general it was less aggressive than had been feared. The last Israeli soldier left Gaza on 11 September. The retiring power gained further international sympathy when the Palestinians trashed greenhouses on ex-settlement territory that American Jews had donated as a gesture of goodwill. Sharon cashed in on this sentiment when, on a visit to the UN, he spoke of his desire for peace and the need for Palestinian rights to be recognized.

At the time much was made of Israel forcibly closing down its own settlements and handing back land it had captured – and it certainly was an important gesture. But it was part of a plan for unilateral disengagement and never more than one small step on a very, very long and difficult road. The Palestinians still had no state; the West Bank remained largely in Israeli hands and was being further settled, divided and isolated; the Palestinians had no right of return to the lands from which they had been driven in 1948–9; two peoples still demanded Jerusalem as their capital... beside all that, the Gaza issue was very small beer indeed.

EXIT SHARON

The autumn of 2005 saw the Fatah–Hamas divide widen still further. Tensions mounted when 20 Gazans died after a car carrying Qassam rockets intended for Israel exploded accidentally during a Hamas parade, and when Hamas outperformed Fatah in PNA local elections. By the end of the year, the two major Palestinian factions were in barely disguised conflict.

While Palestinian divisions may have played into Sharon's hands, ongoing rocket attacks into Israeli territory from Gaza only fanned criticism from those who believed withdrawal from the strip to have been a mistake. The IDF responded to attacks with customary ferocity, thereby making further attacks more likely. By the end of the year, Israelis were accusing the Europeans monitoring the newly opened Rafah crossing between Gaza and Egypt of being less than meticulous in their efforts to prevent Hamas smuggling in munitions.

Amid the growing uncertainty and division, in November 2005 Sharon's coalition administration broke up. With his own party, Likud, decidedly agitated about the unilateral disengagement policy, Sharon made a dramatic but not unheralded move: he left Likud to found a new liberal, centrist political party, Kadima ('Forward' or 'Onward'). A number of leading Israeli politicians, including ex-Mayor of Jerusalem Ehud Olmert, Minister of Justice Tzipi Livni and the Labour leader Shimon Perez, swung in behind a party that made peace with the Palestinians a key plank in its platform.

Many have wondered at this apparent change of tack by Ariel Sharon, the man who had built his 'bulldog' reputation as the scourge of all Palestinians. To this day, there are those who say his conversion to more pacific policies was mere rhetoric. Others explain his new willingness to compromise as prompted by advancing age and a wish to be remembered as the statesman who finally brought the Israeli–Palestinian conflict to an end. There were other, more pragmatic reasons for the change. The Second Intifada had cost at least 4,000 lives, almost one quarter of them Israeli. The country's unemployment rate had risen above ten per cent and it was reported that over 30 per cent of its citizens lived in relative poverty.

Israel was under increasing pressure from Washington, too. By the twenty-first century, the USA was propping up its prime Middle East ally at a total annual cost – adding together aid, loan guarantees and military assistance – of around $3 billion. Moreover, as it slipped deeper and deeper into the Iraqi quagmire, the Bush administration urgently needed all the moral and political support it could muster from Arab governments. The price of their assistance on the Iraqi front was progress on the Palestinian front. To this end, in late 2005 the USA gave Israel a massive $600 million aid package for 'joint defence projects' – but in return it wanted an improvement in its relations with the Palestinians.

At this point, as invariably happens in this tragic impasse, fate intervened to wreck the best-laid plans. On 4 January 2006, Ariel Sharon suffered the first of two massive strokes that left him totally incapacitated. Three weeks later, on 26 January, Hamas gained control over the Palestinian National Assembly, winning 74 seats out of 133. Democracy had spoken: the Palestinian people, tired of Fatah's corruption and failure to produce a Palestinian state, had elected a party pledged to pursue its people's cause with fresh vigour and resolve. To Hamas, surrender of one square millimetre of territory held by the Palestinians at the time of the 1949 armistice was out of the question. Officially, they did not even recognize Israeli's existence.

What would happen next?

Descent into chaos

Sharon's illness and the electoral success of Hamas ended conclusively the brief year of optimism that had been triggered by the death of Yasser Arafat. There followed years of bitter and bloody suffering in which Palestinian divisions widened and Israeli responses to Islamist attacks remained as ferocious as ever. The most tragic development was the deterioration of conditions in the tiny, overpopulated Gaza Strip until it came close to resembling hell on Earth.

FATAH AND HAMAS

As Hamas refused to recognize Israel, so Israel refused to recognize the new Hamas-based Palestinian government formed at the end of March with Ismail Haniya as its prime minister. Its hard-line stance meant further serious difficulties for ordinary Palestinians. Israel suspended various revenues it had been paying, such as tax repayments, and the USA, the EU and other Western and Arab governments stopped their flow of aid. As there was no way the Palestinian National Authority could operate without external funding, it was prevented from total collapse only with money smuggled in from Iran and Russia. Later, some EU funds were also allowed in via NGO organizations, bypassing corrupt PNA officials. Even so, a sizeable proportion of these payments disappeared en route, leaving the plight of the ordinary Palestinians, especially the Gazans, especially parlous.

Relations between the Hamas government and President Mahmoud Abbas remained at best tense. As Fatah still controlled the PNA's security apparatus through its President, Hamas set up an 'Executive Force' of its own. This operated apart from the clandestine Izz ad-Din al-Qassam Brigades, Hamas' military wing. Fatah responded by turning a blind eye to armed groups loyal to itself. As spring turned to summer, conflict between Fatah and the Islamists – primarily Hamas and Islamic Jihad – frequently flared into open violence marked by kidnappings, shoot-outs and assassinations. Such events were almost endemic in Gaza, where the Fatah position became weaker by the month. They were helpless, for instance, to prevent the constant firing of Qassam rockets from Gaza into Israel (about 1,000 in the first half of 2006).

Insight

The Islamist Izz ad-Din al-Qassam Brigades and the Qassam rockets fired into Israel from Gaza are both named after Sunni preacher Izz ad-Din al-Qassam who in 1930, at the time of the British mandate in Palestine, helped found the militant anti-British, anti-Jewish Black Hand movement.

The one glimmer of Palestinian hope came from a letter of reconciliation produced by Fatah and Hamas prisoners held in Israeli gaols. It purported to show that both the major Palestinian factions were united in their aims. The Palestinian Prisoners' National Conciliation Document appeared to recognize Israel and placed the responsibility for the creation of a Palestinian state based on the West Bank and Gaza in the hands of President Abbas. However, as the document failed to meet the criteria of the Roadmap, it attracted little international support.

OLMERT AND OPERATION SUMMER RAINS

After Sharon's incapacitation, leadership of the new Kadima party passed to his deputy, Ehud Olmert. With an election looming,

Olmert put more flesh on the bones of Kadima's unilateral disengagement policy. The route of the security barrier remained highly controversial, especially when it became clear that the proposed withdrawal from the West Bank was not quite as radical as had been expected. The Israelis would maintain a presence in Hebron, for religious reasons, and in the Jordan Valley, for security reasons. Elsewhere, the major settlements of Gush Etzion, Ariel, Kedumim and Maale Adumim (see Figure 11.1 on p. 203) would also be part of the new, definitive Israel. 'The facts on the ground' policy had become a reality: there were now some 400,000 Israelis living in settlements in occupied West Bank.

Olmert reckoned the new frontiers would be ready by 2010. Since the total area of Gaza and the West Bank, without Israeli depredations, was only 22 per cent of the Palestinian state envisaged by the UN in 1948, the Palestinian reaction to the Kadima plan was not hard to anticipate. Nevertheless, it won favour with the Israeli electorate and after elections in March 2006 Olmert remained in power at the head of a Kadima-led coalition. The fact that Kadima won only 29 seats, Labour 19, and Likud and Shas (ultra-orthodox Sephardim) 12 illustrated the growing fragmentation of Israeli society and politics. The low turnout – only 63 per cent – was a worrying sign of disenchantment.

From the start, the Olmert government enjoyed reasonable relations with President Abbas. The opposite was true with Hamas, now the dominant force in the Gaza Strip, and by June 2006, Olmert felt himself pressured to do something about the ceaseless bombardment of Israeli territory by Qassam rockets. Each launch was supposedly earning a US$1,000 reward from Hezbollah. So, after an Israeli soldier was kidnapped during a raid of *fedayeen* tunnelling out of Gaza, the IDF launched a full-scale incursion into the territory. Operation Summer Rains turned into a large-scale conventional war in which the principal sufferers were, inevitably, Palestinian civilians. When the IDF eventually withdrew, they had neither recaptured their colleague nor stopped the summer rain of rockets.

THE SUMMER WAR

Israel's northern frontier had never been exactly peaceful after the IDF's withdrawal from southern Lebanon in 2000. Nevertheless, the occasional cross-border firing of artillery and rockets had been well under control – almost token warfare – when in the summer of 2006 the rules suddenly changed.

For years, backed largely by Iran, the Shia militants of Hezbollah had been building up their forces in southern Lebanon, especially stockpiles of rockets and anti-tank weapons. In June 2006, the group stepped up this cross-border provocation. This may have been prompted by the Iranians as a way of diverting attention away from the row it was having with the UN over its nuclear programme. Be that as it may, when Hezbollah raided Israel on 12 July, killing three soldiers and capturing two more, the Olmert government responded precisely as the Islamists had wanted. Its campaign began with air and artillery strikes against supposed Hezbollah targets deep within Lebanon.

The guerrillas, clearly ready for such action and carefully hidden within areas of high-density civilian population, stepped up their rocket attacks. The cities of Haifa, Tiberias and Safed were hit and 40 civilians were killed. At sea, an Iranian-made C-802 missile hit and damaged an Israeli cruiser off the Lebanese coast. On land, the IDF launched a full-scale ground invasion. Hezbollah proved better equipped, prepared and organized than the Israelis had expected. For the first time, the IDF was not able to sweep all before it at almost no cost. Men were killed, tanks and other heavy armour destroyed, and pockets of Hezbollah resistance proved hard to subdue. Equally serious for Israel, it lost the PR war. TV coverage showing Lebanese civilian casualties and destruction of essential facilities such as roads, bridges and power-plants did not play well to audiences around the world, especially after Olmert had declared that his intention was to 'set Lebanon back 20 years'. Once again, Israel appeared the bully.

Insight

For almost the first time in a major Israeli–Arab conflict, after the 2006 summer war against Hezbollah in Lebanon, Israelis felt obliged to respect their enemies. Opinion polls showed that 74 per cent credited Hezbollah with being able warriors. (Colin Schindler, *A History of Modern Israel*, CUP, 2008, p. 347)

A UN ceasefire eventually came into effect in mid-August. By then some 1,000 Lebanese had been killed, a proportion of whom were Islamist guerrillas. The Israelis lost 120. Hundreds of thousands of Lebanese had been made homeless, the country's economic recovery had been thrown into reverse, the captured Israeli soldiers had not been returned and Hezbollah had not been destroyed. On this evidence, its leadership proudly announced that it had won a notable victory against the oppressor. The entire Arab world rejoiced with them. Over the coming months, Hezbollah used its new-found popularity to press for the dissolution of Lebanon's moderately pro-Western government.

Within Israel, the Olmert government came in for massive criticism from both left and right for its handling of the campaign. Abroad, Israel was blamed for escalating the conflict unnecessarily, for using vastly disproportionate force, for causing unwarranted civilian casualties and for using inhumane weapons such as cluster bombs. In April 2007, the prime minister's reputation was dealt a further serious blow when a report into the Lebanese war singled him out for stinging personal criticism. His alleged mishandling of the war was also condemned from within his own cabinet, and mass rallies were held demanding his resignation and early elections. His position was not helped by persistent charges of corruption against him.

Olmert attempted to restore his battered image by trying to further the peace process. He began by suggesting that the Saudi peace deal, first put forward in 2002 (see p. 250), might be a useful basis for Israeli–Palestinian negotiations. At the end of 2006, he held a summit with Abbas, as much to boost the hard-pressed president's position in Palestinian circles as to further the peace process. The early months of

2007 saw a meeting with Egypt's President Mubarak and a tripartite summit between US Secretary of State Condoleezza Rice, Prime Minister Olmert and President Abbas. However, with neither the USA nor Israel willing to include Hamas, which they regarded as a terrorist organization, in the equation, no substantive progress was made.

THE HAMAS COUP

By the spring of 2007, the humanitarian situation in Palestinian areas had reached crisis point. Things were especially bad in Gaza. Israeli air raids – 270 in the previous year – had destroyed the main power station and killed hundreds. According to the UN, enemy damage, the collapse of the economy caused by the severance of aid, and anarchy among the Palestinian security forces had driven about 80 per cent of the population into poverty. The situation in parts of the West Bank was almost as dire. Commentators talked anxiously of the possibility of a Palestinian civil war.

In the meantime, under huge pressure during talks in Mecca, the PNA had reorganized its Hamas-based administration by taking in moderates to form a shaky 'Unity Government'. It survived just five months. In June, Hamas staged a haphazard, bloody but ultimately successful coup against Fatah in Gaza (the 'Battle of Gaza'), seizing control of the territory and dismissing the European observers monitoring the Rafah crossing that linked it with Egypt. Also into Hamas' hands came thousands of weapons of all kinds with which the USA and others had armed the PNA for its struggle against the Islamists. Power in Gaza was now in the hands of various local leaders, such as the heads of the Izz ad-Din al-Qassam Brigades, Islamic Jihad and Popular Resistance Committees, and the Hamas leadership in exile in Damascus. Among the latter, Khalid Mashal was reportedly pre-eminent.

From this point onwards, there were in effect two Palestinian governments, both claiming legitimacy. Abbas dismissed the Unity Government and appointed a new prime minister, the moderate, US-educated economist Salam Fayyad. As the previous incumbent, Ismail Haniya, insisted he was still in office, the PNA now had two prime ministers! Israel, the Quartet (see page 250) and other influential states recognized only the Abbas administration and imposed swinging sanctions on the Gaza regime. In return, the hail of rockets falling on Israel intensified. It would be difficult to imagine a more complex, intractable or tragic situation than now existed in the land revered by millions as holy.

ANNAPOLIS, 2007–8

Two events marked the late summer of 2007. The first was a mysterious air raid on an installation in eastern Syria. Although a clear violation of Syrian air space and sovereignty, the attack, codenamed Operation Orchard, attracted remarkably little international condemnation. Even the Iranians made no official comment. This silence has been interpreted as implicit approval.

Quite what was done, however, is unclear. Evidence seems to suggest that Syria was building some sort of nuclear facility with the help of North Korea, and it was this that the Israeli jets targeted on the night of 6 September. The USA later released 'before and after' pictures showing a large rectangular building and a similar shaped burned out crater. The International Atomic Energy Authority has since found small traces of uranium at the site, although the Syrian government claims it had housed no more than a stockpile of conventional rockets.

In the autumn, Abbas declared that as the Palestinian Legislative Assembly was unable to function, he was taking it upon himself to change the electoral law to one of full proportional representation. Hamas condemned the move, saying it was merely a way of ensuring more seats in the Assembly for Fatah. The President's argument was that the change would make the Assembly more representative of the people and opinion polls suggested that this was also the belief of the majority of Palestinians.

BACK TO THE ROADMAP

Undaunted by the earlier lack of progress, Olmert, Rice and Abbas had continued to meet and discuss ways of moving the peace process forward. Their efforts culminated in yet another peace conference, this one held in the USA Naval Academy in Annapolis, Maryland in November 2007. President Bush attended, along with representatives from the other countries of the Quartet, Arab states and others.

No great things were expected from Annapolis and it produced no dramatic twist in the long saga of Israeli–Palestinian relations. On the other hand, it did return attention to the Roadmap by setting out a very specific agenda for future progress. It was, moreover, the first conference in which both sides agreed beforehand that the eventual outcome of negotiation was to be a two-state solution based upon the 1949 armistice position, with a Palestinian state comprising the West Bank and Gaza. Abbas outlined the six areas for discussion: borders between the two states, Jerusalem, refugees and the 'right of return', Israeli settlements in the West Bank, an equitable distribution of water resources, and security.

Olmert was prepared to concede that a peace deal had to include the returning of part of Jerusalem to Palestinian hands as their capital city. Such statements were anathema to Jewish activists, who condemned what they saw as a cowardly retreat on the part of their prime minister. On the other side, Hamas and the Iranians were equally vociferous in their criticism of the conference. Nevertheless, such hostility was probably to be expected and when the conference broke up delegates left with a fairly clear idea of where they wanted to go and how they might get there. News was also seeping out of helpful Turkish mediation in discussions over an Israeli–Syrian land for peace deal in relation to the Golan Heights.

Was there really a hint of the sun rising over the horizon?

TRUCE

Whatever talks might be going on in comfortable salons, back on the ground the bitter round of attack and counter-attack persisted. Islamist rockets fell on Israel, the IDF countered with blockades, jets, gunships and assassinations. When, in January 2008, Israel cut Gaza's fuel supplies, Hamas responded by blowing up the Rafah crossing. Within hours, thousands of Gazans were pouring into Egypt to get as many supplies – including live animals – as they could manage. Egypt eventually resealed the border again. When more rockets fell, some no doubt assembled from parts brought in through the shattered Rafah portal, more than 100 Gazans, not all *fedayeen*, died in Israeli reprisals.

Insight

While Israel is held largely responsible for the Gazans' suffering, Egypt too plays its part in keeping the territory isolated. Towards the end of 2009, it was reported to be strengthening its defences at the Rafah crossing by building a steel wall beneath the ground in order to stop tunnelling.

Then, in June 2008, a lull came. Hamas announced an Egypt-brokered *tahadiya* and the storm of rockets slowed to a shower. Hamas explained this as coming from groups beyond their control. A prisoner swap deal was arranged and the blockade of Gaza lifted for a while. It is not certain why the ceasefire was agreed but Egyptian pressure no doubt played its part. As its border with Israel was sealed and its coastline subject to constant Israeli surveillance, Gaza's only reliable access point was the famed Rafah crossing, which Egypt controlled – a hand, so to speak, on Gaza's throat.

While it continued to pursue the 'facts on the ground' policy in the occupied territories by allowing 1,300 new housing units in East Jerusalem, the Olmert government played on the Fatah–Hamas division by allowing Fatah supporters to flee into Israel from Gaza and by supplying the PNA with small arms. Nevertheless, by September 2008 the hostility towards Olmert from all sides had grown so great that he said he would not renew his premiership, and his foreign minister, Tzipi Livni, was elected to replace him at the head of Kadima. When she was unable to form a coalition, Olmert remained in office until a general election could be held in February 2009.

The year ended almost as it had begun, with a note of optimism in the air. In France, President Sarkozy was keen to use his country's traditional links with Syria to help move forward the peace process. November saw the election of another would-be peacemaker, Barak Obama, to the White House. A November meeting of the Quartet in Sharm el-Sheikh reiterated the Annapolis aims and objectives.

All this while, the attacks on Israel that had declined so dramatically in the summer had been gradually escalating. Between 4 November and 18 December 2008, some 340 explosive devices of one sort or another fell on Israeli soil. The Islamist ordnance now included Russian-made Grad or 'Katyusha' rockets, too. So when Hamas announced that the *tahadiya* would end on 19 December, Olmert, Livni and the rest of the Israeli cabinet had a crucial decision to make: try reasoning with Hamas in search of a compromise, or do what many in the Israeli media had been demanding for some time – smash the Islamists of Gaza once and for all.

The shattered picture

2009 dawned just as 1949 had done, with the disputed territory of Israel–Palestine torn asunder by the sights and the sounds of warfare. This time, though, the conflict was limited to just one area, the wretched Gaza Strip. Inevitably, Israel won the battle, just has it had done 60 years before. But it was no closer to winning the war and bringing peace to the land that both sides cherished so dearly. Indeed, by the twenty-first century a considerable number of Israelis and Palestinians believed they were caught up in a struggle that would never end.

Such pessimism was not unfounded. In many ways, the problem was much harder to solve in 2009 than it had been in 1949. After the mass immigration of less liberally inclined Sephardim, Israel was a more divided society. Its slow but steady expansion into East Jerusalem and the West Bank – facts on the ground – made a viable two-state solution all the more difficult. Withdrawing close on half a million settlers from occupied territory to the west of the Green Line – the minimum that a Palestinian leader could expect in a settlement – was becoming harder to envisage by the day, let alone execute.

Palestinian divisions were probably deeper than those of the Israelis. What had begun as a nationalist movement was now also a religious one backed by radical Islamists in Iran and the hard-headed realpolitik of Syria. With Fatah and Hamas both claiming to represent their people, the Palestinian negotiating position was weaker than it had ever been. This did not rule out the possibility of a deal of sorts. But the chances of it appealing to all parties in Israel and the Palestinian territories, and therefore of enduring, were extremely remote.

THE GAZA WAR

Eight days after the ending of Hamas' *tahadiya*, the IDF launched an all-out assault on Gaza's estimated 20,000 armed Palestinians. Operation Cast Lead, named after a song, began with continuous air attacks and was followed up with ground operations involving tanks as well as other armoured vehicles, artillery and infantry. Totally outgunned, Hamas stepped up its rocket attacks into Israel and resisted the IDF as best it could in bitter street fighting.

Around 400 Palestinians had been killed by the end of the year and when the IDF withdrew 18 days later this number had risen by perhaps another thousand. Hamas claimed that 700 civilians, including 400 children, had been slaughtered. The Israelis said overall Palestinian losses were considerably fewer but admitted to having killed around 725 Hamas fighters. Their own losses were just 13, 10 soldiers and 3 civilians. The UN's Goldstone Report of September 2009, which found both sides guilty of war crimes, led to little action by either party. Two Israeli officers were disciplined over the illegal use of deadly white phosphorous in civilian areas.

And what was the result? In some ways the Israelis got what they had wanted, as Hamas called a halt to cross-border attacks. Perhaps, too, the civilian population of Gaza was so battered and starved that it was more prepared to accept a compromise peace than had been the case hitherto. Aljazeera's claim that Hamas never won more than about 20 per cent support in opinion polls could bear this out. As in the past, though, Israel had lost the propaganda war, as the world's media was flooded with graphic images and reports of smashed schools, shelled mosques and bleeding, weeping Gazan children. In contrast, Israel's argument that the misery was self-inflicted because Hamas placed its fighters among the civilian population cut little ice – it did not make good TV pictures.

By the beginning of 2010, little had changed. Gaza's 1.4 million inhabitants, of whom over a million were registered refugees, were sealed into a bleak strip of poverty and hardship. The Israeli blockade remained, the Rafah crossing was less permeable than ever, Gaza's unfinished port was a ruin, its airport a wreck, its roads deplorable, its houses damaged, its people malnourished and its government – such as it was – desperate.

ABBAS AND NETANYAHU

By 2009, President Abbas' term of office had officially ended. He did not stand down, however, and no election was held. After much wrangling between the parties concerned, it was declared that elections for the National Assembly and presidency would be held simultaneously in June 2010. Hamas objected and said it would boycott both and punish any Gazans who participated. When asked about his own position, Abbas repeatedly said he would not stand for re-election unless he could make progress towards a two-state peace deal with Israel, and that could happen only if the occupying power ceased its construction of settlements in East Jerusalem and the West Bank.

Insight

With birth rates almost double that of Israel, the populations of Gaza and the West Bank are growing rapidly to the point when there will be more Arabs than Jews living between the Mediterranean and the River Jordan. This demographic possibility is suggested as one reason why Israel may be willing to accept a separate, independent Palestine.

The Israeli elections of February 2009 to the Knesset gave Kadima the most seats (28). This was only one more than Likud, and the Kadima leader, Tzipi Livni, was unable to form a coalition. President Peres turned to Likud leader Benjamin Netanyahu who eventually managed to gather together enough support from both the right-wing bloc and Labour to form a new Government of National Unity.

Once in power, Netanyahu softened slightly his campaign rhetoric over the issue of a deal with the Palestinians. At a meeting with Presidents Obama and Abbas in September 2009, all three parties agreed that talks should begin again as soon as possible. Five months later, the world was still waiting. Netanyahu had announced a freeze on the construction of new settlements but not on the expansion of existing ones, and he had backed a Knesset law of December 2009 that demanded a referendum before any withdrawal from existing settlements could be sanctioned. Several Arab governments, including Syria, condemned the move as just another hurdle on the path to peace.

THE END OF THE TUNNEL

By the start of 2010, plans for peace talks were once again in the air. Nevertheless, Hamas remained beyond the pale, the Israelis appeared unwilling to contemplate a withdrawal from their West Bank settlements, and President Obama was refocusing his political life on domestic issues after his honeymoon period in office had come to a sharp halt. The Roadmap was still on the table, however, and over the previous decade moderates on each side had come closer to a settlement than ever before. There was discussion, too, of Palestinians within the West Bank unilaterally declaring the emergence of an independent Palestinian state.

Some saw these developments as hopeful, others pointed out that Israelis and Palestinians had been there before, dozens of times. Meanwhile, in the streets and markets, in their apartments and huts, at work in their offices and in their fields, it was the ordinary people who continued to suffer...

10 THINGS TO REMEMBER

1 *When Mahmoud Abbas succeeded Yasser Arafat as President of the Palestinian National Authority, there was optimism in some circles that a permanent peace deal between the Israelis and Palestinians might be possible.*

2 *Following a cordial meeting with Abbas at Sharm El Sheikh at the beginning of the year, in the late summer of 2005 Ariel Sharon's policy of unilateral disengagement led to a total Israeli withdrawal from Gaza.*

3 *After forming a new political party, Kadima, early in 2006, Prime Minister Sharon suffered a massive stroke that left him totally disabled in mind and body.*

4 *The outlook for Palestinians became considerably bleaker when divisions between Fatah and the Islamist group Hamas widened into open conflict.*

5 *In the summer of 2006, the Israeli Defence Force caused widespread damage and loss of life when it launched a massive attack on Hezbollah fighters and positions in Lebanon.*

6 *In 2007, Hamas seized power from Fatah in Gaza, effectively dividing the Palestinian administration in two.*

7 *Led by the USA, the Quartet of powers (USA, EU, Russia and UN) reinstated their Roadmap peace policy with an encouraging Israeli–Palestinian summit at Annapolis, Maryland in November 2007.*

8 *Ehud Olmert, Sharon's successor at the head of Kadima, was forced to step down on account of charges of corruption.*

9 *Early in 2009, the IDF sought to end the threat from rocket and mortar attacks by launching an all-out assault on Gaza. This Gaza War led to around 1,400 deaths and charges of war crimes against both sides.*

10 *In 2009, Likud leader Benjamin Netanyahu returned as Israel's prime minister at the head of a Government of National Unity.*

Glossary

Al-Aqsa Mosque Large mosque on Jerusalem's Temple Mount.

Al-Aqsa Martyrs Brigades Extremist offshoot of Fatah (see pp. 254–5).

Al Qaeda Extremist Islamist organization dedicated to *Jihad* against Israel and the West.

Arab One who speaks Arabic.

Arab League Organization of Arab states formed to promote cultural, economic and (later) political co-operation.

Arab Legion British-trained (Trans)Jordanian army.

Ashkenazim Jews of European origin (specifically from Poland and Germany).

Assifa Fatah battle group.

Balfour Declaration British declaration of support for the establishment of a Jewish homeland in Palestine (1917).

Byzantium Early name of the city that is now Istanbul; also early medieval empire of that name.

Caliphate Empire comprising the entire Muslim world.

Camp David Shorthand for the peace talks and agreement between Israel and Egypt of 1978.

Crusades Wars fought by Christian warriors attempting to wrest the holy places of the Middle East from Muslim hands.

DFLP Democratic Front for the Liberation of Palestine (see p. 137).

diaspora The dispersion of a people across the globe (see p. 151).

Druze Religious offshoot of Islam with separate leaders and emphases.

East Jerusalem Area of the city occupied by Jordanian forces in the 1948–9 war, then captured by Israel in 1967.

Fatah Palestinian nationalist organization with political and guerrilla wings (see pp. 105–6).

fedayeen Palestinian guerrillas of all varieties, widely regarded in Israel and elsewhere as 'terrorists'. Similarly, the British condemned as 'terrorists' the Jews who used violence against their colonial rule. See also 'guerrilla'.

Golan Heights Disputed high ground on the Israel–Syria border (see pp. 146–7).

Grand Mufti Authority on Muslim law and practice (see p. 41).

Greater Israel Israel extending east and west of the River Jordan.

Green Line Arab–Israeli ceasefire line of 1949.

guerrilla Irregular warrior, usually politically or religiously motivated. Frequently denounced as a 'terrorist' by opponents.

Haganah Jewish guerrilla organization of the pre-Israel era (see pp. 51–2).

Hamas Palestinian Islamist party and guerrilla organization (see pp. 208–9).

Hebrew Jewish language. The word 'Jew' derives from 'Hebrew'.

Herut Israeli political party of the far right (see pp. 186–7).

Hezbollah Shia Islamic Lebanese political party and military organization fiercely opposed to Israel (see pp. 185–6).

IDF Israeli Defence Force.

Intifada Palestinian uprising against Israeli occupation.

Irgun Hard-line Jewish guerrilla organization of the pre-Israel era (see pp. 51–2).

Israel An alternative name for the Old Testament figure Jacob. Technically speaking, the modern country is the State of Israel.

Islamic Jihad Anti-Israeli Islamist guerrilla organization (see p. 230).

Islamist Militant Muslim accepting the need for *Jihad* against Israel, the USA and their allies.

Jihad Muslim holy 'war', interpreted as a physical or spiritual battle.

Kadima Israeli political party of the centre-right founded in 2005.

Katyusha rockets Soviet-designed missiles of World War II.

Knesset Israeli parliament.

Lehi Extremist Jewish guerrillas of the pre-Israel era.

Likud Israeli right-wing political party (see pp. 186–7).

Mandate Territory being prepared for statehood by an imperial power.

Mapai Israeli Labour party (see pp. 68–9).

MIG Soviet jet fighter.

Mizrahim Jews of Middle Eastern or Central and Southern Asian descent (see Sephardim).

Muslim Brotherhood Long-standing Sunni Islamist organization.

National Water Carrier Israel's principal irrigation channel.

Negev Desert area in southern Israel.

NGO Non-governmental organization.

OAPEC Organization of Arab Petroleum Exporting Countries.

Occupied Territories Lands on the West Bank of the River Jordan, and around Jerusalem and Gaza City, conquered by Israel in 1967.

Orthodox Christianity Form of Christianity adopted by the Eastern Church, not headed by the pope.

Orthodox Judaism Fundamentalist and traditionalist form of Judaism.

Oslo Shorthand for the accords between Israelis and Palestinians, 1993–5.

Ottoman Empire Former Turkish Empire.

Pan-Arabism Movement for Arab unity.

PFLP Popular Front for the Liberation of Palestine (see pp. 164–5).

Phalange Right-wing Lebanese Christian paramilitaries.

PLA Palestine Liberation Army.

PLO Palestine Liberation Organization.

PNA Palestine National Authority (often simply Palestinian Authority, PA) established in 1994 as an interim government for the Palestinian people.

Qassam rockets Home-made Palestinian missiles.

Rafah Crossing point between Egypt and Gaza.

Resolution 242 UN Security Council Resolution calling on Israel to exchange land for peace (1967).

Resolution 338 UN Security Council Resolution calling for a ceasefire and implementation of Resolution 242 (1973).

Revisionist Hard-line Zionist position that called for an exclusively Jewish state on both banks of the River Jordan.

Right of return Right of Palestinian families and their descendants who had left their homes (now in Israel) in 1947–9 to return there.

Roadmap Peace process drawn up by the USA in 2003.

Security Barrier Fence, wall and barrier erected by Israel in various parts of the West Bank to prevent *fedayeen* attacks.

Sephardim Jews of eastern origin, once used specifically for those of Spanish, Portuguese or North African origin but used here more loosely, as is customary, for all those not of Ashkenazi origin (see Mizrahim).

Sharm El Sheikh Popular Egyptian Red Sea resort frequently used to host talks.

Shebaa Farms Small area on the Lebanese–Syrian border claimed by both countries.

Shia Minority branch of Islam centred around Iran.

Sinai Largely desert peninsula between Israel and Egypt.

SLA South Lebanese Army, a largely Christian militia backed by Israel.

Soviet Relating to the USSR.

Sunni Majority branch of Islam.

tahediyeh Ceasefire (loosely).

Temple Mount Holy site at the heart of East Jerusalem.

terrorist See *fedayeen*.

Transjordan Original name for the state of Jordan.

UAR United Arab Republic, a short-lived union between Egypt and Syria.

USSR Union of Soviet Socialist Republics, the former communist empire based on Russia.

West Bank Land on the west bank of the River Jordan, inhabited mainly by Palestinians, captured by Israel in 1967.

Zionism Movement for the establishment and maintenance of a Jewish state.

Taking it further

Objective history of the Israel–Palestinian conflict is often hard to come by. Readers are advised to consult as many sources as possible. Below are a few starting points. For those wishing to go deeper into the subject, many of the books have full bibliographies.

BOOKS

Aburish, S. K. (1999) *Arafat: From Defender to Dictator*, London: Bloomsbury.

Carter, J. (2007) *Palestine: Peace not Apartheid*, New York: Simon and Schuster.

Fromkin, D. (2003) *A Peace to End All Peace: Creating the Modern Middle East*, London: Orion.

Gelvin, J. (2007) *Israel–Palestine Conflict: One Hundred Years of War*, Cambridge: CUP.

Gowers, A. and Walker, T. *Arafat: The Biography*, London: Virgin

Harms, G. and Ferry, T. (2008) *Palestine–Israel Conflict: A Basic Introduction*, London: Pluto.

Kimmerling, B. and Migdal, J. S. (2003) *The Palestinian People: A History*, Cambridge MA: Harvard UP.

Kolers, A. (2009) *Land, Conflict and Justice: A Political Theory of Temtory*, Cambridge: CUP.

Laqueur, W. and Rubin, B. (eds) (2008) *The Israel–Arab Reader*, London: Penguin.

Meital, Y. (2006) *Peace in Tatters: Israel, Palestine and the Middle East*, Boulder CO: Lynne Rienner.

Pappé, I. (2006) *The Ethnic Cleansing of Palestine*, Oxford: Oneworld.

Pappé, I. (ed.), (2007) *The Israel/Palestine Question: A Reader*, London: Routledge.

Ross, D. (2005) *The Missing Peace*, New York: Farrar, Straus & Giroux.

Sabbagh, K. (2006) *Palestine A Personal History*, London: Atlantic Books.

Schulze, K. (2008) *The Arab–Israeli Conflict*, Harlow: Pearson.
Shindler, C. (2008) *A History of Modern Israel*, Cambridge: CUP.
Shlaim, A. (2001) *The Iron Wall: Israel and the Arab World*, London: Penguin.

WEBSITES

Al Jazeera: www.aljazeera.com
Arab world: www.arab.net
BBC: http://www.bbc.co.uk/news/world/middle_east
CNN: http://www.cnn.com/WORLD/meast/archive/
Chronologies, etc: http://www.securitycouncilreport.org/site/
http://www.mideastweb.org/timeline.htm
History in the news: www.albany.edu/history/middle-east
Israeli government website: www.israel.org/mfa
Modern history sourcebook: www.fordham.edu/halsall/mod/modsbook54.html
Palestinian sources: www.politicalresources.net/palestine.htm
Peacewatch: www.mideastweb.org/history.htm
UN: www.un.org/unrwa/english.html

Index